STRANGE COUNTRY

STRANGE COUNTRY
A Study of Randolph Stow

Anthony J. Hassall

University of Queensland Press

ST LUCIA • LONDON • NEW YORK

First published 1986 by University of Queensland Press
Box 42, St Lucia, Queensland, Australia

Typeset by University of Queensland Press
Printed in Singapore by Kok Wah Press (Pte) Limited

Distributed in the UK and Europe by University of Queensland Press
Dunhams Lane, Letchworth, Herts. SG6 1LF England

Distributed in the USA and Canada by University of Queensland Press
5 South Union Street, Lawrence, Mass. 01843 USA

Cataloguing in Publication Data

National Library of Australia

Hassall, Anthony J., 1939–
  Strange country.

  Bibliography.
  Includes index.

  1. Stow, Randolph, 1935–   – Criticism and
interpretation. 2. Australian literature – 20th
century – History and criticism. I. Title.

A823'.3

British Library (data available)

Library of Congress

Hassall, Anthony J.
  Strange country.

  Bibliography: p.
  Includes index.

  1. Stow, Randolph, 1935–   – Criticism and
interpretation. I. Title.

PR9619.3.S84Z7   1986   823   85-8510

ISBN 0 7022 1866 9

For Doug and John
and in memory of Harri

Contents

Preface

In 1979 Randolph Stow received the Patrick White Award, the aim of which is "to recognize Australian writers . . . whose achievement has not been adequately appreciated". Few of the recipients of the award have fitted this description so clearly. Stow has been publishing novels and poems for almost thirty years. He has won a number of awards and prizes, and there have been enthusiastic reviews, a few perceptive articles, and one book, but there has been no sustained critical attention commensurate with his achievement. The *Australian Writers and Their Work* series saw fit to devote only a quarter of a slim monograph to Stow in 1974, and the recent *Oxford History of Australian Literature* (1981) speaks of his "disappointingly slender accomplishment".

This study has been undertaken in the belief that Stow is a more important writer than is yet generally recognized, and that he is the only Australian novelist of recent decades whose best work bears comparison with Patrick White's. Stow's reputation, like White's, is not of course confined to Australia – he has published in England from the beginning and he now lives in and writes of East Anglia – but his formative experience was Australian, and he has written of that experience with such sensitivity, such insight, such elegiac celebration that he will continue to be seen importantly though not exclusively as an Australian writer.

The time has therefore come for a serious assessment of Stow, and in the pages which follow I offer a critical reading of all of his works to date. Writing a critical study of an author in mid-career is not, however, without its hazards. Later books and subsequent events have a habit of changing our views, and of rendering our assessments even more the sport of time than those made when the author is himself beyond change. The task is nonetheless worth attempting, and if this study contributes to the eventual recognition of Stow as a major writer it will have fulfilled its purpose.

Acknowledgments

It is a pleasure to thank the people who have helped me to write this book. I owe a special debt of gratitude to Randolph Stow for his unfailing courtesy and kindness in answering my queries about his work over a number of years and in saving me from many errors. I would also like to thank Mrs Mary Stow and Mrs Helen McArthur who talked to me of their memories of Randolph Stow as a son and brother in the Geraldton years and after, and William Grono who reminisced about his friend's undergraduate years in Perth. Mrs Gay Moustaka, Mrs Mavis Geddes, Mrs Margaret Cobley and Mr and Mrs Eric Sewell gave generously of their time, hospitality and memories during my visit to Geraldton in 1983. Bruce Bennett and Michael Lanchbery gave me expert advice, and my colleagues and students at Newcastle and James Cook universities suggested many of the ideas which found their way into the book. I would also like to thank the editors of *Australian Literary Studies, Southerly, Meanjin, The Age Monthly Review, Westerly, LiNQ* and *Perspectives 79* in which earlier versions of parts of the book first appeared.

The manuscript was expertly typed and patiently revised by Mrs Marise Greenland, Mrs Gloria Sargent and Mrs Marie Hill. It was read by Elizabeth Perkins, Dorothy Green and Gina Goulder, all of whom made valuable comments and suggestions. John Burrows and Dianne Osland read many versions of the manuscript, and improved everything they read. My wife Loretta gave me invaluable criticism, encouragement and support throughout the work.

Chronology

1935   Julian Randolph Stow born in Geraldton on 28 November. Parents Cedric Ernest Stow and Mary Stow (née Sewell). Sister Helen born 1937.

On both sides of the family, Randolph Stow belongs to the fifth generation resident in Australia and the third generation born in Australia. The Stows came to Australia from Hadleigh in Suffolk, and the Sewells from the nearby Maplestead Hall in Essex. The Stow family is connected to the Randolphs of Virginia, to Thomas Jefferson and (allegedly) to Pocahontas. The Reverend Thomas Quinton Stow (1801–62), Randolph Stow's great-great-grandfather, arrived in South Australia in 1837. His descendants were distinguished lawyers and judges in that state. Cedric Stow was a lawyer, and Randolph Stow enrolled in Law at the University of Western Australia in 1953, later transferring to Arts. George Sewell (1816–91), Randolph Stow's maternal great-grandfather, arrived in Western Australia in 1836, following his brother and followed by their parents, and moved with his family to Geraldton in 1866, having taken up Sand Springs station in the 1850s. Sand Springs, the model for Sandalwood in *The Merry-go-Round in the Sea*, remains in the family, and is now owned by Eric Sewell, one of the models for Rick Maplestead.

Geraldton, one of the principal provincial centres in Western Australia, lies on the coast five hundred kilometres north of the capital, Perth. It is the port for a considerable fishing industry, and for a major grain-producing area. The hinterland to the east includes the Murchison goldfields and the towns of Cue, Wiluna, Yalgoo, Day Dawn and Sandstone, the models for Tourmaline. To the west of Geraldton lie the Abrolhos Islands, where the *Batavia* was wreck-ed in 1629, leading to one of the bloodiest episodes in the early history of Australia. The Geraldton of the 1940s and the surrounding sea and countryside are precisely and affectionately described in Stow's early poems and novels, especially the semi-autobiographical *The Merry-go-Round in the Sea* (1965).

1941–47   Geraldton Primary School.

Educated by correspondence in the bush during the Japanese scare of 1942 and the resulting evacuation of Geraldton.

1948–49   Geraldton High School.

1950–52   Guildford Church of England Grammar School, Perth.

1953–56   St George's College, University of Western Australia, Perth. Initially a Law student, later (1954) changed to Arts.

1954–55   *A Haunted Land* written at Geraldton in the university summer vacation, November 1954 to February 1955.

1955–56   *The Bystander* written at Geraldton in the summer vacation.

1956   *A Haunted Land* published by Macdonald in London and (1957) by Macmillan in USA. Later translated into German, Dutch and Danish.

B.A. degree from University of Western Australia with majors in French and English.

1957   *The Bystander* and *Act One* published by Macdonald in London. *The Bystander* later translated into Danish. The Gold Medal of the Australian Literature Society awarded to *Act One*.

Worked as a storeman at the Anglican mission to the Umbalgari people at Forrest River near Wyndham in the far north of Western Australia for some months early in the year.

Tutored in English at University of Adelaide in the second half of the year.

Wrote *To the Islands* in Adelaide and Geraldton, September 1957 to February 1958.

1958   Studied Anthropology and Linguistics at University of Sydney.

To the Islands published by Macdonald in London and (1959) by Little, Brown in USA. Later translated into German. Awarded the Gold Medal of the Australian Literature Society, the Miles Franklin Award and the Melbourne Book Fair Award for *To the Islands*.

1959   Worked in Papua New Guinea, as assistant to Dr Charles Julius, the government anthropologist, and later as cadet patrol officer, mainly in the Trobriand Islands, where he learned the Biga-Kiriwina language. *Visitants* (1979) is set in the Trobriands.

Contracted malaria, and was invalided back to Australia.

Cedric Stow died.

1960   Visited England and signed contract for the publication of *Outrider*.

1961   Began work on M.A. on Conrad at University of Western Australia.

Temporary lecturer in English at Leeds University 1961-62 academic year. Wrote *Tourmaline* on the boat to England and in Leeds.

1962   *Outrider* published by Macdonald in London.

Interviewed by Russell Braddon while spending winter 1962-63 in Scottish Highlands. Braddon's experiences as a prisoner-of-war of the Japanese in World War II, building the infamous Burma-Siam railway, later used by Stow in "Thailand Railway" and *The Merry-go-Round in the Sea.*

1963   *Tourmaline* published by Macdonald in London, and (1965) by Penguin in Melbourne.

Summer in Malta.

Temporary lectureship in English at University of Western Australia 1963–64.

Edited *Australian Poetry 1964.*

1964   Travelled through United States, visiting forty-six states, on Harkness Fellowship.

Wrote *The Merry-go-Round in the Sea* in Aztec, New Mexico in November-December.

1965   *The Merry-go-Round in the Sea* published by Macdonald in London and (1966) by Morrow in USA. Later translated into Hebrew and Swedish.

"Stations", commissioned by the Poetry Society of Great Britain for the Commonwealth Festival of the Arts in London, written in Maine (in the shack in the woods described by Jacques Maunoir in *The Girl Green as Elderflower*).

Attended Summer School on Indonesian language at Yale.

Visited Alaska.

1966   Renewed friendship with Peter Maxwell Davies, then composer-in-residence at Adelaide University. Davies and Stow later collaborated on the Music Theatre works *Eight Songs for a Mad King* and *Miss Donnithorne's Maggot.*

Received Britannica–Australia Award.

Midnite written in April-May in Perth.

Returned to England with Peter Maxwell Davies, visiting Thailand and India.

1967   *Midnite* published by Macdonald in London, by Cheshire in Melbourne, and (1968) by Prentice-Hall in USA. Later translated into Japanese, Dutch, Danish, German, and Swedish.

1969   *A Counterfeit Silence* published by Angus & Robertson in Sydney.

Eight Songs for a Mad King premiered at Queen Elizabeth Hall, London. Later recorded by Julian Eastman and The Fires of London.

Moved in May to East Bergholt in Suffolk. The Suffolk countryside, to which Stow feels an "atavistic" attraction (both sides of his family came originally from Suffolk/Essex area) is portrayed with Stow's usual sensitivity, and fine eye and ear for detail, in "Outrider", *The Girl Green as Elderflower* and *The Suburbs of Hell.*

The first three parts of *Visitants* written between August 1969 and April 1970.

The Grace Leven Prize for Poetry awarded to *A Counterfeit Silence.*

1973   Visited University of Aarhus lecturing on the Australian novel.

1974   Returned to Australia with Commonwealth Literary Fund grant.

Miss Donnithorne's Maggot premiered at the Adelaide Festival.

Recorded *Randolph Stow Reads from His Own Work* for the University of Queensland Press Poets on Record Series.

Returned to England via revolutionary Portugal and the Azores.

1978   Visited University of Aarhus, mounting exhibition on *Terra Australis Incognita.*

1979   *The Girl Green as Elderflower* written in East Bergholt in January.

Visitants completed in March.

Visitants published in autumn by Secker & Warburg in London, and (1981) by Taplinger in USA.

Received Patrick White Award.

1980   *The Girl Green as Elderflower* published in spring by Secker & Warburg in London, and by Viking in USA.

1981   Revised edition of *To the Islands* published by Angus & Robertson in Sydney, and (1982) by Secker & Warburg in London, and by Taplinger in USA.

Tystnadens landskap, a selection of poems translated into Swedish, published by Cikada in Gävle.

Moved from East Bergholt to Old Harwich in Essex.

1982   Attended Commonwealth Literature conferences at universities of Pisa and Gothenburg.

1983   *The Suburbs of Hell* written in Harwich.

Tourmaline reissued by Secker & Warburg in London, by Taplinger in USA, by Angus & Robertson in Sydney, and (1984) by Penguin in UK.

1984   *The Suburbs of Hell* published by Secker & Warburg in London, by Taplinger in USA, and by Heinemann in Melbourne.

The Merry-go-Round in the Sea reissued by Secker & Warburg in London, Taplinger in USA, and Angus & Robertson in Sydney.

Midnite reissued by the Bodley Head in London with new illustrations by Ralph Steadman (the original illustrator).

Miss Donnithorne's Maggot recorded in London by Mary Thomas and The Fires of London. Released 1985.

1   The Landscape of the Soul

Hard to say whether the subtle sky-rim of our tenure
   or the home-paddock heart is more unexplored.
         "A Helicopter View of Terrestrial Stars", Les A. Murray

Il n'est d'histoire que de l'âme.
                                    "Exil", St-John Perse

In *The Girl Green as Elderflower* Randolph Stow retells the
legends of four medieval figures, three of them children, who
find themselves transported from their own countries into alien
worlds. Those who survive live sad, lonely and disoriented lives,
haunted always by memories, hearing the grievous music of the
lands they have left behind. They seek love, but are hindered by
their foreignness, and although some of the natives are kind, any
love they find is transitory and fragile. All of Stow's work is
peopled by such visitants, by those who are strangers and afraid,
in landscapes which are alien, and yet which reflect that
strangeness they also find when they look inwards, seeking an
inner home. The theme is familiar in the twentieth century,[1] and
the condition is intensified for the writer of European descent
born in Australia, where the landscape looms, both familiar and
alien.[2] "The writer", Judith Wright wrote in 1965, "must be at
peace with his landscape before he can turn confidently to its
human figures";[3] but the harmony with the country enjoyed by
those few Aborigines who have not been forcibly dispossessed is
not yet widely shared by European Australians.[4] Stow is neither
at home nor at peace with his native landscape, but it has so
possessed him that he describes it more sensitively, more surely
and more poignantly than almost any other writer.[5] His
protagonists too are acute observers of outer and inner landscapes, seeking like Voss and Captain Quiros to find the truth of
one in the other:

Terra Australis you must celebrate,
Land of the inmost heart, searching for which
Men roam the earth . . .[6]

Stow is both a celebratory and a searching writer, seeking to find an abiding home, within and without, "in reach of God's hand".[7]

Our own time has seen an increase in many different kinds of alienation: tribal, racial, urban, geographic and religious. Stow draws on all of these, making particular use of the alienation of native people in European colonies and former colonies like Australia and Papua New Guinea, and the post-colonial alienation of settlers, which he, like Martin Boyd and Henry Handel Richardson, depicts as a European consciousness fretting in an Australian landscape.[8] Christopher Koch describes the dilemma: "A writer who is a native of such an island comes quite soon to the problem of trying to match its spirit with the spirit of the ancestral land in his head – the lost northern hemisphere. It's possible to love both, but matching them up isn't easy: the task of a lifetime, in fact".[9] And Andrew Taylor has pointed to the Australian hostility to the harshness of the country, which contrasts markedly with the American inclination to romanticize nature. There is no Australian equivalent of *Walden* which, though harsh enough at times, does not see nature as Lawson sees the bush – as hostile and dehumanizing.[10] The challenge is to master this unyielding terrain, and only a writer who has come to terms with that can begin to look confidently at the human figures within it.

The aridity of the Australian continent for Stow is due partly to the absence of the "lovely lumber"[11] of European culture – hence the anthology of European poetry that Heriot somewhat incongruously carries around in his head – and partly to the loss of local deities, those ghosts and genii that accumulate in a lived-in country over the centuries. Ironically these abound in the Aboriginal culture which the European settlers largely ignored, leaving themselves with a country that was both physically and spiritually depopulated. In his first two novels Stow wishes his country *was* haunted, as the East Anglia of *The Girl Green as Elderflower* and *The Suburbs of Hell* is haunted, and as even Tourmaline is haunted by its green past. For the Europeans, Australia before their arrival knew only the "tremor of nomad fires",[12] and those nomads have since become the ghosts of Onmalmeri. Stow's country then, as Harry Heseltine has pointed out, is haunted "less by the ghosts of the past than by the unquiet spirits of the present".[13] Crispin Clare, who treats his post-colonial disease by recreating some of the ghosts of Suffolk, would have found such ghosts less easy to come by and less friendly in Australia.

In addition to the outer landscape, the Australian writer is also driven to explore the inner landscape, and Stow is very conscious of the shifting boundary between the two:

> The boundary between an individual and his environment is not his skin. It is the point where mind verges on the pure essence of him, that unchanging observer that for want of a better term we must call the soul. The external factors, geographical and sociological, are so mingled with his ways of seeing and states of mind that he may find it impossible to say what he means by his environment, except in the most personal and introspective terms . . . The environment of a writer is as much inside him as in what he observes.[14]

As this early remark suggests, Stow sees the individual's inner landscape and his perception of the outer landscape as images of one another. Heriot, like Voss, explores the two simultaneously, and in terms of one another. His final statement, "my soul is a strange country", thus becomes the consummation of both the journeys to the islands that the book describes. Laura's final comment on Voss that "perhaps true knowledge only comes of death by torture in the country of the mind"[15] is both more extreme and more assured than Stow is prepared to be. The deaths of Heriot and Cawdor are hedged about with more uncertainties than the death of Voss: they both see their visions near the end, but these are less clearly defined than those that White's visionaries see as they encounter death. In *Midnite* Stow pokes some fun at White and himself, at desert journeys and death among the bones, but he clearly believes that the perception of the self and the perception of the landscape condition one another, and that to explore one is to explore both.

Stow is a private rather than a social novelist, less interested in interpersonal relationships than in his characters' relationships with themselves and with God. His love poems describe not the joy of union but the "ache and waiting" between the lovers' few and infrequent meetings.[16] And the major characters in his novels seldom sustain close relationships for any length of time. From the disintegration of the Maguire family in *A Haunted Land* and the failure of Patrick and Diana's marriage in *The Bystander*, through the severing of Rick's attachments to Hughie and Rob in *The Merry-go-Round in the Sea*, to the "refusal" of Cawdor's wife in *Visitants*, Stow portrays isolation and loneliness as the inescapable lot of man. He is fascinated by men like Heriot, the Law and MacDonnell who are old and alone, adrift in the outback, the desert, or the jungle, and still in search of peace with themselves and with God. But if loneliness is inescapable it is also, paradoxically, the soil in which love may grow:

> The love of man is a weed of the waste places.
> One may think of it as the spinifex of dry souls.[17]

In one of the most perceptive essays on Stow, Jennifer Wightman argues that loneliness is "the condition that Stow uses to reveal his characters' capacity for love".[18] And Heriot certainly discovers his love for Rex in the course of his lonely journey, when Rusty reminds him that intending to kill Rex and actually killing him are very different things, at least to Rex: "then new thoughts moved behind Heriot's eyes like yachts on an empty sea, and for the first time he remembered Rex alive, and what it must have been to be Rex, to take pleasure in clothes and women".[19] The yachts that move on the empty sea of Heriot's solipsism are a haunting image of man's separation from his fellows. There may be islands in that empty sea, or there may be only yachts, the passing images of other lives, of what it feels like to be other men. Stow, like Virginia Woolf, is a poet of silence, of "the things people don't say".[20]

Silence is a temptation as well as a theme for Stow. Joyce's Stephen Dedalus chose it, along with exile and cunning, as one of his strategies for escape from the island of his birth. And Patrick White, who returned to the island of his birth, has expressed his distrust for language and his preference for the silence between words: "Part of me is austere enough to have conveyed the truth, I like to think . . . If I believe this today, tomorrow I may feel that truth is the property of silence – at any rate the silences filling the space between words, and over those I sometimes have control".[21] This is a sentiment that Stow, who has counterfeited silence in his poems, is inclined to share:

> If my words have had power to move, forget my words.
> ....
> In the silence between my words, hear the praise of Tao.[22]

These final words of *A Counterfeit Silence* were followed by a decade in which he published very little, and he has certainly not made of writing the career that was open to someone with his gifts. In *Tourmaline* he wrestled with the Taoist dilemma of whether to choose speech or silence. The book amply demonstrates his fine ear for dialogue and his sure psychological insight: Deborah and Kestrel are acutely observed and their unlikely relationship is entirely credible; but his real interest is elsewhere, with the tortured diviner Michael Random and with his chronicler the Law, both of whom are isolates, struggling with themselves and with God. Self-exploration, self-realization, and the agonized search for a personal God in "*le silence éternel de ces espaces infinis*"[23] characterize the progress of his protagonists, who also sometimes stumble upon love in the course of their largely silent journeys.

In addition to the unease with landscape, and the failure to sustain love, there is portrayed throughout Stow's work a radical unease with the self, a failure to accept the innermost landscape, which produces the most basic alienation of all. Heriot, Random and Cawdor are tortured by forces within themselves that they do not want to recognize and cannot accept. Heriot's murderous hate, Random's sexual revulsion, and Cawdor's schizophrenic "visitant" are all fiercely resisted, and the resulting psychic turmoil leaves the characters even more isolated. In "Strange Fruit", one of Stow's densest and most private poems, he writes of psychic conflict in terms of a once-united Adam and Eve separated by Eve's fall: "Alone for an hour, in a thicket, I reached for strange fruit".[24] Now the fever-ridden Eve stalks the unfallen Adam, determined that he too "*shall try strange fruit*". The poem is haunted by fear of a lost and alienated psychic partner returning to wreak vengeance, a vengeance that will lead, as with Cawdor, to a "suicide of the night". The poem reflects not only a self-destructive inner alienation, which is its essential subject, but also the failure of love — "Did we ride knee to knee down the canyons, or did I dream it?" — and the deserted, hostile outer landscape:

> the great
> poised thunderous breaker of darkness rearing above you,
> and your bones awash, in the shallows, glimmering, stony,
> like gods of forgotten tribes, in forgotten deserts.

It thus includes, in brief compass, much that is central to Stow's writing.

This then is the territory that Stow explores. There is the outer landscape of Australia, which is "neither kind, tutelary nor companionable",[25] which contrasts disconcertingly with that of the cultural homeland — the East Anglia of *The Girl Green as Elderflower* and *The Suburbs of Hell* — which is nonetheless loved because it is the experience of childhood, ineradicably imprinted on the writer's sensibility. There is the other lost world of love, which has been visited briefly, but never inhabited, except in the special dispensation of childhood. And there is the silent, inner landscape, where the dialogue of self and soul has been at best intermittent, and all too often hostile. Stow writes of this triple alienation in a manner that is both celebratory and elegiac. There is the generous domain of the Maplestead clan as well as the emptiness of Heriot's continent. There is the recovery of Crispin Clare as well as the bitter heritage of Malin and Tourmaline. And it is all described with a fine, poetic intensity, in a spare yet richly evocative style that recreates the sense-impressions, the ambience of a landscape with extraordinary vividness and imaginative power. Like his pioneering ancestors in America and Australia, Stow has claimed new territory. He has annexed his native Western Australia, explored and charted the European experience of it, and added it to the known literary world.

2 A Bitter Heritage

Early Fiction

Le passé n'est pas fugace, il reste sur place.
A La Recherche Du Temps Perdu, Marcel Proust

One doesn't belong before one's body is shaped from the dust of one's ancestors.
A Chain of Voices, André Brink

Randolph Stow's first two novels, *A Haunted Land* (1956) and *The Bystander* (1957), were written while he was an undergraduate at the University of Western Australia, and published by the time he was twenty-one. The books, which display a remarkable command of narrative, great imaginative intensity, and a disturbingly acute insight into the condition of alienation, are compulsively readable. It is hardly surprising to find that there are also faults in the work of so young a writer, who has not yet developed his personal style. There are occasional overstatements, infelicities, and failures to realize or to dramatize, and the sympathies of the reader are not as clearly focused as they might be. But the overwhelming impression created by these first two novels is that they are the work of an immensely gifted writer in the making.

If Stow had not yet perfected his method, he had certainly zeroed in on his subject matter. The novels portray the settlement of the harsh, alien, yet haunting land of the Geraldton district in Western Australia by psychically-displaced Europeans, who are tortured, restless and bitter. Their ambition is to found new dynasties in this oldest, newest of lands, but they are doomed to failure by their self-destructive impulses, and by the black Celtic melancholy which isolates them from the mainstream of colonial life and leaves them lonely outsiders. Representative of their fate is Patrick Leighton, the bastard descendant of the Maguires, who accumulates properties but has no heir to inherit them. And so in the end only the land remains, haunted by the unquiet spirits of the Maguires and Leightons. It is a bitter heritage for those who follow.

Stow explores that heritage — the world he himself

inherited as a fifth-generation Western Australian – in his first two novels. And he was conscious that he was a literary pioneer. "His country was pretty", Rob reflected in *The Merry-go-Round in the Sea*, "but impossibly far from other more beautiful, more soul-filled countries, that had earned the right to be written about in books".[1] The few books of literary distinction written about Western Australia were little known and difficult of access, and this lack of a visible literary tradition compounded the difficulty of writing about a country only recently settled by Europeans.[2] Patrick White has described the problem: "Writing, which had meant the practice of an art by a polished mind in civilised surroundings, became a struggle to create completely fresh forms out of the rocks and sticks of words."[3] It is, however, easy for contemporary Australians to forget how recently and how spectacularly the tradition has consolidated. Stow has pointed out that poetry readings would have been "unthinkable" in his undergraduate days, when he was writing his first two novels and the poems in *Act One* (1957). The editors of a Western Australian anthology in the late fifties "reluctantly decided to make it an all-fiction collection, rather than show up the West as a State with no more than two or three poets".[4] As well as learning to write, Stow was going to have to do without much help from the local tradition.

Naturally enough he looked for what he could borrow from older literary traditions to help him shape his response to this new world, a world itself conditioned by a European cultural heritage, and by the sometimes parallel experience of America. Geoffrey Dutton has listed some of the writers who influenced the young Stow: "the Jacobean dramatists, the Brontës, certain Spanish poets, the American tradition dealt with by Leslie Fiedler, Patrick White . . . the Elizabethan pastoral poets and Keats".[5] Characters like Anne in *A Haunted Land* and Heriot in *To the Islands* (1958) quote frequently from European literature, and if this sometimes seems self-consciously literary, it reflects the unease of the explorer, signposting the country through which he travels with familiar names. Rob Coram, whose "handsome young great-great-grandfather . . . had left Byron his bed to die on, and gone back to England with a bit of a poem called *Don Juan* in his pocket",[6] is taught Scottish ballads by his Aunt Kay and Australian ballads by his mother. At the same time he feels a peculiarly Western Australian alienation from the literature of his own country: "the poems she [his mother] liked were poems about Australia, about sad farewells at the slip-rail and death in the far dry distance . . . Deep inside him he yearned towards Australia: but he did not expect ever to go there".[7] Stow, like Rob, felt a double alienation.

The connections between *A Haunted Land* and *The Bystander* recall those between Faulkner's Yoknapatawpha books, and Stow's later books attempt, though on a smaller scale than Faulkner's, to encompass the history of the regions they portray. Stow and Faulkner share a profound love/hate attachment to the land and its people, a consciousness of the brutal European taking and exploitation of the land, an oppressive sense of the weight of the past — "The past is never dead. It's not even past"[8] — and a conviction that "life holds the mirror up to melodrama".[9] The Maguire family disintegrates like the Compson family, and Keithy and Benjy share the agony of adult children who lose the objects of their primal affections. The styles of the two writers, however, are strongly contrasted. Stow's mature style is spare, lucid, understated and resonant, and while it is not always achieved in his first two novels, there are unmistakable signs of its emergence. Even so severe a critic of Stow as Leonie Kramer finds much of the writing in *A Haunted Land* "lucid and self-effacing . . . sensitive".[10] And in his later work he has refined and simplified further, relying more on ellipsis and the bare, suggestive detail. Faulkner developed in the opposite direction, from the succinctness of *As I Lay Dying* to the fulsome rhetoric of the Snopes trilogy.

A Haunted Land is an ambitious first novel in which Stow combines naturalistic observation of the Western Australian scene with a dreamlike story that is violent, passional, and surreal. The combination made a good many critics, used to more stereotyped novels, uneasy, and they puzzled over its mixing of modes, its lack of consistent "realism", and its affinity to "dramatic poetry" and "romance".[11] They might, I suppose, have expected a mid-twentieth-century novelist to write in a less Romantic and more psychological manner, though the period has its Gothic masters, like Faulkner and Patrick White. What they encountered was a spare, primary narrative which built to a bizarre yet inevitable climax. While there is not much overt character analysis, the insight into family relations is acute. And if Stow has not succeeded entirely in uniting the ordinary and the exceptional — he was to do that later in *Visitants* — he has certainly made a brave beginning. Maguire, like Cawdor, is seen mostly through his effect on others. Both are enigmatic, but Cawdor captures the reader's sympathy in a way that Maguire — and other characters like Adelaide — do not, and it is this failure to engage the reader's affections, more than any mixture of fictional modes, that limits the success of *A Haunted Land*. It remains nonetheless a striking first novel, full of promise, and executed with daring, intensity and an already impressive style.

The book opens with a prospect of the country around Malin, and of the homestead itself, some fifty years after the main action takes place. Jessie, Martin Maguire's wife, returns to the west, and to the homestead that was never her home. Why she goes back to Malin is not spelled out, but her life has been scarred by her involvement with the Maguires, and if fifty years and a second marriage have not laid her private ghosts, she may hope that a return to Martin's home will bring some understanding, and perhaps some release. The country through which she travels is familiar:

> And suddenly she saw the great red cliff of Malin Pool rise up in front of her, the wide water and the white gums, and this was true changelessness . . . The shade of the gumtrees was cool there and the rushes moved gently in the hot breeze. Somewhere a mullet jumped; a wild duck flapped low across the water. Peacefully the wind ruffled a wild hibiscus mirroring its pale mauve flowers in the pool. (10)[12]

If there are memories here, however, there are no ghosts. And when she reaches the house there is nothing for her: "I am as much a stranger now, she thought, as I was then. I never knew them; they have left nothing here for me" (12). This quiet opening suggests that it is the people who are haunted, not the land. The people — almost all of them — have gone, but the land remains. The struggle of pioneering, the dream of affluence that built the grand houses, the slow decline into disrepair and abandonment have all passed the country by, and it has reverted to its native peacefulness.

The narrative which follows this prologue is, however, anything but peaceful. It begins with the death of Elizabeth Maguire in 1892, sixty years before, and the sending of the three younger children to school in Melbourne. The scene between Andrew Maguire and his dying wife, which is overheard by the nine-year-old Adelaide, is an abrupt introduction to an intense relationship:

> "What devilry are you planning? What are you going to do to me?"

Her breathless voice whispered against his ear: "I'll haunt you till you hate me. You'll never forget me, Andrew."

"No," he said, and the sound was almost a groan. "Oh God, I need you, Beth."

The coughing was worse and he would have released her. But she cried: "No! Hold me closer! Andrew, if I have to die, let me die of you." (16)

Because we see only this fragment of the couple's life – it is the end of another story rather than the beginning of this one – their feelings appear extreme and their relationship improbably Gothic.[13] Adelaide is a mute spectator. Her parents' love is not an expansive one, and the children are excluded. In the next chapter, ten years later, when Adelaide, Anne and Patrick return from Melbourne, they might seem to be making a sentimental journey back to a half-forgotten childhood, but they are immediately embroiled in the family warfare, which compulsively re-enacts the violent, possessive passion that joined Andrew and Beth, and that still torments Andrew, as Beth had promised it would. She possesses her husband like a visitant from beyond the grave, and in the year which follows, each of the children in turn becomes a casualty of the resulting conflict.

Martin and Nick, the two sons who have remained at Malin with their father, are already locked into a destructive ritual of trying to win his approval by alternately moulding themselves to his wishes and rebelling against him. His interest in his sons is selfish, exploiting them as drinking companions, depriving them of contact with the outside world for fear they will leave him, and projecting on to them his own and his dead wife's image of a fearless, liquor-holding masculinity. When Martin is bitten by a snake, his father reveals how warped his sense of priorities has become. While Nick and Adelaide try to extract the venom, Maguire looks at his son with contempt: " 'Keep your voice down,' Maguire said sharply. 'Do you want the Crosses to know you're scared?' " (96). The incident prompts Martin's attempt to escape from his father by marrying Jessie Cameron and moving to Strathmore, but Maguire kills whatever chance the marriage has by telling Martin that his children are likely to inherit insanity. As a result, Martin's marriage does not become a sexual relationship, and it is soon not a marriage at all. Martin's fate is laconically narrated in the prologue: "I don't know the whole story, but apparently he ran away from her and came back to live in a cottage at Malin. He was a drunk; an honest old-fashioned drunk" (11).

Nick also tries to escape from Malin. In his farewell note to Addie he blames himself rather than his father: "I know you'll all be happier when I'm gone, because it's his disappointment in me that makes him so snappish and when I'm not here he'll pretty soon forget me" (153). This simplistic misreading of the true relationship between father and son – "snappish" is a very inadequate description of Maguire's abuse of his children, especially Nick – is strangely at odds with Nick's "vicious and brilliant" caricature of his father as a snake, which makes even Adelaide realize: "you hate him, Nick" (134). Maguire has obstructed Nick's musical and artistic development, and the rest of his life, like Martin's, is an empty postscript to a wasted childhood.

The third son, Patrick, is clung to even more desperately. When Martin and Nick have gone, Patrick is the last son left, and Maguire is determined to keep him. Patrick's ten years away, however, have left him less dependent upon his father, and able to love Jane Leighton in the only successful sexual relationship any of the children achieves. When Maguire learns of it we get a rare glimpse into the workings of his mind:

> His mind shrieked, down its dark grooves, of ingratitude and treachery and his eyes held a flare of hatred for Jane, Edith's daughter, in whom he saw her mother. For Edith had stolen Nick from him, and because of that theft Martin was lost, and now here was her daughter scheming, treacherous, soothing away the loyalty of the last and best-beloved, of Patrick who was most his son, who had his hair and his face and the young wildness which Beth had most loved in him. His hands about the rifle were strong and vicious with hate for Edith and Jane. (183)

While this provides an insight into Maguire's insane possessiveness, it does not carry the conviction of the rest of the scene, presented dramatically, in which he disguises his real motivation behind an appearance of generous, parental concern. He offers to approach Jane's mother Edith, ostensibly to help smooth the way for the lovers, but really to ensure their separation. Though the stratagem fails at the time, Maguire is eventually instrumental in the death of Patrick and so in the ending of the relationship. Maguire had forced Patrick into the fatal struggle with Tommy Cross with intemperate accusations of cowardice: "I should never have let you leave Malin to become what you have become: a degenerate, a coward, a pampered schoolboy not fit to mix with your brothers . . . You're not a Maguire! And you're not your mother's child either, because she wasn't afraid; there wasn't a thing she feared in the whole world" (57). The reaction is typically excessive: Beth may not have been afraid of anything, but Maguire is certainly afraid that her fearsome standard will not be maintained by their children. It comes as no surprise, then, that Maguire's violence finally kills – and that it kills his remaining son, of whom he demanded so much.

Anne, the daughter who looks like her mother, and who will die like her mother of consumption, is also tormented. In her case it is not by Maguire's expressed disapproval, but by her knowledge of what that disapproval would be if her father knew she had allowed the Aborigine Charlie to make love to her. She tells Patrick what happened – an edited version – and in a parody of what he imagines Maguire would want, Patrick shoots Charlie. Nursing this double guilt Anne withdraws into herself, and so she too is lost to her father, and alienated from the family.

At the end of the book Adelaide alone of the children is left, and it is she who comforts her father with the lie that the destruction he has wrought is not his fault. Adelaide has been lonely and isolated throughout, trying to relate to the others, and trying unsuccessfully to relate them to the outside world. We do not see her living alone with her father when all the others have gone, but it could not be other than a sterile relationship, with nothing ahead to live for, and the past oppressively present.

Maguire's personal heritage is a complex, disabling mixture of genetic instability, family misfortune and neurotic dependence. His grandfather, he says, was mad, and his grandmother, who raised him in Ireland after his mother died when he was born, feared for his sanity. He learned early that "we Maguires can't live in a crowd, and the crowd can't live with us" (23). His wife gave him the courage to marry, and have children: "Before, I should have been afraid of having a brood of idiots and consumptives" (20). But the relationship was a dependent one, and the dependency is transferred to the children after her death. Maguire's cruel threatening of Martin with the family insanity ensures that the fear he himself has ignored will poison his son's marriage. Even the wife he loved for her fearlessness seems to have been cruel and selfish – her sister calls her "very strong-willed" (19), while her daughters recall her brutal treatment of her son Nick, and her poisoning of wild dogs. In the final chapter of the book, Adelaide realizes her mother's cruelty and her father's weakness: "always underneath he must have been so lonely, so little and lonely without her, a deserted child. So much like Nick" (250). She tries to comfort him, but the damage has been done, the children are locked into the prison of the past, and, as we learn in *The Bystander*, even Adelaide, the least injured of them, dies relatively young and childless. If Maguire has suffered, he has at least known some fulfilment: his children, who know none, reap a bitter inheritance.

Though Maguire is the central character in the book, and the effects of his maimed personality pervade the lives of his children, he remains an enigmatic figure. There are occasional dramatic scenes where he comes fully to life, like the new year's eve dance at Strathmore where he taunts Edward Cameron for fighting the Boers, but for much of the book he is seen through the largely uncomprehending eyes of Adelaide, who seldom perceives his motives. In one of his more bizarre gestures he drives a stake into the earth above Tommy Cross's coffin, and when Adelaide asks Anne if he is mad, she is told he is drunk. Her genteelly inadequate response −" it seemed to her sordid and degrading for a man to be drunk in the early afternoon" (225) − portrays her as conventional and unimaginative, but it sheds little light on Maguire. The narrator is also reluctant to explain his characters directly. We are told, for example, of Maguire's "terrible drunken grief" (47), but with occasional exceptions we do not see into his mind, and are confined to observing the actions that his suffering prompts him to take. The driving of the stake expresses his grief for Patrick, his last remaining son, whom he has killed. The reader cannot help wondering how accidental the shot was. Maguire has already destroyed his other two sons. Perhaps there was some deliberation, or some unconscious will, in his shooting of Patrick? The narrator offers no explanation of his state of mind at the time, and while the reader is free to speculate, the absence of information makes Maguire less defined, and hence less sympathetic, than he might have been.

The reader's sympathy is, in fact, largely undirected in *A Haunted Land*. Whether the author is narrating directly, or through Adelaide or Anne, there is the unusual combination of an intense imaginative engagement with a dispassionate emotional distance. This is partly though not entirely due to the choice of Adelaide − the least typical of the Maguires − as the main narrating character. She is less involved than the others in the family's internal conflicts, and the last to find out what is going on. She looks on bewildered at the family she left, with Anne and Patrick, when she was nine, and to whom she return-ed ten years later. As the other two are drawn into the vortex of their father's violence, she tries ineffectually to run a normal household. The reader often knows more than she does, but the dramatic irony is not exploited, and she seems therefore to be limited both as a narrator and as a character. Anne, the other narrating character, is preoccupied with her own guilt over Charlie, and most of her narration is concerned with herself. While she is more quick-sighted than Adelaide, she is less interested in other people, and cares deeply only for Patrick, who shares her secret. Nick, the artist of the family, and the most perceptive and vulnerable of the children, might have made a more interesting narrator. As it is, the story is imagined with great power, but no corresponding intensity of feeling for the characters is generated in the reader, who is held spellbound, but not deeply involved.

The best scenes are presented dramatically, like the discussion between Anne and Adelaide after Martin's wedding. The coolness between the sisters is evident, and when Adelaide offers conventional sentiments — "it was rather a nice wedding . . . Jessie looked quite beautiful" — Anne is irritated into expressing the opinions of a true Maguire: "I'm only interested in weddings like Lorna Doone's and Jane Eyre's. I was half hoping that Father would jump up and shoot at Jessie, or else disclose that she was already married to Tommy Cross" (189). Anne's liveliness and humour contrast with Adelaide's lacklustre banality, and she perceives clearly what drives both her father and her brother:

> "Martin doesn't want to be made cheerful and comfortable. He's grown up in such a way that what's really necessary to him is to have someone to admire and follow round, someone harder and cleverer than he is to give orders and to praise or blame him when he carries them out. He doesn't even care about injustice, so long as he has this . . . over-ruling power to drive him." (190)

Even at this early stage, Stow was conscious of the mutually corrupting effect of one person taking charge of another's life, a theme he was to develop in *Tourmaline*. Anne is not much interested in others, however, and she retreats into her private world, telling Adelaide a fairytale she invented as a child, which dramatizes the death of her mother and her own impending death. She also explains why she has never written down any of her stories:

> Because I won't destroy them, she was thinking, because there's too great a gap between the imagination and the word and I won't destroy what takes me away from me and makes me greater, as love should

do when love is large enough. No, I'll keep my child-dreams in my mind, where they are whole, and sink down in them as I dreamed of sinking down through the sea, watching the sun grow small and pale above me, and no one else can and no one will know what it is to be me as I drown in that private world. (193)

This is the silent country of the soul that Stow was to make very much his territory in the books which followed. The isolation is intense, dreams predominate, drowning is a recurrent image, and love is a distant, longed-for liberation. The family means little to Anne here, though it has shaped her private world as well as her public world. She is characterized effectively in the few pages of this chapter: the contrast with Adelaide, the mixture of dialogue, storytelling and interior monologue, and the wit and evocativeness of the writing all contribute to the depth and authority of the portrait.

Her father needs an opponent, and with her acuteness and her mother's spirit Anne might have been a worthy opponent for him, had she not been restrained by her feelings of guilt and defilement. In the scenes where he is opposed Maguire becomes more credible. His argument with Edward Cameron over the Boer War has already been mentioned. And at Adelaide's picnic he clashes with Edith, who is irritated by his criticisms of her matchmaking, and who shakes his composure with some bitter home truths:

> "You know quite well that you wouldn't let your children marry anyone. You want to keep them to yourself for ever. I know you, Andrew; you're the most contemptibly selfish man I've ever met . . . Nick has told me how you refused to let him go away to study music. Pat mentioned in a letter before he left school that you wouldn't allow him to take up law." (114)

Maguire's discomfiture here reduces him from the demon-like figure of Malin to human dimensions, but for most of the book he has no real opponent, there is no Tom Spring to challenge, however quietly, his Michael Random. This leaves the book unbalanced to a degree. Like the Maguire children, the reader knows whom to fear, and whom to pity, but can find no one to love.

Maguire is the first of a series of characters in Stow — Heriot and Random are others — whose apparent strength is derived from weakness. Their evident will and determination spring from fear of themselves, and fear of failure. Though they try to suppress signs of weakness they remain vulnerable, and their vulnerability adds, ironically, to their charisma. The self-contained strength of a Tom Spring, by contrast, attracts few disciples, and in Stow's first novel it is only the land which exemplifies the Taoist wisdom of yielding, accepting, enduring, and which stands in mute challenge to the frenzy of self-destruction at Malin. The land is lovingly described, in all its moods and seasonal changes, and it remains in the reader's mind when the people who fret its surface have faded.

Keithy in *The Bystander* is the first Taoist character in the novels. While he is no match for the wilful and knowing "adults" who dominate his world, he retains his innocence, his simplicity, and his uncomplicated emotions, and he knows how to draw his strength from the land:

> That afternoon he went walking, far away from the house, in a lonely gulley that all his life had been his favourite haunt when he was in trouble. It was a long defile between two lines of hills. All around him dense scrub, bright with the orange flowers of poison bush and the pink heath, climbed up the slopes to shut him off from the world. There was utter silence in that narrow valley. He walked along with his hands in his pockets and his head down, following the small trickle of water that led to a creek.
>
> He came at last to the rock pool where the creek received its tributary and lay down on the grass to rest his legs from walking, his brain from thought. It was very peaceful there. Across the water a tall wattle in full bloom hissed a little in the wind and spread a ruffled golden image of itself across the stream. Green-eyes and wagtails fussed and fluttered in its branches, and a crow called far away. Turning on his back, he could see the everlastings springing from the rocky bank behind him.
>
> He did not know what he was thinking. He lay on his back and stared at the sky.
>
> Small fairweather clouds drifted calmly between the wide sky and the huge green land. A hawk, coming into view suddenly, stopped in the air, motionless, resting on the breeze. He saw the light on its wings and tried to name the colour of them; but they were golden and pink and brown and were always changing.
>
> He rolled on his side and shut out the universe.[14]

Keithy here immerses himself in his private part of the world, but he is not drowning, like Anne, in the private world of the self. Anne's gaze is turned inwards as she tries to escape from the outside world. Keithy absorbs and reflects what is about him. He can empty his mind of everything else and find peace.

The other alternative to Maguire's destructive assertion of will is the fragile mutuality of love, exemplified in the novel by Patrick and Jane. They find a refuge at Old Malin, a former childhood playground, and it is a shared, not a private retreat. Their son Patrick Leighton is conceived there, and the sterility of Malin is challenged by the hope of new life, and a new generation. While their love is short-lived, and fails to withstand Maguire's fierce opposition, it nonetheless challenges his determination to involve all his children in his own obsession with the past. Finally only Patrick Leighton survives, an orphan, raised by grandparents locked into the past, unaware of the love that united his parents, and heir to the ghosts of all the Maguires. His story, told in *The Bystander*, is of the failure of the search for love, and of the ultimate triumph of sterility. He is the last of the Maguires.

The story in *The Bystander* is less diffuse and episodic than in *A Haunted Land*. Focused on the triangular relationship between Patrick, Keithy and Diana Ravirs, it is better articulated and more surely handled. The characters are more complex and more responsible for their actions, and there is less dependence on psychological determinism and arbitrary fate. As a result *The Bystander* is more dramatic, more suspenseful and more emotionally compelling than its predecessor. While it is a bleak and bitter book, in some ways more pessimistic than *A Haunted Land*, it also has relaxed and humorous moments which qualify and humanize the starkness of its vision.

The opening sequence is typical of the more dramatic method adopted in *The Bystander*. In place of the formal prologue in *A Haunted Land* is a direct beginning *in medias res*. Diana Ravirs has just woken from sleep and is unsure of her identity. Officially she is a "displaced person" and she is also psychically displaced, a victim of war and alienation. We see her first at her most vulnerable, travelling by train at night: "Waking out of the brief sleep into which she had fallen, she lay and listened to the wheels of the train under her until they seemed to be questioning her – name, age, place of birth; weight, height, colour of hair – and she lay analysing her life into words that could be written along dotted lines" (9). She is on her way to a new job, "the old hated business of settling down, fitting in again". Outside the window of the train is the moonlit countryside as a sleepy passenger might see it.[15] When the train stops at a station she hears a song on the station's radio, the last line of which, "I just want something for ever", sticks in her mind and becomes, as Geoffrey Dutton noted, a signature tune which recurs throughout the book.[16]

As a new arrival at Lingarin, Diana introduces the reader to the world in which the novel is set. The Farnhams' station adjoins Malin, and the other Maguire properties of Koolabye and Strathmore, and while it is more homely and less Gothic than Malin, it provides a link with the world of *A Haunted Land*. Diana's arrival seems to her to be calculated to embarrass and humiliate her, and when she realizes that Keithy, for whom she is to keep house, is "a fool" she decides to leave. Ironically it is Patrick who persuades her to stay, with the promise of a home of her own for a year.

The story develops from this vivid introductory sketch, which anticipates later events. Diana learns that she has reason to fear Keithy's simplicity. And both she and Patrick ignore, to their cost, their first impressions of one another: she dislikes his quick insight into her motives, while he finds her "the coldest little bitch this side of the rabbit-proof fence" (29). Their motives for marrying despite these impressions are essentially self-interested. Diana later thinks to herself: "Admit that you deceived him for what he had and you had not, a place for ever" (212). She does not seem to have considered Patrick, who wants an heir from Diana to inherit his properties, and all the family memories:

> "Someday I'll die . . . and there they'll be, sold to a pastoral company or split up into little farms. They won't be Koolabye and Malin any more . . . and we'll all be resting in our old cemetery at Malin, with other people's ploughs running round overhead, probably. – God, a hundred years and four generations isn't long for a dynasty to last."
>
> "You are blaming me. You are not fair."
>
> "I don't blame you, you know that. What right would I have? I was resigned to this long before I ever saw you. I never expected to get married; by the time I was thirty I'd been turned down by three girls and I'd stopped thinking about it. Then I met you, and the idea of having a family was just a pipedream that lasted for about a month." (176)

Patrick's denials here do not hide his hurt, which Diana perceives, and which is caused not only by the loss of an heir, but also by the loss of that other dream of love: "when a man looks at a woman and sees that she doesn't feel anything but disgust for him – well, what do you think that man feels for himself?" (177). Patrick and Diana are both isolated, and the defences they have erected to shield that isolation ironically prevent them from giving and receiving the love they both desire. As Diana says: "We are two people on islands" (222). With Keithy they make a strange lovers' triangle. As she watches them leave for the pictures Kate Farnham reflects: "I don't suppose three such lost lonely people ever set out together with ideas of enjoying themselves" (126). It is, however, precisely such lost, lonely people that interest Stow.[17] Each of the three is locked, like other Stow characters, into a solitary world, a private history, from which it is ultimately impossible to escape, though all of them try to break out in their different ways.

It is one of the puzzles of the book that we are told so little of Diana's experiences in the war, though we are asked to accept that they have left her emotionally and sexually cold. Like Anne, she feels unclean, defiled: "I am not clean. I will never be clean. Oh, Patrick, the things I have seen! – the things that men and women do. You do not know how I have lived. And the people, Patrick – the women selling themselves for cigarettes – and in the camp, the girls giving themselves to guards – to women like men – for food. How can you say that I am clean?" (129).

Even the unobservant Frank Farnham notices her aloofness: "She was certainly good-looking; handsome, cold and lonely" (12). Had Patrick taken more notice of his own similar observations, and of Diana's warning when he proposed to her, he might have been less bitter about her inability to make the marriage into a sexual relationship. She asks for time to allow that to develop, but Patrick is too sensitive, too wounded in his self-regard by Diana's evident distaste, to be patient with her, and his resulting bitterness blocks her efforts to make the marriage at least an emotional union. On the night of the storm, for example, when the Norfolk Island pine at Koolabye is struck by lightning, Diana tries to woo Patrick out of his bitterness: "I must learn, you must give me time. There are things in my mind that must heal – " (177), but Patrick refuses to be mollified. As a result, the marriage itself becomes a prison for her, and she tries once more to escape. The marital discord is convincingly dramatized, but her motives remain enigmatic, and this costs her much of the sympathy she engaged at the beginning from the reader. She is clearly unhappy, and in her own way as much a victim of the past as Patrick, but his past is realized while hers is not, and this leaves her less believable. She is a very isolated figure at the end, having lost her "something for ever".

Her relationship with Keithy is even more destructive than her marriage. Her first reaction to Keithy, which he senses, is dislike, but it changes with time: "she was beginning quite genuinely to like him, to like his loneliness and self-sufficiency and the air of pathos which he quite unconsciously possessed" (64). Ironically it is that very self-sufficiency that is destroyed, first by Diana, and then by Diana and Patrick's marriage. The turning point comes when Keithy takes Diana to Malin, and tries to kiss her. She realizes that he is not just an overgrown twelve-year-old boy: "his face was intense and purposeful as any man's" (77), and she rejects him physically as she is later to reject Patrick. Keithy does not understand why his love is rejected. Nor does he understand why Diana later wants to marry Patrick and not him. Patrick, who is unaware of Keithy's abrupt maturation, expects his anger at the forthcoming marriage to pass: "I wouldn't expect him to be involved with us enough to care much what happened" (144). Diana, however, knows that this is no longer the case, that Keithy's noninvolvement has ended. When she tries to reassure him about the marriage, he responds with bitter accusation: "he'll take you away from me and you'll take him away from me . . . I won't have you or Patrick or anything and it'll be like that always" (139). Keithy is thus excluded, to begin with, from the marriage; but when the quarrels become more open, he is drawn into what has become a conflict. Without thinking of the effect it will have on him, Diana self-indulgently complains to Keithy about her marriage. Keithy takes her talk of going through fire literally, and he attempts the "ordeal" in which he dies trying to gain her love.

In the final scene Diana tells Keithy that she loves him "much more" than Patrick, but when he picks her up she screams, and when he puts her down so that he can run through the fire she thinks: "you too, even you, would destroy me for yourself" (238). It is Keithy who is destroyed, not Diana. And how he might have destroyed her is not made clear, since we do not see enough of her thoughts to know what it is that she fears. It may be the loss of the self in love, the loss of the identity she has struggled so hard to regain in a foreign country after the war – but we cannot be sure. The point of view moves away from Diana as the book progresses, and we see more of what Patrick and Keithy think, and less of what she thinks. In addition there is not much attempt by other characters, except the simple Keithy, to imagine her thoughts. Patrick, whose view of the marriage is the predominant one, is too busy nursing his wounded self-esteem to try to understand his wife. The result is that, as her role in the action becomes more important and she moves to the centre of the stage, her character becomes not less but more opaque. We do not see her private thoughts, her private anguish. The infrequent times when we see her talking or thinking frankly do not win her enough sympathy, and though she tries harder than Patrick to make the marriage work, she seems, finally, to have damaged whatever she has touched, and to be less forgivable because she is less understandable.

Patrick, by contrast, is first seen through the hostile eyes of Diana. He parades his illegitimacy and his limp, insisting that she know the worst of him from the beginning. She detects the bitterness and the self-ridicule behind the display, and when Kate Farnham apologizes for the "wrong impression of himself" (22) that he gives, Diana realizes that it is in fact a right impression, and deliberate. Koolabye, where he lives, and which he has inherited with Malin, is filled with family photographs and bric-à-brac, and the weight of the past is heavy: "They were all there. There was no one in the room who was not dead" (38). As the book progresses this past is elaborated, and it does much to explain his pride and quick temper, his isolation and sensitivity, his obsession with his family. The shifting of the point of view towards Patrick and away from Diana also helps to make him more sympathetic to the reader.

Why he wants to marry Diana, however, is far from clear. There is a sense in which, despite his bitterness, he is comfortable enough with his life, or at least resigned to it, before Diana arrives. She later accuses him of entirely selfish motives:

> "He would never give up anything for me. It was always his land and his child and his family and his land, and there was never room for me. He wanted his pleasure, and he wanted a son for his land and his family, and would never listen to me or understand me or care. He would not stop a minute to know what I was thinking. Everything was him and I was nothing." (228)

All Patrick himself says at the time of the proposal is: "I've got something for ever" (130), which seems to support Diana's accusation, but the reader cannot be sure. Diana is young and attractive. In her menial situation she is unlikely to get a comparable offer, and so is unlikely to refuse, and, as Nakala observes, she encourages Patrick. Perhaps he seeks an escape from the past in the hope for a future. Certainly their brief courtship consists of a cleaning out of the rooms at Koolabye devoted to ancestor worship. Patrick at first is hesitant about disturbing the family relics, which he shows to Diana with "a half-ironic, half-sentimental pride" (97), but after the first porcelain urn is accidentally broken, he sets about smashing them in earnest, with a sense of liberation.

His thraldom to the past is not, however, replaced by a new-found freedom, but by a marriage offering no sexual love, no son, and no family future. Having dreamed his dream, Patrick feels doubly cheated, and his bitterness towards Diana, while in a sense impatient and unfair, is understandable. And in any case the past cannot so easily be put aside. The conflict between the old and the new surfaces on the night of the storm, when Patrick is torn between staying with Diana, who is anxious for a reconciliation, and going out to see the fallen tree, which epitomizes the hold the past has on his imagination: "My great-grandfather planted that tree. It was as old as the house. I can't – imagine Koolabye without it; it's part of the place, almost. Why do things like that have to happen? . . . God, I hate time. You can't keep anything safe from it. Not the tree, not Malin, not Koolabye" (175-76). Diana takes a more pragmatic view: "It was old and rotting, it would have died. Nothing will last for ever" (175), and Patrick is driven for sympathy to Nakala, who shares his view: "I want to keep everything the same for ever . . . I couldn't bear a change at Strathmore. Sometimes I look at those hills and thank God that no one can do anything to them" (181). A child might have enabled Patrick to reconcile his past and his marriage, but there is to be no child. By the end of the book Patrick has lost both Diana and Keithy, but still has the past to live in, and we can imagine him turning back to it, like other long-term prisoners, with resignation and even some relief.

Keithy is the book's ultimate victim, imprisoned, not by the past, but by his limited mind, and by the false expectations other people have of him. He has not been gelded, like Benjy Compson, but he is treated as if he were still twelve years old, physically as well as mentally, and the effect is not dissimilar. Like Benjy, what he wants is love, not sex; but even Diana, who is afraid of sex, does not see the difference, and recoils in fear from his expressions of affection. Keithy is isolated by the other characters. Whether they baby him, like his mother, prescribe for him, like Mrs Charles, dislike him, like Nakala, or patronize him, like Patrick, they all treat him as less than human, and the cruelty is real, if often unintentional. Until the arrival of Diana, however, he is comparatively self-sufficient. His mother, who is anxious about her trip back home to England, wants Keithy and Diana to get on: "She does love you, Keithy", she says, when he confesses their mutual dislike, " 'And you must love her. You will, won't you?' 'Okay,' he said serenely" (30); and he does what he is told. Diana is also instructed: " 'There's one thing about Keithy – he will probably become rather fond of you when you've been here awhile; he always does. I hope you'll let him.' 'I shall not care,' Diana said coolly" (46). In the event Keithy does love Diana, and she does not care, or not at least until the damage has been done, and Keithy's frail self-sufficiency is gone.

Like Rob at the end of *The Merry-go-Round in the Sea*, Keithy is overtaken by feelings that break in upon the simpler affections of childhood, and that he neither wants nor understands:

> There were other things that he loved – his animals, his parents, Patrick – but that was a feeling that was somehow different. The girl made him possessive and angry. She had made him hurt her by rejecting him and running away, and he could not understand how that had happened. There was no other thing that he loved in the world that he could have brought himself to hurt. (80)

Stow is remarkably successful with Keithy, as this passage indicates. He portrays his simplicity as an emotional directness unmediated by adult thought, as an isolation from much of the business of adult living, and as a haunting alienation from other people. Keithy dislikes being treated as a less-than-human object, and when Mrs Charles discusses him clinically with his mother, he asks bitterly: "Had your sixpenceworth?" (90). When the Robson boys take him to town at Mrs Charles's insistence he remains separate and resentful, wandering down to the beach alone while they play billiards, and roughly pushing off Betsy, the girl who tries to arouse him. In his own world Keithy is accepted – outside it he is a freak. It is hardly surprising that he wants to stay in it, to remain accepted and safe, and that he resists the events that force him outside it.

Diana, who comes from outside, initiates the break-up of Keithy's world. Her decision to stay at Lingarin allows his parents to leave on their trip. She arouses in Keithy for the first time an adult desire that she is unwilling to reciprocate. And her relationship with Patrick excludes Keithy from an old, longstanding friendship. When the three go to town together Patrick and Diana leave Keithy to watch the second film by himself, while they go off courting. He does not understand the "emotional tangles" of the film (130), but he understands the feelings of the lovers: "He climbed in beside Diana and did not speak, and when they did not try to draw him out he knew for certain that they no longer cared about him" (131). Their marriage uproots Keithy from Lingarin:

> He was lost at Koolabye. He wandered from place to place like a cat in a strange house. He tried to talk to Fred, and found Fred sullen and still resentful of Diana. He tried to talk to Patrick and found that Patrick seemed uninterested in him. And yet, whenever he tried to get near Diana, Patrick was always there, proposing something new that he and Keithy could do together, leaving Diana outside . . . Neither Diana nor Patrick guessed that he was more unhappy there than he had ever been in his life. (166)

When Patrick and Diana quarrel, Keithy is unfairly drawn into the conflict, and while he does not understand its subtleties, he certainly grasps the essential emotions. Feeling unwanted at Koolabye, he goes back home to Lingarin, and refuses to live anywhere else. Even there Fred kills his carpet snake, and Patrick shoots his dog Mac, after Keithy has accidentally run over him. Finally Diana tells him that she wants to leave Patrick and go away, and Keithy's world is all in pieces. His "ordeal", his attempt to keep Diana, only results in his death.

The abruptness of the ending of *The Bystander* suggests some uncertainty on the author's part about what to do with his characters, and how to direct the reader's sympathy. Stow commonly ends his books in an unresolved manner, avoiding neat conclusions, but *The Bystander* goes beyond this – its story peters out, like the Maguire dynasty, in bitterness and sterility. The difficulty with the characters is that Stow has found the people he wants to write about, but not the method best suited to exploring them. Keithy is a typical Stow protagonist in his loneliness and alienation, and Patrick and Diana also belong in this category. The most interesting thing about such solitary people is, however, their inner lives, as the creator of Robinson Crusoe remarked: "Our Meditations are all Solitude in Perfection; our Passions are all exercised in Retirement; we love, we hate, we covet, we enjoy, all in Privacy and Solitude".[18] But in *The Bystander*, as in *A Haunted Land,* Stow does not give us much of the private lives of his characters, choosing instead to present them largely through dialogue and interpersonal relationships. The result, as G.A. Wilkes has observed, is something of a vacuum where the central interest should be.[19] Stow wants to write about silence. But people do not talk about silence, and the novelist has to find a way to present the inner life. Stow is further hindered by his attraction to a very different kind of writing, the depersonalized, cinematic manner of Robbe-Grillet, which strives to record precisely what the senses observe, while leaving the reader free to speculate about feelings, thoughts and motives. The reticence this induces has kept Stow from making the inner life his entire subject, as Woolf did in *The Waves* and as Joyce did with Molly Bloom. The compromise he reaches in his mature work − a typical attempt to reconcile opposites − is to use the observed world as an objective correlative for the inner life. The landscape, described with "fanatical" realism, [20] is used to suggest the mind of the viewing character in all its privacy. In his first two novels, however, Stow is only beginning to reach towards this eventual, very personal style. While he already writes with great power and evocativeness, he has not yet matched his method to his subject, and the more conventional methods he employs do less than justice to the intensity of his vision.

3   Lost Man's Country

To the Islands

Time strips the soul and leaves it comfortless
and sends it thirsty through a bone-white drought.
                              "The Harp and the King", Judith Wright

In my end is my beginning.
                                        "East Coker", T.S. Eliot

With *To the Islands* (1958) Stow took a major step towards
maturity as a writer. The dust jacket of the revised edition (1981)
calls it a "classic Australian novel", and for once this is no more
than the truth, the passage of twenty years having tested and
endorsed that status beyond current questioning. Where the
earlier novels had been "absolute for death", *To the Islands* sets
this pessimism against a more hopeful view of human destiny,
and Stow is able to explore the ongoing struggles between hope
and despair, love and hate, and life and death that dominate his
later fiction. Earlier characters like Patrick Maguire and Keithy
Farnham, who try to escape from their tortured worlds, are
destroyed by stronger opponents so possessed by spectres from
the past that they deny life in the present to themselves and
those about them. Heriot is also haunted – by the ghosts of his
family and the victims of Onmalmeri – but he is not destroyed
by them. After hurling the stone at Rex he leaves the mission
with the apparent intention of suicide, but finds himself instead
on a journey of self-discovery. And by the time he faces death at
the end of the book he has experienced peace, love, and reconciliation, as well as terror, despair, and self-disgust. His conflict
is not with the others who would kill him but with himself, and
he ultimately comes to realize the strangeness of the soul he has
never faced. *A Haunted Land* and *The Bystander* generate tragic
emotions at times, but are too negative, too monochromatic to
sustain them. *To the Islands*, however, moves inevitably to a
climax of tragic intensity. Stow has given Heriot positive human
potential for growth and self-understanding, and from the
conflict between that potential and the despairing bitterness of

the earlier novels, which is still powerful in *To the Islands*, he creates and sustains tragedy.

The quality of Stow's achievement in this book was quickly recognized. *To the Islands* won a number of prizes when it was first published, including the second Miles Franklin Award (1958) – the first having gone to Patrick White's *Voss* in 1957.[1] These first two winners of Australia's most prestigious fiction prize are linked in a number of interesting ways. Perhaps as a result of an influential essay by Vincent Buckley, which describ-ed Stow as working in the shadow of White, the impression grew up that *To the Islands* had been influenced by *Voss*.[2] This was not the case, as Stow is understandably anxious to point out in the preface to the revised edition, his manuscript having been delivered to the publishers before *Voss* appeared in Australia. It is, however, a good deal more significant that two such books should have appeared independently of one another at about the same time, than it would have been if one of them had influenc-ed the other. The time to begin the exploration of the unprofess-ed religious factor in Australian life had clearly arrived, and a journey through the inner and outer landscape seemed to be the way towards the truth.[3] Stow disliked "the tyranny, in Australia, of social realism",[4] while White "was determined to prove that the Australian novel is not necessarily the dreary, dun-coloured offspring of journalistic realism". Both writers sought "the mystery and the poetry" that lay behind the lives of ordinary men and women.[5] Believing that a key to the Australian soul lay in the Australian landscape, they took their protagonists away from the European huddle on the fringes of the continent to seek its meaning, and their own, in the empty desolation and silence of the interior. And if Stow was later to poke some light-hearted fun at *Voss* and the "Cosmic Symbolical Desert" in *Midnite*, it was the rueful humour of one who had been there in his time.[6]

The two books signalled a crucial move in Australian fiction away from social realism towards the more experimental and internalized fiction of major twentieth-century novelists like Faulkner, Woolf and Joyce.[7] The dominance of social realism in Australia had obscured for a time the real direction that modern fiction had taken, and one has only to read the reviews of *To the Islands* and *Tourmaline* to be reminded how staunch an orthodoxy was maintained, and how little deviations from it were tolerated by the sterner "realist" critics.[8] Anticipating his reviewers' problem, Stow began his note to the first edition by declaring that "this is not, by intention, a realistic novel". In the very different critical climate of the 1980s, Stow has modified this bald statement which, he says, "has been misinterpreted as a sort of manifesto". "In the 1950s", he continues, "novelists . . . were supposed to concern themselves with Statistically Average Man, and he did not interest me. But in other respects I aimed, as I always have, at the most precise description I could achieve of things I had experienced with my own senses. Except in the choice of subject-matter, I have always been a fanatical realist."[9]

It comes as no surprise to learn that Stow sees himself as a realist. His marvellously vivid account of the Forrest River country is immediately and persuasively authentic. And relations between the races at the mission are acutely observed and sensitively recorded. Stow combines the detachment of an anthropologist with a novelist's imaginative sympathy, and the result is an impressively clear-eyed depiction of the limited but real success of the mission in offering an alternative to the massacres of the old days, and to the squalid life of "drink, prostitution, violence and gaol" in contemporary Wyndham (viii). J.J. Healy praises the "stark visibility of fundamental moral questions implicit in a situation of race" in *To the Islands*,[10] but not all of Stow's early critics would agree, and a good deal of ink was spilt asserting the primacy of the "realistic" novel, and deploring his attempts to combine such "realism" with mystery and poetry. Young as he was he was wise enough to ignore such advice, sharing what Dostoevsky described as "an understanding of reality and realism entirely different from that of our realists and critics . . . what the majority call almost fantastic and exceptional sometimes signifies for me the very essence of reality".[11] Dostoevsky enjoyed pointing to newspaper accounts of a Raskolnikov-like murder, and Stow no doubt enjoyed telling John Hetherington that the monstrous Tommy Cross was the only character in *A Haunted Land* who was not fictitious.[12] But if the critics were a little slow to recognize the arrival in Australia of the modern novel, they did sense the importance of Stow's third novel. At the age of twenty-three he had ceased to be a promising beginner, and had in fact written a novel that could stand comparison with *Voss*, the most important Australian novel since *The Fortunes of Richard Mahony* (1930).

An increase in technical skill is evident from the beginning of *To the Islands*.[13] Stow narrows his focus to a single character in place of the trio of *The Bystander* and the family of *A Haunted Land*,

and he moves a good deal further into the private, inner life of that character. *To the Islands* opens with Heriot in the foreground, and the emphasis remains squarely on him throughout – he does not fade, like Diana Ravirs, nor turn out to be quite minor, like Jessie Scott. The book is better constructed and more deliberate than the earlier novels, the pace is brisker, the detail more selective, and the "carefully angled"[14] episodes are cinematically juxtaposed. Characters discuss one another and the landscape, and there is less authorial narration, except when it is necessary to give an inside view of the characters. At the same time it is clear that Stow's central interest is in Heriot's internal conflicts, and that, being internal, these can be dramatized only partly. The mission has been Heriot's life, and Stow portrays one in describing the other, making, in characteristic fashion, the external surroundings an image of the inner landscape.[15] As a result Heriot is more complex than any of Stow's previous characters and more successful. We see more of his inner life yet he also remains an enigma, to himself and to the reader. Believable and yet strange, he commands our attention and our sympathy throughout.

In the preface to the revised edition, Stow reflects on the ambitiousness of his portrayal of Heriot: "Nowadays I should hardly dare to tackle such a *King Lear*-like theme; but I do not regret having raised the large questions asked here, and so wisely left unanswered" (vii). Not all of Stow's critics, however, have been able to command a comparable negative capability. Leonie Kramer, for example, suggests that the last line of the book, "my soul is a strange country", should be at the beginning, not the end.[16] The end of *To the Islands* is, however, a beginning for Heriot, as well as an ending, a beginning of self-acceptance, a surrendering of will, and a freedom at last from hope and fear. Not even death is a resolution for Stow, as *Visitants* also makes clear: his protagonists are not granted the kind of final illumination that comes to so many of Patrick White's spiritual adventurers shortly before they die. Heriot does not even die at the end of his book, but reaches instead a point of bewildered self-illumination as he nears death.

Heriot was the undoubted success of the first version of the novel, and his part of it needed little reworking. Stow was less satisfied with other aspects of the book, however, and in his revision sought to detach it from its origins as "propaganda on behalf of Christian mission-stations for Aborigines". He therefore omitted "a good deal of talk by the white characters about their difficulties and hopes, and even a very tepid love-interest, introduced not for its own sake but to suggest that at least two Europeans would remain committed to the Mission" (vii). Terry Dixon and Sister Helen Bond remain in the story, and they still decide to marry, but the longish scene between them at the end of chapter nine, and a related scene between Helen and Bob Gunn in chapter seven, have been omitted. Earlier discussion of the mission has been reduced, and the scene between Helen and Bob in chapter one has been rewritten a good deal more tightly.

A number of youthfully luxuriant images have been pruned. Some, like "a shining bird, stout as an abbot of Boccaccio's", or morning standing at Heriot's bed "like a valet", probably deserved to go; while others, like "the failed faith, so long a swag on his back to be humped by night over the hard countries of his privacy", might have been retained.[17] Almost all the quotations from European poetry which clutter Heriot's thoughts are retained, though they upset many of the book's first critics, who thought that Stow was showing off his own learning, not characterizing Heriot. Stow has added a brief section on the first page, "on the shelves of the rough bookcase Heriot's learning was mouldering away, in Oxford Books of this and that, and old-fashioned dictionaries";[18] but he has wisely resisted omitting the fragments which Heriot — a European consciousness adrift in the alien landscape of the Kimberleys — has shored against the ruins of his identity, and which are an integral part of his self-awareness.

Revision is always a tricky business, particularly after a period of twenty years when, as Stow says, the younger author "no longer seems to be myself" (vii). There will be readers who prefer the earlier version, accepting its youthful flourishes as part of the consciousness which created the book. I prefer the revised edition, which is a little tighter, a little plainer, more focused on Heriot, but not essentially altered. And the new epigraph — a passage written by a brother of Stow's great-grandfather who explored "the islands" — is hauntingly suggestive in the best Stow manner, and a real addition to the resonance of the story and its title:

Still islands, islands, islands. After leaving Cape Bougainville we passed at least 500, of every shape, size, and appearance. . . . Infinitely varied as these islands are — wild and picturesque, grand sometimes almost to sublimity — there is about them all an air of dreariness and gloom. No sign of life appears on their surface; scarce-

ly even a sea bird hovers on their shores. They seem abandoned by
Nature to complete and everlasting desolation.

Jefferson Stow: *Voyage of the Forlorn Hope*, 1865

If there is a still point in the human story which is set against
such a wild, unpeopled landscape it is Justin's account of the
Onmalmeri massacre. This is presented in the book in the same
words that Daniel Evans used when he told Stow of the Umbali
massacre of 1926.[19] The sorry history of race relations in
Australia is littered with such horrifying stories, and in transferring an actual account of one into a fictional setting Stow engages
powerfully the guilts that haunt the descendants of those responsible for such outrages. The mission, like Heriot's life, is a
gesture of reparation. It is uncertainly motivated, grudgingly
funded, and mostly ignored; but imperfect as it is, it is clearly
superior to any existing alternatives, and that is why Stow was
making propaganda on its behalf in the first edition of the book.
The mission is, however, still pervaded by racial tension, and the
conflict of wills between Heriot and Rex is in many ways a re-
enactment of Onmalmeri. Heriot is enraged because Rex will not
leave the mission – *his* mission – as Mr George is enraged
because the old Aborigine will not leave *his* cattle run. Heriot
regards Rex as a worthless native and troublemaker, again like
Mr George, and his rage provokes Rex into throwing the stone,
which in turn provokes Heriot's overreaction of "killing" Rex. At
this point the stories part, however, because Heriot has been
obsessed by Onmalmeri, and he believes that he has repeated
the very crime he has spent most of his lifetime trying to expiate.
He has indeed pulled down about him the world he has tried to
create, and suicide seems the only choice left.

When Heriot disappears, the people at the mission, who know
so little of him that they do not know his first, "Christian" name,
assume that he will have gone to Onmalmeri – where he has
said he would like to be buried – and they send the first search
party there to look for him. When Terry Dixon arrives, he finds a
haunting landscape:

> At the edge of the cliff, on an overhang above the water the country
> filled his eyes, beauty struck at him, and in a strange stillness of mind
> he recognized it. He looked at a land of rock, a broad valley between
> cliffs and hills, even the floor of it studded with broken stone. But the
> pools were bright blue under the sky, and the endless hills blue also.
> In some places the water was almost obliterated by lily-leaves and

grass, in others fringed with dense trees and pandanus. Below him, many miles down, he thought, lay the Onmalmeri pool, shrunken by distance, dark, dark green among its thickets of wattle and pandanus, its creeper-choked gums. He picked up a stone and threw it far out, and it swerved and landed with an echoing clatter in the clump of pandanus at the cliff foot. A cry of birds broke out.

On the far bank, beside the smoke of his fire, a tiny man, Gregory, looked across at the noise. The toy horses started and stared.

What am I thinking? Dixon asked himself. But it'd be easy to give up here, to get out on an overhang and drop into the water. That'd be a death to die, you could easily do that, with the water just about calling you on. Wonder if those little crocs would eat a dead man, they don't touch live ones. (59)

Dixon is mesmerized by the landscape: massive, empty, unpeopled, overwhelming. It seems to invite him, the most unlikely of suicides, to an easeful death. Earlier it had reminded him of his alienation:

Walking behind the native he felt, suddenly, regret at his own awkwardness, for Stephen moved over the rocks with the sureness of a bird, but he stumbled and slipped, having always to plan his next step, to tread carefully. He saw himself for the first time as a stranger, cast without preparation into a landscape of prehistory, foreign to the earth. Only the brown man belonged in this wild and towering world. (58)

The white man Dixon is an alien in his adopted land, to which he does not belong, and in which he has not yet learned to live like a native, without a complex life-support system. He recognizes the beauty of the country, and regrets that he is not more at ease within it. The brown man Stephen has been forcibly dispossessed of his land, and made an alien in it. His alienation expresses itself in despair, or in Rex's angry refusal to cooperate with the rules and schemes of Heriot. The white man's alienation expresses itself in violence towards the land, the natives, and himself. Even the mission, which has sought to redress racial violence, has been a violent place, "spreading civilization with a stock-whip" (4). And the landscape itself, while not responsible for the crimes of the people who inhabit it, is seen by Stow as an image of their tormented minds, and as violent in its own right. In the confrontation between Heriot and Rex, for example, it might well have been the cyclone which wounded Rex, and it certainly exacerbated Heriot's already raw and overstrained nerves. Onmalmeri, by contrast, seems eerily quiet and peaceful, except for the bird: "There was a bird which he had never seen but which he hated savagely, it was there now in the trees or hidden in the pandanus, making its sound like a baby's crying and answering itself with a madwoman's laugh" (57). But this place also invites self-violence, and if Heriot had gone there it would have been to end his journey.

Onmalmeri draws into focus the dominant themes of *To the Islands*: the relationship between the indigenous blacks and the immigrant whites; the relationship between the Europeans and the alien land they have settled, but not come to terms with; and the relationship of Heriot with himself, with the conflicting and contradictory forces which drive him. These three concerns are worked out in terms of one another, and Heriot unites the three, beginning as an alienated European, driven by guilt for a violence which he cannot exorcise even from himself, and ending, like Cawdor, "a black man true",[20] having achieved at least a temporary reconciliation with himself, with Rex, and with the country.

When we first meet Heriot he is old and tired, a prisoner in the cell he has constructed for himself over the years:

> He smiled at himself in the mirror. But it was wrong, the muscles of his face were stiff, and the twist of his mouth was no smile. How long, thought Heriot, covering his mistake with lather, it must be since I have laughed.
>
> And the mirror was broken, the wooden shutter of the window broken. Broken, broken. He saw himself as a great red cliff, rising from the rocks of his own ruin. I am an old man, an old man. *J'ai plus de souvenirs que si j'avais mille ans.* And this cursed Baudelaire whining in his head like a mosquito, preaching despair. How does a man grow old who has made no investment in the future, without wife or child, without refuge for his heart beyond the work that becomes too much for him? (2)

Some of his staff at the mission think he is going troppo; but he is faced with the dilemma of wanting to resign from a life's work which has given meaning to his existence, and having, again like Cawdor, nowhere to go, no family to live with – the mission has taken his family – no retirement he can imagine. Like Lear, he cannot step out of his role and survive, but the role has become oppressive, and he longs for release from it. "Home? What is home?" (10) he asks, when told that Bob Gunn wants to go home at the end of his year at the mission. Heriot is trapped: he cannot bear to stay, and yet he cannot leave.

As the pressure within him builds, the conflicts he has suppressed begin to surface. His conversations with his staff are an awkward mixture of frankness and withdrawal, which they find disconcerting. He wants both to confess and to conceal his frustration and despair. Helen, who has been treating his insomnia, is made to feel "bumptious" when she loyally takes his side against the "smug little bunch of clerics and do-gooders by proxy" (9) who have failed to find a replacement for him. And Father Way is surprised to have a serious discussion with Heriot about the future of the mission and the Aborigines:

> Never before in their uneasy, sometimes angry association had they been so much at peace with one another as at that moment in the shadow of the baobabs, watching the man's slow movements on the roof, listening to the slower ring of hammers echoing from beneath it. In Heriot's eyes Way had suddenly grown, had become a figure of hope and of foresight, fit, if he should propose himself, to take over the torch, the helm, whatever rhetorical term you liked to apply to it, of the small world so long of Heriot's governing. And Way, for his part, discovered without warning such springs of warmth and depths of seriousness in Heriot that he was left silent for a time with the awe of revelation. (32)

Having thus shared his mind with Way, however, Heriot abruptly retreats into a frigid politeness, and when he finds that Rex is not working, he flies into a rage, accusing Way of ignoring his orders. Way is left regretting "that the veteran chief of a moment ago should have shrunk so catastrophically into a petulant child" (33). Such wild swings of mood and emotion testify to Heriot's instability, and his crumbling self-control.

The return of Rex with Stephen triggers the series of outbursts that lead to Heriot's explosion of hatred in the cyclone. He believes that Rex is responsible for the death of Esther, the beloved foster daughter he adopted as a replacement for his dead wife. Rex denies responsibility for Esther's death, and it seems likely that at least some of Heriot's feeling is inspired by jealousy of the man who stole away his child. He makes no secret of his feelings when he finds Rex back at the mission:

> "I wish to God," said Heriot, "Stephen had killed you."
> The tall man, who had been standing partly stooped, hoping to placate Heriot a little with this attempt at humility, straightened and looked at him uneasily.
> "I know," Heriot said softly, "that sounds strange from me. But I'm very bitter, I'm very bitter, Rex. And I'd see a thousand of you dead if it could bring back Esther." (15)

If these are hardly the words of a Christian missionary, they do express Heriot's deep and bitter resentment at what he feels the mission has done to him as a private man — taken his wife and child, and Esther, and left only the disappointment of Stephen and the troublemaking of Rex.

Heriot orders Rex to work, threatening a whipping if he disobeys, but the threat is empty, and displays only Heriot's impotence, his inability to impose his will:

> Twenty years ago, or even fifteen, this threat from Brother Heriot might have been dangerous; but the old man was weak now and had changed, or perhaps all white men had changed, at all events the whip was gone, and the old man's almost unheard-of weapons of ex-pulsion and wage-stoppage were powerless against Rex. They watched him, their clever black kinsman, climb with leisurely in-solence towards them, and struggled with a mounting laugh. (33)

Heriot's feelings about Rex, like his feelings about Way, swing wildly: he resists the appeal of his counsellors that Rex be allowed to stay, yet when he next talks to him it is quietly, with no assumption of authority: "I'm not boss of this mission any more. I'm not ordering you" (44). There is even some fellow feeling when they meet in the oncoming cyclone, and when Rex insists that he will stay, Heriot says only: "We'll speak about it again . . . later, Rex, when it's calm" (44). But when he feels the stone strike his leg, all his murderous hate rises within him, and the conflicting forces which have motivated his life rush into his mind: "But he would be no martyr, not submit to these flailings, as if owning himself wrong, he would strike back, godlike" (45). In thus responding, Ahab-like, he re-enacts Onmalmeri, as we have seen, and so cancels out, in a moment of rage, the "expiation" of his years at the mission, which he had used in self-pitying justification for his refusal to let Rex stay:

> "Yes, my wife, you remember her. Sister Margaret. She had beautiful hands. You remember her hands, don't you, tying up your sores and bathing your eyes and playing with you when you were children. You haven't forgotten that. And when you were young men, you remember her getting thinner and thinner and not smiling much and going to bed and dying . . . while I sat there beside her . . . trying to believe I couldn't have saved her by taking her away from this country . . . I've given half my life," he said softly. "My wife gave all of hers. I've lived in poverty, half-starved at times, been lonely, been overworked, been forgotten by everyone in the world except you." (38–39)

While Heriot immediately repents this outburst to his

counsellors, recognizing that he is boasting of his sacrifices to "bludgeon them for their gratitude" (39), he indicates the resentment that has been festering within him, and that Rex's return brings to the surface. It is only when he finally expresses his resentment that he begins to understand his feelings, and the extent of his alienation. He has told himself he was motivated by charity, but, swinging to the other extreme, he now believes that it was only a self-indulgent desire to be rid of guilt. In his self-castigation he believes that he has continued to use the methods of the perpetrators of the massacre – spreading civilization with a stockwhip. His unthinking violence in "killing" Rex makes him feel that his charity has been a fraud, and that his years at the mission have been wasted.

It is not only charity that he finds himself alienated from, but faith as well: "I believe in nothing" (42), he says in his quarrel with Way, "for years I set myself up as a philanthropist and was really a misanthrope all the time. Ironic" (41). And he is very humanly nasty to the unwilling recipient of these painful admissions:

> "Does it sometimes occur to you that I'm a lonely old man who needs someone to discuss his problems with him?"
> "Yes, it does."
> Heriot ground out his cigarette. "It's like your smug impudence," he said viciously. "I need no one." (41)

There is no longer affection for the mission, either. Heriot would like to destroy it along with himself, and when Way points out reasonably that "it's not yours to smash", Heriot replies with bitterly acute self-assessment:

> "I'm the only one of the builders left. All the others are dead. They had my ideas, they made my mistakes, they used the whip sometimes, they were Bible-bashers and humourless clods, they were forgotten while they were alive and attacked when they were dead. You don't like the work we did – very well, we'll take it back." (42)

In thus admitting that he does not like what he has been, and what he has done, Heriot takes his first major step towards liberating himself from the self-imposed hypocrisy and pretence of his public role, which over the years has become a substitute for whatever inner life he once had. He now believes that he has not really been a builder at all. The mission he wants to tear down, and the self he wants to destroy – they are images of one another for him – are the constructs of bitterness and self-distortion, and they need to be destroyed, or at least sloughed off, if he is to explore and learn to live with his estranged soul.

When he believes he has killed Rex he has a number of choices open to him. He may wait for justice to take its course, or he may anticipate it and kill himself, or he may leave the mission and wait for some resolution to emerge from the turmoil. The first is too passive a course for Heriot, and he lacks the singleness of mind to carry out the second — though he is tempted by it. He therefore opts for the third, indeterminate course of action. Whatever happens later, he does not set off into the desert, like Voss, in a premeditated search for self-understanding. If he is not exactly troppo before he leaves, he has certainly lost his sense of direction, and the events that occur, while they have origins in his long-nurtured discontents, rapidly acquire a momentum of their own. He takes only a rifle and a box of cartridges with him, and it is not clear whether these are for self-defence — he later tells Rusty "they'll send a revenge party after me . . . That is always done" (89) — or for suicide, a motive he admits to Justin. Heriot is acting impulsively, with mixed, conflicting motives. He has told Way during their last quarrel that he knows, in Aboriginal manner, that his time for dying has come. And the islands of the dead of Aboriginal legend are clearly in his mind, since he speaks of them in his tactless conversation with Galumbu early in the book, and again in his meeting with Justin as he is leaving. But he does not have a clear plan of action. The point is worth emphasizing because critics have tended to stress the pattern of Heriot's journey and to disregard its randomness and fortuitousness. If it is a parable of sorts,[21] it is also a very convincing study of a man near the end of his tether, stumbling from one purpose to another, uncertain of what is happening to him, of where he is going or why.

Justin provides the stabilizing force that gives some direction, and some chance of success, to Heriot's initially almost aimless quest. The two complement one another admirably, black and white, native and alien, tranquil and febrile, quiet and talkative, adept at survival and helplessly self-absorbed. Shortly before they attempt to swim their horses across the flooded river, Heriot praises Justin in a style which embarrasses him:

> "I'm afraid I've never made the best use of you. But I do know your value, I do know that."
> Justin scowled. "Brother — "
> "Yes?"
> "I don't want to talk so much. I too hungry for talking."

> "I'm sorry," said Heriot humbly.
> "White man always talking and never listening."
> "That's true," Heriot admitted. "Very true."
> "Whatever you say to white man, he always got something else to say. Always got to be the last one."
> "We call it conversation," Heriot said, and bit his lip as soon as the words were out. (97)

Not even goodwill saves Heriot here. He tries to agree with Justin, but in the end behaves exactly like a white man, winning a pyrrhic victory of articulateness over his taciturn companion. It is a splendid cameo of their relationship, and indeed of black-white relations in Stow's work as a whole.

If some things stay the same between Heriot and Justin, others certainly change. When Justin first joins him, for example, Heriot protests his isolation and independence: "There's nothing you can do, I don't want you or need you. Or your food or blankets. I need nothing at all" (47). Then abruptly, in one of his series of insights, he realizes that he does need Justin: "'Welcome, my Good Deeds,' whispered Heriot. 'Now I hear thy voice, I weep for very sweetness of love'" (47). Like the returned explorer of "The Land's Meaning", Heriot finds, at the end of his years of aloneness, that he needs to share love. This is possible, however, only between equals, and in winning the struggle for the rifle Justin overcomes Heriot's white superiority – a major barrier between them. Soon after Heriot announces that he is "No more white man. I'm a blackfellow, son of the sun" (68), and they travel on in something like equality, Justin at home in the country, Heriot searching inside himself for peace and reconciliation.

As their journey continues, Stow alternates descriptions of it with scenes from the mission and from the search parties. He does not use separate chapters for the different locations, as White does in *Voss*, nor does he run them together like Robbe-Grillet or Claude Simon. Instead he cuts from one scene to another in cinematic manner, usually using a larger than normal paragraph break to signal the transition.[22] The most striking example follows the organizing of the second search party at the mission:

> There was Rex, lying awake on a dark veranda, crying in his mind: "Ah, brother, where you now, eh? Where you now?"
> And there was Heriot, asleep below his rock. "Oh no, no, I couldn't take a life. An old, weak man like me? And such a strong young life, Rex's."

And between them plain and hill, rock and grass and tree, mildly shining in the warm dark.

"I did wrong, the worst wrong a man can do. Who could have foreseen this, who could have thought this of *me*?"

"And might be I done wrong. Might be that girl dead 'cause of me. Ah, brother. Might be I ought to be dead."

At Onmalmeri a dingo slunk out of shadow, hungry, scanning the valley with eye and ear and nostril for a hint of prey. And if it should kill, or, more conveniently, if it should come upon the putrid victim of a rival and steal it, what morality was infringed? How should that impede an easy sleep among the warm rocks?

"Ah, brother — They hating me now — "

"Oh, Rex, Rex, Rex. You will never go out of my mind." (83)

The transitions here are not signalled in the usual manner because the author is bringing the two characters together in a kind of communication that is not quite the telepathic link of Voss and Laura, or Rick and Rob, but that indicates the love that is the obverse of the hate between them. The addition of the dingo at Onmalmeri echoes Heriot's preoccupation with the "preying" which he finds so distressing a part of life, but which, as Crispin Clare is later to recognize, is "the way of the green god".[23] The rapid alternation draws the three locales together, and emphasizes the real, if fragile links between the human characters.

The alternation of different strands of the story works best when, as in the above example, the thematic connection between them is clear. Chapter six juxtaposes three strands of the story — Heriot and Justin, Dixon in town, and Rex and Helen at the mission — with mixed success. Awaking in the bush to the "harsh outcry of crows" (68), Heriot feels his alienation: " 'Why is the earth so hungry?' Heriot protested weakly. 'Where is God?' " (69). We then switch to Dixon lonely in town and feeling that his work at the mission has separated him from his former friends: "He was foreign everywhere, and disliked it, being a friendly man and anxious to be in no way different from the rest of the human race" (70). The mission Aborigines also feel foreign in town, though they are clearly more tempted by its squalid pastimes. In the third scene Helen carries out her intention of telling the convalescing Rex that his wound was inflicted by Heriot. As she had guessed, Rex does not remember the incident, and might have been told the official version, that he had been struck by a piece of iron in the cyclone. But she is determined to tell him the truth, so that a reconciliation with Heriot can at least be attempted, as she explains to Dixon and Gunn:

"I don't believe in heaven and hell, but I believe in sin, and sins that aren't wiped out on the earth stay on the earth forever echoing and echoing among the people left behind. We're trying to wipe out the sin of the white men who massacred these people's relations, but we can't ever quite do it, because we're not the same white men. And Mr Heriot has to come back, he's the only one who can wipe out his hatred of Rex. They'll come to see that as hating and rejecting all of them . . . we have this chance to bring them back and reconcile them. That's heaven. But if we fail, their hate will go on spreading and growing forever, and that's hell." (53)

While these three scenes are certainly diverse, the quoted passage articulates the themes of alienation and reconciliation that link them together and that underlie the entire book. Later in the chapter the scene switches back to Dixon, discussing his mission job with a Queenslander in a pub. The transition here is less successful, because the Dixon scene is positioned in the middle of Justin and Heriot's encounter with Alunggu and his people – one of the bleakest scenes in the book – and it seems trivial by comparison, despite the authenticity of its dialogue. Had it been added to the previous town scene it would have suffered less by contrast, and would not have interrupted one of the book's most powerful moments.

The positioning of the final reconciliation, however, is precisely right. As the book draws towards its close, the focus is more and more on Heriot, who cannot complete his journey until he is reconciled with Rex. In the penultimate scene of the book Heriot's presents, his knife, watch and rifle, are given by Justin and accepted by Rex:

"Hard to believe it's over," Gunn said. "Hard to believe. Nothing will be the same again."

High on the hill, overlooking the reconciliation of Heriot, his foster-father, Stephen bent his head. "No," he said quietly. "Nothing going to be the same," he promised. (124)

The way is then clear for the final stage of Heriot's journey, in which he confronts the ocean, and searches for his islands within the setting sun.

The earlier meeting with Alunggu brings into focus white attempts to distribute Christian charity to the Aborigines, who take it but are not always grateful to receive it. Alunggu, who used to be at the mission, has chosen to go back to the bush, and his people "don't like white man" (74). Justin shoots a kangaroo for them, however, while Heriot feeds one of their precious tins of meat to an old, blind woman. In a later conclusion to this powerful scene, Heriot sings — over the voices of the Aborigines — three stanzas of "A Lyke-wake Dirge":

> If ever thou gavest hosen and shoon,
>> Every night and all,
> Sit thee down and put them on:
>> And Christ receive thy soul.
>> (77)

Before he falls asleep for the night he reassures himself: "I've given hosen and shoon . . . Haven't I? And meat and drink. And a wife. And many years of my life . . . I will pass" (77). While Heriot's hope that his charity may have earned him salvation is an advance on his earlier despair, it still suggests doing the right thing for the wrong reason. When he wakes, he finds that the Aborigines have taken advantage of his generosity by stealing his tucker-bag. He has thus — albeit unwillingly — given them everything, yet without true charity.

Sam, whom Heriot meets later on his journey, says of his mission: "Nothing but trouble we ever had with them natives. Didn't like the whitefellow, see, weren't going to take nothing from him — excepting clothes and tucker and tobacco and the like of that, of course. Take any amount of that" (111). By this time Heriot is tolerant, not resentful like Sam, recognizing the predicament of an indigenous, "primitive" people, who learn to live off the white man as they live off the land, and who covet the "somethings", the cargo of white society, but not its ideas, values and customs. Unless they adopt the latter, they cannot produce these goods for themselves, and must therefore either abandon their culture and assimilate, or else accept handouts. And while giving charity may be good for the soul of the giver, it robs the recipient of dignity and self-respect, reducing him to client status. Alunggu prefers to go back to the bush.

On the first night that he spends at Alunggu's camp, Heriot dreams of being pursued across the plains by a surf of light. He is guilty: "My hands . . . My quick, malicious hands"; and he is afraid to die: "I am old and weak, too weak to bear annihilation" (78). He may think he believes in nothing, but his subconscious cries out to God to preserve him. He is trapped at the foot of a cliff by "the boiling light . . . flowing and fractious", and tries to escape by clawing his way up the cliff. The contradictory imagery — a surf of light, surging across a desert — has the sur-realistic cogency of a nightmare, and recalls the Nolan illustrations in *Outrider*. Heriot's fear is followed by a moment of stasis:

> The sun was blinded with the spray of them, time died, there was nothing but the light and the agony of waiting.
> Now I become nothing, whispered Heriot, now and forever, for ever and ever, I am no more. He closed his eyes, waiting, clinging to the rock. No more, no more. (78)

And this in turn is followed by a reversal in which death, the loss of identity, is accepted with "astonishment and joy", as he merges with the pursuing light: "All elements and colours in him were resolved, each to return to its source below the enormous swell. And under the surf and into annihilation sank the last of Heriot's wild white hair" (78). Half-waking, Heriot watches to see if anything of himself will be left when the tide ebbs back from the cliff: he cries out in fear that there will be nothing, and wakes both himself and Justin.

The dream dramatizes the primal emotions which are driving Heriot. First there is his guilt, made up of a general guilt for belonging to the murderous human race, a group guilt for the Onmalmeri massacre, and his personal guilt for the attack on Rex. Then there is his terror of death, of annihilation, which is partly overlaid by a contradictory longing for it — the conflict being caught in the oxymoron: "the intolerable sweetness washed over him". And finally there is his hunger for God in what he fears is a vacant universe: *"Le silence éternel de ces espaces infinis m'effraie"* (60).[24] Heriot, alone in his dream in a wild and alien land, confronts these emotions. His psychic conflicts are projected on to the landscape and, as he recognizes by the end of the book, the land and the sea he seeks and fears and explores are himself.

If there are no other people in Heriot's dream world, there are some in the country he travels through by day. When he first meets Rusty, shortly after leaving Alunggu's people, Heriot is hostile and preoccupied, and Justin has to introduce him. In the conversation which eventually ensues Heriot talks almost to himself, while Rusty responds in the plain and earthy manner of Fred in *The Bystander*. If he does not exactly play the Fool to Heriot's Lear, he certainly provides a contrasting pragmatism and humour that places and intensifies Heriot's lonely self-preoccupation. "What d'you do", Rusty asks, when Heriot quotes scraps of poetry in half a dozen languages at him, "Schoolteacher?":

"Missionary."

"Jesus, why?"

"I don't know. I had nothing to do and I was restless."

"Funny sort of life for a man."

"Once I was sick in hospital, one summer, and there was a sunset, one of those gaudy southern sunsets, and I looked out and saw a nun watching it, quite still, with a bedpan in her hand. I thought if I were a nun I'd feel like that, as if I'd earned the sunsets for myself."

"You need a shave," Rusty said, "if you're going to be a nun."

"Then I met a woman who had — that goodness. And I married her."

"Happy ending, eh?"

"We weren't young. No. And she died after a few years. That was twenty-one years ago. But," said Heriot with surprise, "she was young, young to die."

"You have stiff luck," Rusty said.

"No," Heriot protested. "I didn't say that. I'm not sorry for myself, not now." He fixed his awakened eyes on the man. "You're wrong."

"Okay, okay," said the stranger irritably. "I wasn't getting at you, mate."

"No. No, I'm sorry," said Heriot with remorse, "forgive me."

"She's right," Rusty said. (88)

The scene is a particularly effective one. As Rusty is drawn in from his initial laconic scepticism to dispute Heriot's notion of God, and finally to confess that he too is a murderer, the authentically Australian dialogue locates Heriot's metaphysical speculations in a familiar and recognizable world. Rusty provokes Heriot into reviewing his life, and the review reveals that he has become a missionary, and even married his wife, to capture goodness, and to earn what he saw as salvation. Rusty later disputes Heriot's chain of reasoning which implicates God in the killing of Rex, and puts a more conventional view:

"The stone I killed him with," said Heriot, "was full of God."

"Yes," said the man in an empty voice.

"God was an accessory. He always is."

"No," said Rusty violently. "God forgives you."

"Your fingers forgive you, before you've used them. God is like that."

"No. He pays us back for what we done."

"We pay ourselves back. You know that. Because you know our crimes are like a stone, a stone again, thrown into a pool, and the ripples go on washing out until, a long time after we're gone, the

whole world's rocked with them. Nothing's the same again after
we've passed through."

"I don't believe that," Rusty said. "No." (89–90)

Heriot's conviction is, however, a thing of the moment, and the
scene ends with him saying: "We're all lost here" (91). Knowledge
of the crimes of others is no help in trying to resolve one's own
guilt. Rusty and Heriot share a camp, food, and tobacco, they
even confess their murders to one another; but they remain
separate and alone, passing quickly into that "solitary land of the
individual experience, in which no fellow footfall is ever
heard".[25]

The meeting does, however, bring Heriot to two crucial
realizations. The first is that Rex is a man like himself, and not
just a criminal idea in Heriot's mind:

> "I wanted to kill someone," Heriot said quietly . . . "That was my –
> that brought me here."
>
> The other's eyes moved up his face, puzzled, looking for decep-
> tions. "Wanted to? Didn't you do it?"
>
> "But that isn't important," said Heriot, with faint surprise. "It makes
> no difference at all."
>
> "Except to the bloke."
>
> Then new thoughts moved behind Heriot's eyes like yachts on an
> empty sea, and for the first time he remembered Rex alive, and what
> it must have been to be Rex, to take pleasure in clothes and women,
> to be sullen and rebellious and know the causes, to suffer injustices
> and to invent injustices in order to resent them. He thought of Rex
> dancing by canegrass fire and delighting in the rhythms of his body,
> or subsiding into sleep under shade at midday, or swimming, or
> hunting, or sitting round a fire at night talking or singing to a guitar.
> Rex's life presented itself whole to him, the struggle against sordor,
> and then the defiant return to sordor, and the bitter pride underlying
> it; the old tribal grievances, real or inflated by legend; the fights and
> the humiliations, the quick gestures of generosity and the twists of
> cruelty; all the ugly, aspiring, perverse passions of a living man.
>
> "Now I know," he said from a great distance, "I know why I'm going
> on." (93–94)

This discovery of Rex's humanity gives a new meaning to
Heriot's search for the motives and passions which have
governed his own life. His second realization, which follows immediately, is that murder is inescapable in human life: "It was
because of murders my first amoebic ancestor ever survived to
be my ancestor" (94). Heriot cannot take the guilt for Onmalmeri,
however appalling, upon himself – that too is egotism disguised
as idealism or expiation. This realization is a further vital step in

Heriot's escape from the self-concern, the self-obsession, that has oppressed and blinded him.

Heriot's next meeting is with Sam in the deserted mission of Gurandja. When he first sees the township, Heriot, thinking it populated, is ready to abandon his journey, and give himself up to others: "They'll know what to do with me" (104). But he is not to be allowed the luxury of having others take charge of his life, like Theodora at the end of *The Aunt's Story*, or the people of *Tourmaline*. Like so much else in Stow's Australia, Gurandja is empty, unpopulated except by ghosts and a solitary refugee: "Not a town, no, an abandoned mission. A ghost mission. Gurandja, fifteen years dead" (105). Heriot's own, personal mission has also been dead for years, and Gurandja gives back the image of his emptiness and desertion. Sam, the only inhabitant, is a bystander, a gardener at the former mission, who observed its passing:

> "Ah, the missionaries, they was a bit hard, maybe – you know, holy, not what you'd call laughing men. And some of the natives went off on stations and come back again hating the white men there. They was too clever, you see, too big for their boots, not right for stations."
> "What were they right for?" Heriot said.
> "Couldn't tell you, mate. I know this, but – they wasn't right for here. Just one blow-up after another, all the time I worked here. Then we got the real blow-up that finished it off."
> Tenderly feeling the welt on his shin: "What was that?" asked Heriot.
> The old man looked at him disbelievingly. "You heard about that, mate. Don't tell me."
> "I can't remember. My memory's not good now."
> "The bomb," Sam said patiently. "You know, the bomb the Japs dropped here. Fell in a trench, killed three of the only four white blokes we had here."
> "And that was the end," said Heriot. "I remember." (112)

It is a measure of Heriot's growth that he can find some sympathy for the Japanese pilots: " 'Imagine it,' said Heriot dreamily, 'setting out with a load of bombs for a country you'd never seen and wanted to conquer, and when you got there – nothing. Nothing at all for hundreds of miles. And then a few little houses that no one would want to destroy. They must have felt lonely at first' " (112). The senseless violence of the Japanese bombing reflects the violence that Heriot finds endemic in human existence, and that so troubles him in himself – as when his encounter with Sam begins by threatening violence.

In his first talk with Sam, Heriot is again drawn to explain his

life as a missionary. Sam eventually goes to sleep without having
understood, but Heriot is clearly beginning to understand
himself, and why he has lived with guilt all his life:

> "I was a missionary," Heriot said.
> "What for?" asked Sam . . .
> "Expiation," said Heriot. "Yes. This is my third life. My third
> expiation."
> "What was the others?" asked Sam incuriously.
> "I suppose it was my birth, as a human being, that drove me to
> charity. Yes, that was the first. Then there was the massacre, done by
> my race at Onmalmeri."
> "I heard of it," said Sam.
> "That was the second. It drove me to the mission. And then at the
> end there was my – my hatred."
> "What'd that drive you to?" murmured Sam.
> "That?" said Heriot pensively. "That has made a lost man of me."
> The old man scratched himself. "Haven't you ever been happy?" he
> demanded, with disapproval.
> "Happy? Yes, sometimes. But in all my – expiations, there's never
> been a reconciliation. And what less," asked Heriot, "what less could I
> hope for now?" (108)

This conscious self-scrutiny confirms the subconscious evidence
of Heriot's dream. The reconciliation he seeks will, he hopes,
finally expiate his guilt, and free him for the death he both fears
and desires.[26] His journey through the bush is a last attempt to
find that reconciliation, which has eluded him throughout his
life, and without which he cannot die in peace. He is afraid that
he will not find it before the wave of death overtakes him, before
he finds the islands to which his soul can migrate.

Stow's expert use of dialogue in Heriot's encounters is particularly evident here. Sam, like Rusty, begins with laconic
defensiveness, and he articulates the reader's reluctance to
overhear Heriot's metaphysical probings, but eventually he is
drawn to speak of his sins, and of the worth of his life:

> Heriot peered at him through the flickering light. "You're an old
> soldier," he said. Their eyes met and slid away, distrustfully.
> "That's right," said Sam.
> "I am, too," Heriot said. "I am, too."
> "All right," said Sam harshly. "What do you want us to do? Sing
> songs together?"
> "No. Anything but that."
> "Took a lot of time to forget those days," Sam said. "A lot of time."
> "I know that, Sam."
> "You say it ain't easy to die. It ain't easy to kill, neither."

"No, harder, much harder."

"And when you get to want to do it – "

Heriot said sharply: "Don't say that, Sam."

He had broken something then. A stillness fell over them, and they were wrapped in memories; Sam, on his chair at the table, head bent over his hands, scrawny profile outlined by firelight; Heriot on the sagging bed, his face turned to the dark floor. Outside, the silence of the moon.

"What are you thinking, Sam?"

The old man licked his lips. "Thinking we was all animals, that's all. Just animals. No, worse."

"And suffer more for it. We have pity, and conscience, and reason. Those things hurt."

"I made a muck of my life," Sam said.

"That's something animals don't do," said Heriot.

"Nothing ever turned out right. I never *done* nothing. And these days – "

"You sit and rot," said Heriot, "like an old buggy in a shed."

"What did you do?" asked Sam. "Anything?"

"I did a little," Heriot said. (112–13)

One of the most influential things that Heriot has done is, ironically, to depart so spectacularly from his role as head of the mission. This action challenges both the people he leaves behind at the mission, and the people he meets on his journey, to re-examine the meanings of their lives. Helen Bond reflects on the damage sin does, and continues to do, unless it is recalled by the sinner making peace with his victim. Bob Gunn decides to continue working at the mission. Justin learns the possibility of a genuine brotherhood with the white man. And Rusty and Sam confess to killing, and even to liking killing. Heriot's contacts are brief and tangential, but he activates reason, conscience and pity in others. Heriot's gift to Sam in the above meeting, a gift which Heriot himself needs, is an acceptance of the complicity of all men in the violence inseparable from human life.

Heriot's three encounters on his walkabout draw out and dramatize his inner life. That is not their only purpose, however, since there is also a chemistry of interaction in each, and Heriot is changed as well as revealed by each meeting. He is led to examine the recurring themes of his life: the mission work, the alienation, and the killing; the attempted expiation, and the search for reconciliation and ultimate salvation; and, underlying all of these, the guilt, the fear, and the loneliness. There is clearly a sense in which Heriot moves towards self-understanding and self-acceptance, but it is not a one-way progress, and he remains

very humanly contradictory and uncertain to the end.[27] The
large questions asked along the way are, as Stow says, wisely left
unanswered; but they are explored, and not only by Heriot.
Justin enables Heriot to survive, and so to learn about
brotherhood, and such reconciliation as is possible between the
races. Alunggu causes him to ponder the real motives for his
charity and sacrifice. Rusty brings him to accept the inevitability
of killing. Sam provokes his reassessment of his three
"expiations". And together they help him to recover the human
sympathy stifled by his adopted role, and liberated by his
contact with others outside that role. It is his human sympathy
for Rex that saves Heriot, if indeed he is saved at the end.

Justin is Heriot's continuing link with the world outside his
own mind. Like Rusty and Sam he functions as a surrogate for
the reader, receiving Heriot's more vatic utterances with a mixture of unease, irritation and tolerance; but he is also a character
in his own right, loyal, practical, living his life with good
humour and a sense of proportion. He embodies, as L.T.
Hergenhan says: "the values of kindness and spontaneity . . . in
such a human way as to carry him far beyond Heriot's allegorical
label of his 'good deeds' ".[28] When Heriot soliloquizes, Justin is a
less than enthusiastic listener:

> Climbing the hills again in the morning he shivered, and cried out
> to Justin for reassurance. "We're very small," he said.
> "You big bloke, brother," Justin said kindly.
> "No, no, you don't understand. Think of it. This world. A little
> molten pebble spinning in air. This rock we walk on, a thin skin,
> changing every second. And the trees, what are they?"
> "They just trees, brother."
> "A little fur, less than the bloom on a peach. But we creep under
> them. And in the split seconds between the heaving of the earth
> millions of generations of us are born and grow and die."
> "Might be, brother," Justin allowed. (115–16)

But if he does not much like fielding rhetorical questions, he
does respond to genuine emotion, even when it is couched in
awkward, formulaic language:

> "It would be futile, wouldn't it, to try to tell you how much your
> companionship has meant to me. And how deeply it's touched me to
> think that I – had a hand in turning out a man like you."
> "You don't have to say nothing."
> "No. Because you know everything now, don't you. We've become
> – close enough."
> "I never forget you."

"Nor will I forget you," said Heriot. And they held each other by the eyes, words being of no use to them at the time of farewells. (121)

Justin's effect upon Heriot's rhetoric here — and throughout their .journey — is to reduce him from pomposity to simplicity, and then to silence. Like Lear's Fool or Sancho Panza, he functions as a touchstone for the simple verities, and forestalls any failure of sympathy with Heriot by at once sharing it and transcending it. With the truly Jamesian skill that he was later to demonstrate so effectively in *Visitants*, Stow uses Justin to refract the enigma of Heriot.

At the end of the book Heriot is finally left alone to face death. He farewells Justin in an economical, and very moving scene:

> Slowly Heriot stretched out his hands and laid them on Justin's chest. "This is how to say good-bye," he said, "among your people."
> "I can't touch you, Stephen. My hands all bloody."
> "All our hands are bloody," said Heriot bitterly. "Say good-bye." (122)

Justin then returns to enact Heriot's reconciliation with Rex, and to bear his final message: "It's my only defence. It's the world's only defence, that we hurt out of love, not out of hate . . . It's a feeble defence . . . and a poor reconciliation. But we've nothing better" (122). Having made such peace as he can with other men, Heriot is left to seek peace with himself, and to look for God in what he fears is a vacant universe. His own contradictory impulses remain until the end. When he finally reaches the sea, and can see no islands, in disappointed rage he hurls a rock down the cliff and into the ocean:

> He stared out to sea and saw nothing but the sun on the water; his dreams and his fears all true, and there were no islands.
> He turned, blinded, away, and saw on the ledge beside him a block of stone fallen from the cliff. And he stooped, straining, and lifted it in his arms. He knew suddenly the momentousness of his strength, his power to alter the world at will, to give to the sea what the sea through an eternity of destruction was working to engulf, this broken rock. Truly, he would work a change on the world before it blinded him.
> Poised on the ledge, he threw the stone, and it floated slowly, slowly down the huge cliff face, and crashed against it; and slower and slower entered the sea, in a tiny circle of spray.
> And watching it, he staggered, and stepped back towards the cave, shaking in the legs, and in his head following the enormous fall into the waves. (125)

Throwing the rock of himself into the sea,[29] where the wave he has feared in his dream engulfs it, is a last defiant, wilful act, which takes the place of his suicide, and leaves him ready for death. All of Heriot's bitterness, disillusion, and violent self-assertion appear in this passage. Yet having expressed these feelings, he seems to find peace, and even new hope that "there, in the heart of the blaze, might appear the islands" (125). The Jefferson Stow epigraph, which Stow says was much in his mind as he was writing the book,[30] suggests that if Heriot had seen the islands that he sought, he might have found them bleaker, even, than the empty sea.

The sense of closure is strong in the final pages of *To the Islands*, yet it is balanced by an open-endedness that eludes easy definition. The book ends but Heriot does not die; he does and does not find God, or Wolaro; the islands may or may not exist; Heriot is reconciled to Rex, but only by proxy. His last words, "my soul is a strange country" (126), take us, and him, to the point where self-discovery begins rather than ends. And yet it is a satisfying ending. Stow is an exploratory writer, even in his most recent work. He offers deeply meditated and thoughtfully framed questions to which he knows only a series of possible answers — there is no need to deconstruct *his* interpretation to see the full complexity of the book. Like Patrick White, he is a religious writer without a defined ideology, and it does not do to press the text for certain certainties. The final vision of Heriot high on his cliff, staring out into the sun, and searching for meaning in death, has become one of the unforgettable images of the Australian experience. He may be dying, but he has escaped from the European cell of himself into the landscape, and hence into a spiritual freedom to travel towards, if not necessarily to arrive at, a destination.

4 The Single Soul – A Derelict Independence

Tourmaline

This land was last discovered; why? A ghost land, a continent of mystery: the very pole disconcerted the magnetic needle so that ships went astray, ice, fog and storm bound the seas, a horrid destiny in the Abrolhos, in the Philippines, in the Tasman Seas, in the Southern Ocean, all protected the malign and bitter genius of this waste land. Its heart is made of salt: it suddenly oozes from its burning pores, gold which will destroy men in greed, but not water to give them drink.

Seven Poor Men of Sydney, Christina Stead

There is not any burden that some would gladlier post off to another than the charge and care of their religion.

Areopagitica, John Milton

After the critical success of *To the Islands*, Stow, who had published four books in three years, decided to abandon writing for a "non-literary career", and went to Papua New Guinea in 1959 to work as an assistant to the government anthropologist and as a cadet patrol officer.[1] His interest in anthropology had been pursued at the universities of Sydney and Western Australia, and at Forrest River Mission – the background for *To the Islands*. His life was restless and unsettled in the years which followed *To the Islands*, and he told John Hetherington towards the end of 1961 that, except for a handful of poems, he had done no writing for three and a half years. But he also said that he had been turning *Tourmaline* over in his mind for five years.[2] By 1962 he had returned to writing, and in that year he published *Outrider*, his second book of poems, and completed *Tourmaline*, published in 1963. This was the first of his novels to undergo a long gestation period – as all of his novels since have done – and the first with which he remains reasonably satisfied.[3] If *To the Islands* was his first major success, *Tourmaline* was his first fully mature novel, a deeply-meditated and deliberate work expressing his personal religious vision. Given the enthusiasm with which his youthful work had been greeted, he might well have expected it to enhance and consolidate his reputation as a major new writer.

It was not to be, however. *Tourmaline* won no awards or prizes, and while there were some warm and enthusiastic reviews, there was also a good deal of bewilderment expressed by its first readers.[4] Australian reviewers, who might have been expected to show some special sympathy for the work of an Australian author, were in fact unsympathetic and uncomprehending, so much so that "The Tourmaline Affair", as A.D. Hope christened it, became one of the less illustrious chapters in the history of Australian criticism.[5] The reasons for the Australian critics' failure to greet the book with any of the warmth it attracted in England and America included their dislike of speculative religious writing, and a tendency to overreact to the success of local authors. The playwright David Williamson experienced this reaction when *The Removalists* won two prestigious English literary awards:

> My experiences underlined what the novelist Tom Keneally had once said about the dangers of being a writer in Australia. You were discovered, given premature canonisation, the artistic hopes of Australia placed on your shoulders, then if you happened to have a critical reverse you were subjected to savage retribution and you spent the rest of your life wandering from bar to bar wondering why you weren't Dostoievsky. I felt as if I knew what he was talking about.[6]

Dostoevsky would have understood the religious debate carried on in *Tourmaline*,[7] but it was not much understood by those critics who prefer photo-realism to the imaginative, religious vision of Stow or White. Kylie Tennant, for example, said in a review of *Voss* − and it might just as well have been *To the Islands* or *Tourmaline* − that: "when the book strikes off into the deserts of mysticism, I am one of those people who would sooner slink off home".[8] Dorothy Green is one critic who laments this all-too-common attitude:

> One of the great weaknesses of Australian criticism has always been its refusal to take religious ideas seriously. If they are forced on the critic's attention by an obvious symbolic system, as in the novels of Patrick White, or specifically labelled, as in the poems of James McAuley, they are given some patronising attention, but it soon becomes clear that the critic is concerned not with the truth or falsity of the ideas themselves, nor with the notion that anyone could possibly live by them, but with the techniques of presenting them, with their usefulness as literary material, or because they are "psychologically engaging".[9]

In the case of *Tourmaline* this reluctance to engage seriously with religious ideas was compounded by an unfamiliarity with Taoism, one of the schools of religious thought that inform the book. Although Taoism has been known in the West, to some degree at least, for many years, and there have been a number of recent translations of its holy book the *Tao Teh Ching*, it is very much less familiar than the Christian revivalism with which it is contrasted in *Tourmaline*.[10] Partly as a result of this, *Tourmaline* has been the least understood of Stow's books — certainly until recently — and yet it is the most important for an understanding of his work. Like E.M. Forster's *The Longest Journey*, it illuminates the thinking which underlies all the other books.

The most severe review came from Leonie Kramer, who attacked the book for its "quasi-religious ideas", only some of which she recognized as "specifically Australian", and all of which she found "less than satisfying".[11] Taking up a theme begun by David Martin, she attacked the alleged "want of human interest" in Stow, arguing that any novel that is not "realistic" in its characters is doomed to fail — the virtue of novelistic characters being their individual realism, which is undermined if "ideological significance" is attached to them.[12] Kramer's review was followed by an article in *Southerly* in which she briefly surveyed all of Stow's work to date, finding little to admire beyond a "realistic" talent for the "exact evocation of landscape", and suggesting that: "*Tourmaline* is the *reductio ad absurdum* of the symbolic novel". The article was also an attack on the experimental, "anti-realist" novel of the preceding forty years, which Stow had misguidedly followed, with the result that his "character is swamped by symbol", and his "undoubted talents are led into the wilderness".[13] A critic who confessed to disliking Virginia Woolf because "by the last page one is no better informed than at the beginning; one has felt without knowing", could hardly be expected to read Stow with much sympathy.[14] Unfortunately her strictures have been treated with greater deference than they deserve, and have cast a long shadow over later Stow criticism.

Not surprisingly, Stow was irritated by the reception of the book in Australia, and he fired off some sallies at what he saw as the Hope–Kramer axis in Australian criticism.[15] Some years later, in 1966 — in what Helen Tiffin has described as "a fit of authorial desperation" — he published" From The Testament of Tourmaline: Variations on Themes of the *Tao Teh Ching*", which finally alerted critics to the Taoism in the book, and which led to an awareness of the influence Taoism has had on Stow's thinking in all of his books, not only *Tourmaline*.[16] The pendulum has now swung in the opposite direction, however, and there is some danger that its importance may be overestimated. Stow is an eclectic thinker, a Christian of sorts as well as a Taoist of sorts, who seeks like Tom Spring to "trap and amplify the faint whisperings of God".[17] He is not a committed adherent of a particular ideology, even so unparticular an ideology as Taoism, and *Tourmaline* is built on the conflict between the opposing beliefs of Tom Spring and Michael Random. That conflict was little enough appreciated when *Tourmaline* first appeared, but the resulting "affair" has had long-term benefits. It has indicated just how original a novelist Stow is, and how unexpected and diverse are the perspectives he brings to bear on the dilemma of living in a "new" country with the notebooks of an old and alien culture for guidance.

The author's fondness for *Tourmaline* may well be due in part to its chequered critical career, but I suspect that he also likes it because, with its haunting, richly-textured sense of place and its story hovering like a desert mirage between the real and the surreal, it is so quintessentially a Stow novel. It explores the strange country that Heriot discovered at the end of *To the Islands*, the confused spiritual heritage of the European living in Australia. *Tourmaline* is the ship of the Australian soul, isolated in an inland desert as Rob's merry-go-round is isolated in the sea, and with only the enigmatic visits of the truck to suggest that a world outside the town still exists. It is cut off in time as well as in place, as the "note" instructs the reader: "The action of this novel is to be imagined as taking place in the future" (4). *Tourmaline* thus has something of the feel of Beckett's *Endgame*, and, in another sense, of Nevil Shute's *On the Beach* which is set after a future nuclear holocaust. On the other hand Stow's comment that: "*Tourmaline* could almost as well be in the past as in the future"[18] emphasizes that it is the dislocation of normal time rather than the future setting that is essential to its surreal, dreamlike isolation. One of the points of *Tourmaline* is that the more things change the more they stay the same: "Terrors would come. But wonders, too, as in the past. Terrors and wonders, as always" (221). Another is that the future is likely to be grim, though bearable:

> I say we have a bitter heritage.
> That is not to run it down. (221)

The novel begins with a meditation on the land, and on the relationship between the land and the people who inhabit it. The epigraph from St-John Perse's *Anabase*:

> O gens de peu de poids
> dans la mémoire de ces
> lieux . . .

suggests an alien people, recently arrived, and lacking a time-nurtured bond with the country, and this impression is reinforced by the first words of the narrator: "I say we have a bitter heritage, but that is not to run it down. Tourmaline is the estate, and if I call it heritage I do not mean that we are free in it. More truly we are tenants; tenants of shanties rented from the wind, tenants of the sunstruck miles" (7). The tensions which will shape the book are already evident here. The people have inherited a land which they do not possess, in which they are merely tenants, and it is not easy to accept such a heritage without bitterness, and without despairing dreams of owning and improving the estate. The land is certainly uninviting:

> There is no stretch of land on earth more ancient than this. And so it is blunt and red and barren, littered with the fragments of broken mountains, flat, waterless. Spinifex grows here, but sere and yellow, and trees are rare, hardly to be called trees, some kind of myall with leaves starved to needles that fans out from the root and gives no shade . . . The sky is the garden of Tourmaline. (7–8)

And then there is the town, the human encroachment on the land. Tourmaline lies at the end of the road. There is a war memorial, a store, a hotel, some houses, a stone police station, mine heads, and a church: "It is not a ghost town. It simply lies in a coma. This may never end" (9). The human condition in Tourmaline is comatose: there is life of a kind – the animal functions continue to operate – but the higher functions seem in abeyance, except for the narrator, who is beginning to write his testament.

The narrator, who is known simply as the Law, is an old man, like Heriot, who no longer has an official role to perform. Like Heriot and Diana Ravirs, he has difficulty keeping a sense of himself. He fears a loss of identity now that the voices that used to answer him on the wireless are no longer there at the other end to reassure him that he and they exist. The testament he has begun to write as a record of his and the town's experience is partly a self-reassuring soliloquy, and partly addressed to whatever audience there may still be in the outside world:

Silence is a habit as enslaving as the most delicate vice . . . I find that
there is no speech that is not soliloquy. And yet, always, I sense an
audience . . .

There is much I must invent, much I have not seen. Guesses, hints,
like pockets of dust in the crevices of conversation. And Tourmaline
will not believe me.

But (dear God) what is Tourmaline, and where? I am alone. I write
my testament for myself to read. I will prove to myself there has been
life on this planet.

The cells are unroofed, the bars are gone. Records of intriguing
crimes and acts of justice blow in the yard. In other places, it is
believed that Tourmaline is dead.

There is no law in Tourmaline: this is known there. The gaol abandoned and crumbling, the gaoler dead. So all must assume.

Yet I live on, prisoner of my ruined tower; my keys turned on
myself now all the locks are gone.

The Law of Tourmaline. Guessing, inventing. Ghost of a house fur-
nished and inhabited, tormented by the persistence of the living.
(10–11)

The imprisonment imagery here recalls the Marston epigraph of
To the Islands: "My cell 'tis, lady . . . / Where all at once one
reaches where he stands,/With brows the roof, both walls with
both his hands".[19] Later in *Tourmaline* the Law listens to Kestrel
telling him about his life with Deborah: "as I listened to him I
began to have a good deal of pity for him, because he was the
man he was, trapped in his selfhood as the flies in the bar were
trapped in their small cages" (136). The Law too is a prisoner of
himself, but like Heriot he is seeking a way out, and he writes
his testament to try to find a meaning for his own and Tourmaline's experience.

The use of a Conradian narrator in *Tourmaline* in place of the
omnisciently cinematic presentation of *To the Islands* and *The
Bystander* helps to make it a less active and more meditative
book, and one in which the reader is called upon more than
before to construct his own reading. Unlike the strongly-
characterized narrators of *Visitants*, the Law is not so much an
actor as a sensitive register of the town's experience. He does
join the diviner's religious revival, but soon sees the weakness
that underlies the public charisma, and becomes a private
sceptic, while remaining a public adherent. He does not fully
comprehend Tom Spring's unveiling of his Taoist vision, but he
sees and records enough to enable the reader to form an assessment of it. He is characterized enough to make him credible, but
he remains neutral enough not to distort significantly what is

conveyed through him. He acts as a reliable if limited guide through the complex metaphysical world of the book,[20] and his very limitations – he is often uncertain and even bewildered – invite the reader to see more of that world than the guide does. His poetic sensibility and his elegiac tone certainly colour his narration, but they do not prejudge the issues. And it is because he is neither too explicit nor too authoritative that he is so appropriate a narrator for so exploratory and speculative a book.

The Law's main function is to reflect back what other people project on to him, as Random in his different manner also does. His youth, he comes to realize, was little more than a solemn living up to expectations:

> What could be more wretched than to discover, in one's extreme age, that one has had no youth to remember? I see myself again as a boy; a long solemn face, obsessed with responsibilities never more than an illusion, wearing unreasoned habit like a straitjacket. I was a good lad, alas. A tool, a dupe. What price have others paid for my arrogant simplicity? (142)

When Tom Spring later points out his similarity to: "These black-and-white men . . . these poor holy hillbillies who can only think in terms of God and the devil", the Law protests: "I'm not like that!" and Tom replies: "Aren't you? . . . Well, by heaven, you used to be" (185). Tom at this point is trying to "cure" the Law – who has forgotten that he has been cured once already – of his shallow morality and his susceptibility to Random, who is perceived by Tom as self-torturing, guilt-ridden and destructive. Tom's attempt to enlighten the Law is only partly successful at the time, but it sows the seeds of doubt, and when the Law next meets the diviner he sees for the first time that: "He was not sound. How could I think so, when he did not?" (193). From then on the Law is aligned with Tom as "the elders of the tribe, tolerated, but outside" (194); and they do not participate in the common enterprise of mining Random's gold reef, and worshipping unquestioningly in his church. By the end of the book Tom is dead, and it is the Law who conveys his final message to the reader: "There is no sin but cruelty. Only one. And that original sin, that began when a man first cried to another, in his matted hair: Take charge of my life, I am close to breaking" (221). This indicates that the Law is finally "cured", that he has come to share at least the social part of Tom's vision, and to pass it on, as a warning to the reader. The Law thus espouses, at different times, the hostile ideologies that compete for Tourmaline's allegiance, and he is therefore uniquely qualified to write the history of the town's encounter with the diviner.

The narrative he relates begins with a death and an entrance. Billy Bogada dies – and is buried in a packing-case coffin marked "SPRING PERISHABLE" (9) – and the diviner arrives. Brought to Tourmaline in a state of near-death by the driver of the supply truck, he is immediately adopted by the town with "curious yearnings" (17), and when he tells the Law that he is a water diviner these yearnings begin to take concrete shape. He gives himself the name of Michael Random, the second half of which is recognized as an invention, randomly selected, and the town begins to focus on him wild and intense hopes that he will make the desert blossom, Lake Tourmaline fill with water, and the golden age come again. It is a mutual process, with the town providing the initiative, and the diviner only later finding himself involved in a dream that he did not seek to begin, though he pursues it with increasing conviction.

We never learn where he comes from, or anything about his previous life except for the scars that bear witness to his attempted self-destruction. The Law imagines spiritual journeyings that sound something like Heriot's, but which Random may or may not have had: "But he had been far, so far, in country never mapped, on the border-lands of death. He had been where Kestrel had not, where none of us had ever been. And he brought news" (18). To a less sanguine eye, he might seem to be suffering from severe exposure, physical and psychic, which has left him weak and ill. And it might also appear that he is not a successful diviner, since he was unable to find water when he needed it desperately:

> "I depended on, you know, finding some on the way. I have a – a gift, in that line. I'm a diviner, did I tell you?"
> I remarked that everyone in Tourmaline now knew of it, and looked to him for salvation. He frowned, under his yellow forelock.
> "But you didn't find any water," Byrne suggested. "This is hard country, son."
> "I know it," he said. "But no country's hopeless. Only, I lost my rod, a metal rod – you know? And nothing else would do. When that was gone, the – the virtue went out of me. And I was sick . . ." (39)

The double perspective here enables the reader simultaneously to perceive the narrator's growing enthusiasm, and the absence of evidence to justify it. All that the self-styled diviner can be brought to say of where he has come from is:

> "The other end of the road . . ."
>
> "And what's there?" asked Deborah . . .
>
> He sat twisting in his lap the fingers of his multi-coloured hands, and studying them. Then he said, rather quietly: "Hell . . .
>
> "It's — ah, chaos. Like nothing here. Tom couldn't live. I couldn't live. D'you understand?" And suddenly he was far younger, terribly eager that we should understand, that we should acquit him — but of what? Again he appeared to me obscure, alien.
>
> "And the man who drives the truck?"
>
> "Is a saint, a crazy saint. So they say."
>
> "That bastard?" Byrne said, incredulous.
>
> "It's different," he said, "out there . . .
>
> "Wild beasts are loose on the world," he said, from another place, as it were. "When you know that, you don't need to know much more."
> (44–45)

Tom interrupts this apocalyptic account of "out there" by suggesting that the wild beasts are internal not external: "This room's full of wild beasts, too, that might be let loose at any moment. The question is, what controls them? . . . it might be just a kid's convention, mightn't it? What if the Word was only 'Barleys', after all?" (46). The diviner and the Law both object to this questioning of Christianity by what they see as a destructive nihilism. They both fear the consequences of a loss of faith, since they see that alone as standing between them and the chaos "out there" where Random has come from.

When Tom is questioned about his own belief, he replies: "I'm still waiting . . . Who'd dare say before the end of the road?" (46), a demonstration of negative capability that produces an interesting range of reactions in those present. No one agrees with Tom, and it seems unlikely that anyone understands what he means. The diviner, who had previously addressed Tom "with great trust and happiness" (46), is drained of animation: "All of a sudden he had deteriorated, had become querulous, like an invalid" (49); the virtue, as the Law observes, goes out of him. In the remainder of the book it is clear that Random's belief in himself and his virtue is febrile, intense, and intermittent — the antithesis of Tom's quiet self-possession and doubting serenity. It also requires the reinforcement of others' belief to sustain it. He cannot survive, like Tom, as a single soul. Byrne, by contrast, is dismissive: "What's it matter, anyway? . . . We'll live till we die. Who gives a stuff about beliefs?" (47). Tom's answer: "If we believe we exist, that's enough", is challenged by Deborah, who also needs to believe that two or three other souls exist as well as her own: "It's not enough . . . not if you just believe that *you* exist. You have to believe that Mary exists, or Byrnie, or someone. You've got to believe it in your guts" (47). While the Law agrees with this sentiment, he is surprised by the "ferocity" with which Deborah expresses it. He himself is a believer in "esprit de corps" (44), an old-fashioned phrase for a virtue that is to enjoy a brief new vogue in the town under Random's influence. The discussion of personal beliefs is reminiscent of Patrick White, whose characters are given to abrupt revelations and sudden insights, though Stow has a better ear for dialogue. The dramatic presentation of the scene reflects Stow's preference for exploring questions rather than positing answers. If it becomes clear, as the book progresses, that he has a good deal of sympathy for Tom's views, it is also clear that he sees they are open to challenge, and he does not wish to foreclose on the debate.

Random is the most vulnerable of the characters, and the process by which he becomes, paradoxically, the leader of the town is a curious one. His first action after the discussion of beliefs is to cross the road from Tom's store to Kestrel's pub. His ostensible motive is to thank Kes, but he ends up in an arm-bending contest with Byrnie that exposes his fierce will and his fear of close contact. Byrnie is trying to make contact – physical contact – with Random because, as he confesses at the end of the book, he loves him. But to the diviner arm-bending or wrestling is an opportunity to beat an opponent, and also a threat to his untouchability. So Byrnie ends up, as he usually does, hurt, bleeding and rejected. And the uncertain direction of Random's violence is exposed. Directed outwards, it can make him a leader, dominating others; but directed inwards it is self-destructive, leading, as in the past, towards suicide. In either case it is dangerous since, as Tom has earlier suggested, and as the bar room scene makes clear, he does not himself know how to direct and control it.

The next person to approach him with love is Deborah, and she too is rudely rebuffed. The first time she talks generally of love, asking Michael of his experience. He refuses to answer, and his intense embarrassment is evident throughout the scene. The second time she is more direct, both about Michael and her own feelings. She recognizes, perhaps from her earlier visit, his fear: "Why do you hate people to touch you? . . . You don't want people to do you favours because you don't want them near enough to know you" (111). When she nonetheless declares, "I 'love you", Michael responds with a nasty mixture of fear and hostility, which he converts into a show of righteous superiority, retreating into the role of outraged but beneficent saviour of the town. His strategy here is a paradigm of his behaviour for the remainder of the book. As Deborah perceives, he is afraid of people getting close enough to know him – and his response shows that he has good cause to be afraid, since close up he is not only vulnerable but, as Tom Spring recognizes, poisoned with self-hatred. He can, however, manipulate people from a distance, using his roles as diviner and religious leader – the two merge into one as "diviner" suggests – to remain in aloof control and to hide his personal inadequacies.

In between the two meetings with Deborah, the diviner has recognized his new vocation and undergone a conversion. The recognition comes when he is talking to the Law:

> "Who wants money, anyway? Who wants it here? Or gold, rather."
> "There's the truck," I reminded him. "We're not self-sufficient."
> "Why can't we be?" he demanded. "Get rid of the grog, and so on. A
> – a Utopia we could have, with the water . . . I could save this place,"
> he said . . .
> "From what?" I said. "Save it from what?" (73)

Though the Law's question is pertinent, it is not answered by the diviner. Random is projecting his inner turmoil out on to Tourmaline, as Tom Spring recognizes: "He was having a fight with God . . . Just the two of them. Now he's dragged the whole of Tourmaline into it" (185). He believes he can save himself, that he can "come true" (155), but the way he goes about "saving" Deborah is to create a false need and then to satisfy it:

> "Shall I tell you what's in your mind?"
> "No! You don't know!"
> "I'll tell you," he said . . . he poured into her ears such a stream of
> filth as she had never, and probably none of us has ever, heard, much
> of it dealing with her supposedly unquenchable lust for his, the
> diviner's, body. As he spoke he burned, in zeal and exaltation . . .
> "Do you confess you've been a sinner?"
> "Yes," she whispered. "Yes."
> "Will you come to God?"
> "Yes." (157)

Deborah has to be made sinful in order to be saved: Random's religion is a double act, like the sado-masochism of Kestrel and Byrnie. The Law, however, who does not know the rules of the game, innocently asks Random what Tourmaline is to be saved from. Random does not answer, but he does accept the Law's misinterpretation of his meaning: " 'You can save it with water. Is that what you meant?' 'Yes,' he said. 'That's it.' " (73).

The search for water thus becomes central to the action of *Tourmaline*, though it is not the real search in which the people of the town are engaged. The diviner has a gift for finding water, or so he claims, and the people of Tourmaline believe because they want to believe, just as Cawdor in *Visitants* wants to believe that the universe is not empty, that there must be extra-terrestrial visitants. Tourmaline does not need water. It is in short supply, but there is enough to sustain life, provided it is carefully husbanded. The Law's dream of the "days of hope . . . of tree-lined streets . . . when the verandas of the hotel and other buildings were shaded with vines, and oranges grew in what is now Rock's garden" (92) is the recalling of a primal, golden age that is not even remembered by the younger inhabitants of the town. The real diviners in the book are Tom Spring and Dave Speed, who have found what water there is in Tourmaline country — the waters of silence and contemplation. Random and the others seek it, though they do not realize the true significance of their search:

> Tao wells up
> like warm artesian waters.

> Multiple, unchanging,
>   like forms of water,
>   it is cloud and pool,
> ocean and lake and river.

> Where is the source of it?
> Before God is, was Tao.

> . . . .

> Deep. Go deep,
> as the long roots of myall
> mine the red country
> for water, for silence.

> Silence is water.
> All things are stirring,
> all things are flowering,
> rooted in silence.

These lines in "*From* The Testament of Tourmaline" illustrate the imagistic connections between the Tao, water and silence.[21] Random and his followers seek water, but because they do not understand the nature of their need, the water they seek exists only as a mirage.

What he does succeed in divining is a new gold reef. Gold, like water, is essential to life in Tourmaline: the economy is basic, but such as it is, its currency is gold. There is, however, enough, indeed too much gold without the new reef, as there is enough water. Kestrel takes the town's accumulated gold away with him and buys the equipment he brings back to use in his search for water. The gold from the new reef, which is not even worked for some time after it is discovered, accumulates in the Law's safe. The only real power it has is the potential to further the megalomaniac schemes of the returning Kestrel. The gold discoveries in Australia in the middle of the nineteenth century prompted a dream of affluence that drew an immigrant people to an alien land. Exporting minerals has remained a major economic activity, and metal detecting – high technology divining – is a national hobby. Random's career in *Tourmaline* suggests that the dream of affluence is an illusion, and that gold cannot buy water, which is what the country lacks, though there is enough for survival. The true wealth of the country is the wisdom that Tom Spring and Dave Speed find in its harsh simplicity. This can only be won by living in the country on its own terms, not by manipulating and exploiting it as Kestrel plans to do at the end of the book. Stow suggests, like Xavier Herbert in *Poor Fellow My Country*, that the land and the people are at cross purposes, and the two must attain a common purpose – "Body is land in permutation"[22] – before there can be spiritual progress. Sins against the land, like sins against the indigenous inhabitants, "go on washing out until . . . the whole world's rocked with them".[23] It is not, however, expiation that is needed, as Heriot believed, but the divining of a true identity that will unite the land and its people.

The religion that the diviner discovers for himself, and persuades the town to embrace, is closer to the aggressive Christianity of a colonizing Europe than to the patient Taoist quest for enlightenment in sympathy with the land. Random's conversion to it takes place in the derelict church, with Gloria Day, who has tended the church, the witness who relates what happened to the Law. Like others who get close enough to the diviner to see his weakness and uncertainty, Gloria has her doubts about him, though she believes that God has talked to him, and she identifies him with Mongga, the Aboriginal water and fertility spirit, for whom she has tended the church. Talking to Gloria, Random seems very unsure of himself:

> "D'you believe I've found God?"
> "I dunno," she said. "How you tell?"
> "Through pain," he said — half-laughing, she told me, in a very strange way. "Shame. Weakness. He makes me suffer. Persecutes me. Won't let me go. So I know I've found him."
> He lifted his hand to push back his flopping forelock. His hand was shaking.
> "You don't hate God?" she asked, uncertain.
> "No, no, I love him. Have to. There's nothing else." (96)

Random's need is real, indeed desperate; but his God sounds too much like his *alter ego* Kestrel, a cruel hound of heaven, to inspire much confidence. To confirm his shaky hold on his new belief he needs to involve other people, and so he becomes a priest-like figure. "Preaching is an illness," Turgenev has observed, "a hunger, a desire; a healthy person cannot be a prophet or even a preacher".[24] Random, who certainly fits this description, becomes the high priest of a theocracy in which the people of Tourmaline combine to worship and to work the gold reef.

One of the diviner's first acts as a leader is to enlist the Law as his lieutenant.[25] His approach is aggressive:

> "I've come . . . to tell you your duty . . . for the first time you'll be in touch with headquarters. These are no guesses now. This is certainty . . . You're to become a spring . . . an irrigation channel, if you like, to revive Tourmaline . . . I'm here to wake you up, to tell you what you mean. You're to follow me."
> "What is the water," I asked (all bearings lost), "that's supposed to flow through me to Tourmaline?"
> "Real water," he said, "in the ground. And rain as well. And the spirit of God, in and above all that. The spirit that works through me . . . You're to become the Law again, more truly than you ever were. But I'm to have the real dominion." (166)

The febrile intensity here, and the half-digested vocabulary, indicate the fragility of Random's adopted role. And yet he is persuasive, and at the first of his religious services, the Law is drawn in to share the communal exaltation:

> I looked down, from the height of the stars, and saw us united. All Tourmaline, all together; elbow by elbow, cheek by jowl, singing as one, shouting and weeping as one, praising God, beseeching God, wordless, passionate. I felt the power of our unity rise towards the stars like waves of heat from hot rock . . . That was what he, the diviner, had done for us. There was never before this strength of unity, this power, this tremendous power . . . It was he, it was our faith in him (faith which I, astoundingly, now found myself to share) that bound us, in love and passion, together. (172)

Even at the height of his euphoric involvement, however, the Law realizes, like Rob at the end of *The Merry-go-Round in the Sea*, that communality is an illusion, and that we live and die alone. Like islands, the inhabitants of Tourmaline are separated by "the unplumb'd, salt, estranging sea".[26] Not only Tom and Dave, who refuse to attend the services, are alone; even those who participate most enthusiastically in the common purpose are separate: "And yet, united as we were, we had never been so alone. Each on his small island, crying to be with the others, to be whole. The bell and the guitar and the meandering voices could not effect that reunion" (172). And later the Law recognizes that Random has divided as well as united the people: "I thought about Tom and Mary, about Jack and Dave, about Deborah and Byrne and Kestrel. So many gulfs he was opening, for all his talk of unity" (202). The islands are like stars in a galaxy, together and yet alone, united and yet alienated. The Law speaks of his "terrible loneliness" (41, 92), and there is no character in the book who is not estranged. Deborah tries to talk of love, and the Law thinks that he experiences it:

> Inside the dark houses, behind the blind windows, Tom and Mary, Kestrel and Deborah lay asleep. Moonlight would be coming in, perhaps, falling on the yellowed sheets that would be their only covering; lighting the soft curves of the women, the men's lean folded angles. I could see them, as I walked by the walls that hid them. I could feel the heat of their close houses, I could smell that bedroom smell, of shoe-leather and powder, of cloth and warm flesh, that lapped them. I believe I loved them, without wishing to interfere. (103)

This is at best an elegiac love, however, and if it is free of manipulative self-interest, it is also devoid of animating passion:

> The love of man is a weed of the waste places.
> One may think of it as the spinifex of dry souls.[27]

This paradoxical separateness is even reflected in the diviner's services, which make curiously little use of the conventional rhetoric of religion. Random simply announces that "God is very near", and that is enough for Charlie to hail him as Mongga, and for the Law, to his own surprise, to hail him as Christ. Tourmaline welcomes him as a god because the people of the town crave a leader to take charge of and unite their lives. Random plays the role with considerable skill, and nowhere more so than here, when his reticence encourages the people of the town to project their desire and hunger on to him.

Ultimately, however, Random is the victim of Tourmaline's enthusiasm, of its need for a prophet, and its craving for water. He rides the tide of its fervour, and is broken when it ebbs. As Byrnie says: "Poor Mike . . . He doesn't know what he's up against" (184). The conversion of the Law, for example, Random's chosen lieutenant, does not last long. It is first challenged by Tom Spring, and then undermined by seeing the diviner outside his priestly role. Tom does not openly oppose the diviner — that is not his way. He speaks of his views only when the Law asks him why he does not join in:

> "You must join us. If you could feel the power — the esprit de corps. A whole population with one idea — "
> "A hundred minds with but a single thought," said Tom, "add up to but a single halfwit." (184)

Tom then expresses his dislike for the simplicities that will follow the embracing of this one idea, and he sees the truth of Random's effect on people like Deborah:

> "But she's happy," I said.
> "Happy!" Tom said. "You see a healthy girl turned into a hunchback overnight, and you think she's happy?"
> "But she loves him."
> "Isn't that nice?" said Tom. "And hates herself. And he hates himself. But they both love God. It's as good as a bloody wedding. Ah, he's a bright boy, all right, to do all that in a quarter of an hour. It took Kes years to do the same to Byrnie, and he had no luck at all with Deborah."
> "How can you be so stupid?" I burst out. "To compare *him* with Kestrel — "
> "They're two sides of a coin," Tom said. "Shadows of one another. And how is it, anyway, that you've lived all these years and not seen that a man who hates himself is the only kind of wild beast we have to watch for?"
> "But don't we all? Hate ourselves? In different degrees."
> "We were given this sickness," he said. "By the incurables. Deborah

can be cured, Byrnie can be cured. But not Kestrel, not Michael. There's nothing to be done for them, except ignore them." (185–86)

This is very close to the centre of Stow's vision in *Tourmaline*. If the town is in one sense cut off from the rest of the world by time and distance, in another it is a microcosm, like the mission in *To the Islands*, of that larger world. When Random says earlier that wild beasts are loose in the world outside Tourmaline, Tom counters that the beasts are internal, not external. Random seeks escape from his demons in a frenzied effort towards a common goal, inspired by the Protestant ethic which believes God signals his approval by granting worldly success, like finding gold or water. Tom's is the very different Taoist way of cultivating the single soul, with its independence of mind and spirit, of patiently searching for enlightenment, and of accepting what cannot be changed by religious or technological diviners.[28] His way is lonely and uncertain, and the insights it yields up are tantalizingly difficult to convey to anyone who does not already share them. "Words are no good", says Dave Speed, Tom's only fellow traveller, "Words are crap. Throw 'em away, and think . . . If we talk about it . . . we'll talk crap. This is one of the laws of the universe" (152). And Tom agrees, bitterly comparing his own inarticulateness with Random's familiar language: "Words can't cope . . . Your prophet knows how to cut the truth to fit the language. You don't get much truth, of course, but it's well-tailored" (187). The Law protests that the diviner is not so simple, and he admits that he finds Tom's account of his belief almost meaningless, but it is clear that Tom's words have a lasting influence on him, so much so that when Tom dies at the end of the book, the Law takes over from him as spokesman for the Tao. At the time of their talk, however, he finds Tom's revelation obscure:

> At moments I thought I glimpsed, through the inept words, something of his vision of fullness and peace; the power and the darkness. Then it was hidden again, obscured behind his battles with the language, and I understood nothing, nothing at all; and I let my mind wander away from him to the diviner, at the altar, brilliant by flamelight, praising a familiar God, through the voice of a ritual bell. (187)

The familiar ritual is comforting, especially when compared with Tom's lonely struggles, and the Law turns back towards the diviner.

At their next private meeting, however, the Law begins to see

Random as Tom sees him. He has become "a nocturnal creature, never seen by us except at those barbaric séances" (189), and when the Law goes to see him at his hut during the day, he finds him querulous, hostile, and defensive. He tries to hide the suicide scar, which the Law tells him the town already knows about:

> "How could you do it?"
> "It's my life," he said.
> "And robbed us of you. Robbed Tourmaline . . . you're ours," I tried to explain to him. "Not your own, now. Ours. My poor boy – "
> "I'm God's," he said, simply and sullenly. "Don't kid yourselves."
> "We saved you. We made you. And not for your use. For ours."
> "I'm God's," he repeated. "And my own."
> "I think you're selfish," I said. (192)

There is clearly selfishness on both sides here. The Law's attitude is just as manipulative as Random's – Tourmaline has no right to make someone for its own use – and it becomes increasingly evident that the relationship between the town and the diviner is an unholy alliance of contrary self-interests that find, for a time, a common purpose in the pursuit of a misconceived goal. The Law sees the weakness behind Random's appearance of strength:

> I looked at him, and I felt betrayed. So much health, and hope, and strength, in the look of him; there was nothing I would not have trusted him with, from his appearance. One would have judged him, by his looks, invulnerable; one of those made without a doubt of themselves, without a second thought. And it was all deception. He was not sound . . . If there had been any consciousness of having failed, any regret, my sympathy might have reached him, might have found him human after all. But he had rendered himself almost without qualities; there was nothing to him but his ferocious pride, and his yearning. No creature on earth seemed worth his attention.
> And still he kept his brightness. (193)[29]

In a sense the Lucifer-like Random described here has already left Tourmaline. His gaze has always been directed inward rather than outward, though he does not know himself. His war with God and his suicide attempts are internal conflicts from which he escapes into his priestly role. But the narrator finally sees the egotism and the emptiness that underlie that role. He realizes that the diviner is not sound, and that such a man cannot lead others to the truth.

As we have seen, the services the diviner conducts are

remarkable for their comparative lack of rhetoric, and this gives a special emphasis to the little that is said at them. "God is very near" (173, 188) is his first pronouncement, and it reflects the emphasis in much revivalist and charismatic Christianity on a personal God available to meet the immediate needs of the individual believer. Tom Spring's God, by contrast, is very distant, and much more difficult of access:

> His God had names like the nameless, the sum of all, the ground of being. He spoke of the unity of opposites, and of the overwhelming power of inaction. He talked of becoming a stream, to carve out canyons without ceasing always to yield; of being a tree to grow without thinking; of being a rock to be shaped by winds and tides. He said I must become empty in order to be filled, must unlearn everything, must accept the role of fool. And with curious, fumbling passion he told me of a gate leading into darkness, which was both a valley and a woman, the source and sap of life, the temple of revelation. (186-87)

While this is essentially a Taoist vision, it has similarities with other mystical traditions, including the Christian.[30] For Tom, God is far away, and his voice is difficult to hear – one must empty one's mind, and hope for some "infusion of force and wisdom" (94). It is a long, slow, silent, private process, the very antithesis of the diviner's revivalist services, where God seems near enough to reach out and touch, and communal fervour brings immediate emotional rewards to the participants. One of those rewards, if it can be called that, is the yielding up of responsibility for the conduct of one's own life: "This is what we pray. Take charge of my life, father. Because it's too hard – too hard. And I'm close to breaking" (197). At the end of the book the Law describes this plea as "that original sin" (221), the sin that inspires cruelty in others. And at the service when it is taken up by the congregation, it is roughly challenged by Dave Speed: " 'What *is* all this crap? . . . You won't find no water,' Dave told the diviner. 'You? You ain't a diviner's bootlace. You're either a nut or a flicking con-man' " (197). Dave is forcibly silenced by his son Jack, a believer, and the diviner ends the service with the assertion that: "God is near . . . Maybe nearer than ever" (198). But Dave's challenge has its effect. The diviner realizes that he must try to find the water he has promised.

His attempt to divine water fails, and the failure signals the end of his role in Tourmaline. The fervour of the community cannot be sustained when its leader fails to deliver the promised "cargo", and the mania which has gripped the town is replaced by a depressive torpor. The Law wanders in the Tourmaline graveyard to meditate on the failure that he knows will follow the diviner's final instruction to dig one hundred and fifty feet for water:

> Ah, the love of ruin is insidious. In the middle of regret, in the middle of complaint, it is growing on one. There is ease in dereliction. Action becomes irrelevant; there is no further to fall. Or if, by chance, falling is possible, then only action can make it so; and action is therefore suspect, even frightening. And that I was frightened by the diviner I have not denied. I was not alone, I was with Tom in this. (204)

This is the dark side of Tom's Taoist vision. Inaction may be powerful, but it may also be fearful. Quietism may be a conviction, but it may also be an excuse. And there is a positive side to Random's vision just as there is a negative side to Tom's: "It was some consolation, anyway, to see so much happiness, so much beauty. Nothing is more becoming to the human face than hope . . . the diviner . . . was only a symbol; a symbol for what I believed in, the force and the fire, the reaching unwavering spirit of man like a still flame" (195). And the diviner himself was saved, if only for a time, from self-destruction, and given a sense of purpose, a sense of mission, by the joint will of the town.

The ending of the book is nonetheless bleak. Byrnie, who has loved Michael but not believed in him, fails to persuade him to stay in Tourmaline. He jumps the broken fence at the end of town and runs away "into the gathering wind" (216), which presumably buries him in the dune country along with Leichhardt and Lacey's Find. His antagonist Tom Spring also dies, though he leaves Dave Speed and the Law behind to bear witness to his vision. Kestrel, however, returns transfigured by a new sense of purpose: "His voice was somehow altered, and it struck me that all that uncertainty, all that baffled energy that used to sound in it was gone, that he knew now what he was . . . He was a whole thing, and invulnerable" (209). He will draw people to him, as the diviner, who had also seemed invulnerable, had done, and if his followers will be deluded they will also be inspired by hope. "Some desire", as Imlac says in *Rasselas*, "is necessary to keep life in motion",[31] and that is perhaps why Deborah returns to Kestrel when he returns to Tourmaline. Like Random he is not sound. He has treated her cruelly, has "broken her heart" (47), and when she leaves him after his sadistic beating of Byrnie, she describes him as "not a man. He's partly a baby, and the rest of him's a wild animal"

(124). But she goes back to the new Kestrel, and if it is partly an act of despair — she is pregnant, and Random had treated her just as cruelly as Kestrel — it is also partly an act of hope, the beginning of a new life, the only one in Tourmaline.

Tourmaline is dominated by the sun and the stars. "The sky", says the Law, "is the garden of Tourmaline" (8), and unlike Rock's garden, or the oleander at the church, it needs no water and no cultivation except, that is, in the mind. Like the astral colony in Stow's poem "Endymion", Tourmaline is almost sealed off from outside contact, dry, barren, alien and loveless.[32] And yet wherever there is human habitation both good and evil can flourish. An apparent sterility may conceal a riotous fertility, as in the poem "Dust", and a good deal depends on the eye of the beholder. Dave Speed, for example, prefers the new, arid Tourmaline to the older, lusher version:

> "You and me can remember when that pub veranda was covered all round with passion-vines, and bloody good it was, too, to sit out there at this time of day, with a schooner, in the cool . . . But the place is better now than it ever was then. We've got to the bare bones of the country, and I reckon we're getting to the bare bones of ourselves. If the water comes, it'll be when we've stopped needing it. We're coming true, mate . . . when I was in the grass I liked the look of the desert. And now I'm in the desert I like it even better." (86)

This paradoxical suggestion that true growth is enhanced by shedding the appearances of fertility reflects the Taoist tendency to confute conventional thinking. Dave Speed would be content to be the only colonist on a "dead" star, like the astronaut of "Endymion".

The stars in Tourmaline's garden are cold and very distant: they look down with indifference on the minute affairs of men. And yet "the galaxies outside us" reflect "the galaxies within us" (150), and both contain God. Cawdor sees a similar connection shortly before he dies: "I saw. Timi, I saw. Down the tunnel. My body. Atoms. Stars",[33] and his hunger for contact with the star people parallels the cosmic loneliness felt by the Law, particularly in his Anzac address at the war memorial (149-50). This longing for cosmic contact is reflected in the use of sun imagery to describe Random at the height of his power. The Law, who "can understand all peoples who have worshipped the sun" (201), consistently describes Random as a source of light: "he stood in the middle of the fire. Burning. And Kes ran away" (160); and "the black silhouette of the diviner stood, in a nimbus of fiery gold . . . He turned at the altar, and the light washed over him, blue and golden" (173). As Random's influence increases, Tom Spring, by contrast, fades: "Tom turned his head and looked at him; not smiling, not luminous, but cold and blank, a dead sun . . . he seemed as serene as ever. But all the light had gone out of him; a dead sun" (167-68). By the end of the book Random has also become a dead sun or, perhaps, as Byrnie the poet of Tourmaline suggests, Lucifer, the fallen angel of brightness. The consistent use of sun and star imagery gives a primal, cosmic dimension to the small, isolated drama of Tourmaline, not only by extending the microcosm it represents, but by suggesting that it may well be the last place in the universe where this human cycle will be enacted. One of the "jokers" Kes brings back with him has "no nose or mouth; only teeth" (208), and if he is representative of the wild beasts let loose on the outside world, Tourmaline may be the last place left where there are unmutated humans to repeat the human story.

Taoism teaches the unity of opposites, and *Tourmaline* finally invites the reader to find a unity rather than to despair or to make a choice. It is a new testament, an Australian testament, more Taoist perhaps than Hebrew or Christian, but with elements of all, and it is not a question of choosing between them but of finding a way to reconcile their opposing tendencies. If the writer of the testament is "divided of mind"[34] it is because he sees, like Deborah, the attractions and repulsions of the Spring household, the diviner's mission, and Kestrel's pub. His final words offer a warning, a hope, a lament and an ultimate acceptance:

> Beware of my testament!
> (Ah, my New Holland; my gold, my darling.)
> I say we have a bitter heritage.
> That is not to run it down. (221)[35]

These last words of the book echo the first, as in *The Merry-go-Round in the Sea* and *Visitants*, emphasizing the circular patterns, the cyclic repetitions on which all three books are built. In between there is the birth and death — the rebirth and the redeath — of Michael Random, the failed dream of the rebirth of the town, and the death of Tom Spring, which is not really a death: "Watch out for the flowers on his grave" (152). *Tourmaline* is a meditation on the meaning of these events, these cycles in human life. It is an ambitious work, of "immense and imaginative originality",[36] which compels by its very strangeness and the stark truth of its insights. Stow has explored the country of the soul with a visionary intensity more common in the Russian than in the Australian, or the English novel. But his spare, arid, harsh and yet living desert is unmistakably Australian, and offers a compelling insight into our spiritual malaise.

5 Grievous Music

The Poems and Music Theatre

Across the uncleared hills of the nameless country
I write in blood my blood's abiding name.

"Stations", Stow

Non! nous ne passerons pas l'été dans cet avare pays où nous ne serons jamais que des orphelins fiancés.

"Ouvriers", Rimbaud

While Stow's reputation has rested on his novels, his poems, which are more private and more difficult of access than the novels, have been comparatively unregarded.[1] The difficulty resides partly in the unfamiliarity of Stow's vision – as with *Tourmaline* – and partly in the references he makes to an unusually wide and varied range of reading. The privacy results from his references – often oblique – to people and events in his own life. But if he is sometimes a difficult poet, sometimes a private poet, and often seemingly a reluctant poet, he is also at times a very good poet, and his work is certainly deserving of more serious and sustained critical attention than it has yet received.[2] Stow has written poetry throughout his career, and while four collections have been published, a good deal remains uncollected.[3] There are many interesting connections with the fiction – the most obvious being "*From* The Testament of Tourmaline" – for Stow sees the two kinds of writing as complementary: "my poems and my novels are very closely related".[4] The land and its meaning are again overriding concerns, as in the novels, but the range is wide, and Stow also writes of his childhood memories, of his time in Papua New Guinea, of the search for spiritual enlightenment, and of love.[5]

Because the land is so central to Stow's imaginative vision, "The Land's Meaning", published in *Outrider* (1962), is an appropriate poem with which to begin a discussion of his poetry. It was written in 1960, after *To the Islands* and before *Tourmaline*, and as in those novels the author confronts the inner landscape of Australia, and reflects on the disturbing experience of exploring it. It is a complex, suggestive poem, typically veiled and reticent, which does not readily yield up its meaning, but which haunts the mind of the reader:

> The love of man is a weed of the waste places.
> One may think of it as the spinifex of dry souls.
>
> I have not, it is true, made the trek to the difficult country
> where it is said to grow; but signs come back,
> reports come back, of continuing exploration
> in that terrain. And certain of our young men,
> who turned in despair from the bar, upsetting a glass,
> and swore: "No more" (for the tin rooms stank of flyspray)
> are sending word that the mastery of silence
> alone is empire. What is God, they say,
> but a man unwounded in his loneliness?[6]

The poem is "For Sidney Nolan", who did a series of paintings for *Outrider*, Stow's second book of poems, as well as the dust jacket for *Tourmaline*. The collaboration grew out of a series of "Australian Artists and Poets" which appeared in *Australian Letters* between 1960 and 1968.[7] The painting which accompanies "The Land's Meaning" shows red desert, spinifex, and sky – all empty. The land predominates, "the bloodred, bitter ground".[8] There are no human or animal figures, and the heat haze rising from the land partly obscures what sky there is. Light comes from behind the wave-like ridge, emphasizing the wrinkled, rippling dunes. The "skin-coloured surf of sandhills", topped with a spray of sunlit haze, is reminiscent of Heriot's dream – in country not unlike this – of being pursued by a surf of light.[9] The same images recur in "Strange Fruit", the next poem in *Outrider*:

> the great
> poised thunderous breaker of darkness rearing above you,
> and your bones awash, in the shallows, glimmering, stony,
> like gods of forgotten tribes, in forgotten deserts.
>
> (*CS*, 37)

It is dangerous, challenging country, harsh, arid, and uninhabited. It waits for those few explorers, rejects, loners ("They were all poets, so the poets said"), who cannot forego its challenge, who cannot resist "embracing pain/to know; to taste terrain their heirs need not draw near".[10]

"The Land's Meaning" begins baldly, with striking but at first sight inappropriate images:

The love of man is a weed of the waste places.
One may think of it as the spinifex of dry souls.
(*CS*, 36)

What follows offers an explanation of — or at least a series of
glosses on — this cryptic assertion. Stow has described the poem
as a "wry sermon preached on the text of the solemn first two
lines".[11] The starting point for the trek to the difficult country,
where the truth of the statement might be ascertained, is that
true outpost of white Australian "civilization", a tin bar room,
stinking of flyspray. The speaker of the poem has not yet left on
his trek, except, that is, in the country of the mind, where "the
footprints of the recently departed/march to the mind's horizons,
and endure". Those who have gone send back word:

> that the mastery of silence
> alone is empire. What is God, they say,
> but a man unwounded in his loneliness?

Their words echo, incongruously, through the bar room, that
citadel of mateship, which does not have much to say about the
love of man or the nature of God. The poem is both hesitant and
expeditionary, and if it is uneasy, unfinished and uncertain it
reflects accurately Stow's view of the "meaning" of an alien land.
Like *Tourmaline*, with which it shares its desert landscape, the
poem asks some basic spiritual questions, and even offers some
answers, albeit enigmatic ones. But it is difficult to earn those
answers in the space of a short poem which begins with abstrac-
tions like "the love of man". If the poem is not entirely convincing, then, it is partly because the subject is intractable. The land
will not give up its meaning to those who wait on its fringe,
listening to the stories of others who have explored, but not exploring themselves; and this applies to readers of the poem as
well as to the speaker. The incongruity of the poem and its
images attempts to make this point: that insight cannot be
grasped by reading a poem, by travelling in the mind. It may be
glimpsed in this manner, but true understanding only comes to
one who has been "bushed for forty years". The poem, then, is attempting to communicate the incommunicable, and one of the
temptations for a writer confronted with this contradiction is to
revert to silence — accepting the aphorism that those who speak
do not know and those who know do not speak. It is a temptation
Stow is familiar with — there have been long periods when he
has published little — but in works like "The Land's Meaning"

and *Tourmaline* in particular he attempts to confront, not avoid, the problem.

Whether one journeys into the difficult country or huddles on its periphery, the land remains, a great enigma, challenging, waiting to be explored, and yet alien and indifferent, evoking complex and often contradictory emotions, as *"From* The Testament of Tourmaline" indicates:

> The loved land breaks into beauties, and men must love them.

And yet:

> To move from love into lovelessness is wisdom.
> The land's roots lie in emptiness.
>
> (*CS*, 71)

Stow has located some of these contradictions in a powerful modern version of the Endymion myth:

ENDYMION

> My love, you are no goddess: the bards were mistaken;
> no lily maiden, no huntress in silver glades.
>
> You are lovelier still by far, for you are an island;
> a continent of the sky, and all virgin, sleeping.
>
> And I, who plant my shack in your mould-grey gullies,
> am come to claim you: my orchard, my garden, of ash.
>
> To annex your still mountains with patriotic ballads,
> to establish between your breasts my colonial hearth.
>
> And forgetting all trees, winds, oceans and open grasslands,
> and forgetting the day for as long as the night shall last,
>
> to slumber becalmed and lulled in your hollowed hands,
> to wither within to your likeness, and lie still.
>
> Let your small dust fall, let it tick on my roof like crickets.
> I shall open my heart, knowing nothing can come in.
>
> (*CS*, 41)

The speaker here, as Stow indicated to John B. Beston, is a lone astronaut who has found a moon, an island continent, sleeping untouched in the sky.[12] The neutral colour of the sky in the accompanying Nolan painting captures the absence of sun, and hence of life and growth, on this dead and sterile planet. There is not even the arid harshness of "The Land's Meaning", just muted blue and dusty brown, a dreamscape lost in sleep. The threatening, wave-like cliff rearing up out of the sea and towering above the viewer is, however, repeated, and this motif recurs in the painting, "The Calenture", where it is even more striking. (This has another neutral, or rather jaundiced sky, a feverish not a tranquil dreamscape, and the only human figure in the series – diving, leaping, or perhaps taking a mark?). Stow has called "Endymion" an anti-love poem, which it is, as well as a love poem.[13] It begins, in Donne-like manner, expostulating with the beloved and denying her the attributes that poets traditionally ascribe. This denial of the conventional leads to more elevated praise: "You are lovelier still by far", which is in turn followed in the next two couplets by the rueful self-mockery of the colonist, who plants his shack with hardly a lover-like tact. The tone changes yet again in the sestet: in place of the brisk and forthright lover we find the drugged victim, who has imbibed the landscape like a sleeping draught, and subsided into apathetic somnolence. The poem ends with his chilling embrace of the lifeless, torpid love of his moon-goddess: "I shall open my heart, knowing nothing can come in". Like the God of "The Land's Meaning", he is "unwounded in his loneliness".

"Endymion" is one of Stow's first mature love poems, and one of his best. It uses myth, as many of the later love poems do, as an objective correlative to give resonance to the personal experience on which it is based. The speaker is Endymion as lover and astronaut, and he is also a castaway on the *"costa branca"*,[14] the white coast of Western Australia, a first European visitant to that other empty island continent, the love of which is dangerous, addictive and irresistible. "Endymion" connects the landscape poems, in which the speaker is characteristically alone, isolated and alienated, with the love poems which, for all their echoes of despair, celebrate at least a partial defeat of that lonely isolation. The landscape for Stow is an all-purpose image, reflecting the self, the other than self, and the lover with multifaceted indifference.

"Endymion" suggests that love of the land, of the sleeping virgin continent of Australia, is a kind of death-in-life. Awaking from such a state is painful, as poems like "Jimmy Woodsers" and "Outrider" movingly demonstrate. These poems reflect the dilemma of Rick in *The Merry-go-Round in the Sea*, who knows that he must leave his home, his family, his land, and Rob, but whose sense of alienation from them does not diminish his grievous sense of loss. Rick identifies with Ellenbrook, the chestnut mare he rides home from Marsa: rider and mare have both been scarred by brutal experiences which leave them too neurotic for routine tasks or "normal" life in their own country.[15] Rick's ride home on the mare in the novel is echoed in "Outrider", the title poem of Stow's second book, with its haunting, repeated refrain:

> My mare turns back her ears
> and hears the land she leaves
> as grievous music.

The poem tellingly contrasts fond memories with bitter truths:

> Diseased with memories,
> I starve on lies, recall
> days when I rode abroad
> pursued, pursued with cheers;
>
> when barefoot children raced
> to pester and applaud,
> leaping from shadow to shadow
> over the burning road.
>
> . . . .
>
> But in truth, I think I lay
> on the bloodred, bitter ground,
> watching the centaur children
> canter seaward, away,
>
> and wept, in the draining heat;
> while poincianas shone
> like streetlamps or mocking stars
> on the roofs of the shanty town.
>
> (*CS*, 45-46)

The exile is tormented by contradictory memories, some glamorous, some bitter, some true, some fictive. With its spare four-line stanzas and its piercing refrain, "Outrider" is a stark, vivid poem, beginning in nightmare, haunted by memory, and ending in courageous opposition to the nightmare world.

Stow is very much a poet of nostalgia, and there are many memory-laden poems recalling his childhood, that childhood so unforgettably recreated in *The Merry-go-Round in the Sea*. There are relatively unstructured recollections, like "Seashells and Sandalwood":

> My childhood was seashells and sandalwood, windmills
> and yachts in the southerly, ploughshares and keels,
> fostered by hills and by waves on the breakwater,
> sunflowers and ant-orchids, surfboards and wheels,
> gulls and green parakeets, sandhills and haystacks . . .
> (*CS*, 4)

And there are more formal poems, like "Sea Children", in which the memories are marshalled into stanzas, and the nostalgia is tinged with awareness of time and death. "Child Portraits, With Background", one of the best of these early poems, is a matched pair of portraits, visually conceived and executed, and reminiscent of Blake's pairs of poems in *Songs of Innocence and of Experience*. It is a leisurely poem, slow and timeless as childhood, full of striking images ("the sun/rolled on the land like a horse in a cloud of dust"), yet not without menace:

> And spring
> led him where summer sent the sheep to die,
> and showed him orchids, eyes of a staring skull.
> (*CS*, 10)

The poem is an early instance of Stow's continuing concern with the symbiotic connection between the outer landscape of childhood and "the secret landscape" of the mind. The country of one's childhood, like the country of one's cultural inheritance, is seen to condition irrevocably the inner vision of the child, an inner vision that in turn conditions what the child sees in the landscape. In a feminine land of "greenness and shade and water", it seems that "life is safe and endless" and "all things come again"; in a harsh, masculine land, tyrannized over by the sun, it seems that "life is a white bird, screaming through the hills,/ harsh as brass, fleeting, not to be held". The poet, like other European Australians, knows both heritages, and the contradictions of having to live with both.

The childhood poems in *Outrider* are more thoughtful, more intense, and technically more accomplished than the youthful poems of *Act One*. "At Sandalwood", perhaps the best of them, is a quiet celebration of change in continuity:

> "The love of time, and the grief of time: the harmony
> of life and life in change. – In the hardest season,
> praise to all three."
> (*CS*, 34)

"Jimmy Woodsers", by contrast, as the accompanying Nolan painting suggests, is a bitter poem enacting the choice of exile.[16] The poet would submerge himself in memory if he could, but the country of childhood is now dry and barren, the family pool has been drained, and the poet has said "goodday to time":

> "You must drove your sheep elsewhere.
> My dams are dry. You must leave this waterless country."
>
> (CS, 42)

The sense of loss is more personal in "For One Dying: Miss Sutherland MacDonald, 1873–1956", which is a very moving tribute to a much-loved childhood companion:

> Now, in that place where all birds cease to sing,
> and paths grow faint and melt into the hills,
> you pause, tasting the wind; for it is spring,
> and down on Ellendale's wide water spills
> a dust of petals. In this last September,
> opening your hands to seize the golden light
> (your hands, which flowers and animals remember,
> and trees, and children) you will enter night.
>
> I am no more the child whom you made cry
> so readily with your sad ballad-tales,
> not skilled to soothe the life that prays to die,
> not skilled to pray. But must, since all else fails,
> trust that your Lord, who owes you some amend,
> grant you a quiet night, and a perfect end.
>
> (CS, 13)

Stow uses landscape in the octet as an image of the state between life and death: "that place where all birds cease to sing, / and paths grow faint and melt into the hills". It is an evening scene, an edge-of-desert scene, almost the point of departure for "The Land's Meaning". The memories are given added resonance by the functionally ambiguous use of "remember" and "must", which echo backwards and forwards through the poem. "For One Dying" is a sonnet of deceptive simplicity, rich with intense feeling, and superbly controlled.[17]

Like *The Merry-go-Round in the Sea*, Stow's poems recalling his childhood, collected in *Act One* and the first half of *Outrider*, offer few difficulties. Alongside them in the first half of *Outrider* is a new kind of poem, private, cryptic, dense, and less available. This new style is first evident in "The Embarkation", one of many "sea voyage" poems, which describes a difficult departure, and a new and ambivalent psychic beginning:

> Parent or kinsman, wake,
> come to the sea's dark lip,
> cry me farewell: who glide
> white arm into black tide
> and strike, for life or sleep
> (that sleep for living's sake)
>
> *through waves, to the dead ship*
>   (*CS*, 29)

The poem is filled with images of decay and ruin: "the salt white ribs of boats", and "My house is a ruined cell/embattled" – the latter recalling a key image of *Visitants*, the body as house, as well as the Marston epigraph in *To the Islands*. The ship that the speaker finally swims to is "dead", and there is a pervasive sense of inevitability and despair. The environment, both beach and sea, is unyielding, destructive, indifferent; but it must be confronted, an attempt must be made:

> The weak must dare to drown,
> and harvest as they can
> the salt, enormous field.

While the poet wrestles with his demons, the reader, who is overhearing, not being addressed, is almost an intruder. "Landfall", the last poem in *Outrider*, forms a pair with "The Embarkation", and describes the return from the voyage begun in that poem, repeating many of its images: "I shall anchor, one day – some summer morning/of sunflowers and bougainvillaea and arid wind". Having returned to his starting point, which sounds very much like the Geraldton coast, the poet will "unlade" his eyes "of all their cargo"; but there will be no traveller's tales:

> And when they ask me where I have been, I shall say
> I do not remember.
>
> And when they ask me what I have seen, I shall say
> I remember nothing.
>
> And if they should ever tempt me to speak again,
> I shall smile, and refrain.
>   (*CS*, 48)

The reader is thus, in a sense, denied access to the poet's experience, unable to penetrate the silence, the reticence, which preoccupy Stow. And yet between 'The Embarkation" and "Landfall" there are eighteen poems which do constitute the cargo, the traveller's tales, of this strange, intriguing voyage.

They range from the sonnet-like "Wine", a finely-imaged reflection on the cruelty of April and new growth ("I rejoice in the spring. I strike the intolerable window./ Another year, and the bubbles rise bitterly in my veins"), to the tortured density of "Strange Fruit", in which one part of the personality stalks another, threatening to engulf it in sleep, and to involve it in its fall, as Eve involved Adam in the original fall by offering him strange fruit. The second half of *Outrider* is made up of a group of related poems which depict aspects of the severe illness, precipitated by a bout of malaria, that Stow experienced in New Guinea in 1959, and which forms an important part of the background in *Visitants* and *The Girl Green as Elderflower*. "Kàpisim! O Kiriwina", which uses many of the images of *Visitants*, is one of the most powerful and haunted of these poems.[18] The boat driven by a storm to an unknown island is both a boat and the poet's malaria-wracked body, and that body is further transformed, through the mists of fever, into a village:

> And bleeding, bleeding,

> I looked down the street of my body, and people were waving;
> "The village is dying," they smiled. They were waving good-bye,
> as the lugger with all aboard her drove for the headlands –
> with tears, with such tears of joy – with such blood and trembling.

> But an old dark woman prayed in the village church.
> And your piety – ah, your piracy, *inágu!* –
> beached me, and bore me again. Into fear and trembling.
>
> (*CS*, 40)

In *Visitants*, it is Cawdor's house that is bleeding, both the resthouse in which he dies and his body. The novel and the poem share a sense of dislocation, of watching one's reified body from a distance, like a spirit already departing, and also the sense of being forever watched and in public, even in one's most private moments, so that death "that brings a gift, the final privacy,/time to oneself"[19] becomes a wished-for release, and rebirth into life a frightening ordeal.

One of Stow's most anthologized poems from *Outrider*, "Ruins of the City of Hay", is a gently ironic account of the dreams of the Western Australians. The primal vision of the West as a new Eden is compared, not to the moon as in "Endymion", but to the

city of "lovely Petra", built of yellow hay.[20] Being built of hay, the
city has proved ephemeral – "The wind has scattered my city to
the sheep"; but if its life was inevitably brief, it was real while it
lasted:

> This was no ratbags' Eden: these were true haystacks.
> Golden, but functional, our mansions sprang from dreams
> of architects in love (*O my meadow queen!*).
> No need for fires to be lit on the yellow hearthstones;
> our walls were warmer than flesh, more sure than igloos.
> On winter nights we squatted naked as Esquimaux,
> chanting our sagas of innocent chauvinism.
>
> (*CS*, 35)

This is part mocking, and part affectionate. While the "dreams/of
architects in love" may not produce substantial, practical houses,
you may get a lovely, improbable Opera House, or a mansion of
hay. Another Western Australian poet, Dorothy Hewett,
describes the chauvinism that the poem depicts: "When the rest
of Australia gave up, or at least, grew misgivings, we still went
on building in our dreams that perfectly new vitalist society
washed clean in the hard white light of a western Paradise,
where our luck would never run out. This is the real Australia,
we said".[21] But Petra's luck did run out, and in the latter part of
the poem its destruction is mourned with a grief untouched by
mockery. This lost and lovely city in the desert may have been
real only in the dreams of its inhabitants, but that only heightens
the sense of loss for the poet, the lone survivor, contemplating
the ruins.

Stow's third book of poems, *A Counterfeit Silence* (1969), includes
a selection from his two previous books, and some new poems
under the heading "Stations".[22] The new poems include a number
of love poems, "Western Wind When Will Thou Blow",
"Ishmael", and "Persephone", and three sequences of poems,
"Stations", "Thailand Railway", and "*From* The Testament of Tourmaline". "Persephone", which is a good example of the love
poems that Stow has increasingly been publishing since *A
Counterfeit Silence* appeared, is perhaps the best of the short
poems. Like "Endymion" and many of these recent poems,
"Persephone" uses myth to echo and to objectify personal experience, as Stow has explained: "The speaker one is to imagine
is a mortal lover of Persephone, who's fallen in love with her
when she's in the upper world in Spring, and then tries to go and

rejoin her in her Winter world. In this case Hell is a city much like London, it has a pewter-coloured river, it has train-shrill tunnels, and so on. This is quite literal description of a personal experience".[23] The welding of the mythic and the personal is very skilfully done – the personal narrative dominates the surface of the poem, and it is only the title and the emphasis on seasonal imagery that alert the reader to the mythic parallel, which provides a haunting echo without obscuring the personal emotions. The poem uses the two-line unit that Stow has made peculiarly his own, particularly in his love poems. The form, which is looser and more varied than a conventional couplet, and more isolated, more separate from its context, is an economical unit which allows the poet to generate a range of rhythmical effects within a simple formal pattern:

> And every street threatened irremediable meetings;
> in every train-shrill tunnel the winter faces
>
> promised to turn upon me your winter face,
> saying winter words. And love, I was afraid.
>
> Yet I would have you know I have been, and gone.
> I would have you think of me on another island
>
> where it is never quite spring, but an ache and waiting,
> foreshadowed nostalgia, voices once heard half-heard.
>
> (*CS*, 56)

The hesitant rhythm here enacts the "ache and waiting" of the lover very effectively. And the oxymoron of the last line, "foreshadowed nostalgia", encapsulates the conflict, the dilemma of the lover, who is forever anticipating or remembering, living outside the present.

Parting, loss, separation, the memory of brief episodes of love, and the half-despairing hope that these will return in some future springtime, these are the themes that recur in Stow's love poems. "Western Wind When Will Thou Blow", with its echo of the sixteenth-century lyric,[24] recalls "five nights of love" with fierce longing. The Hebridean setting of the poem is sharply evoked, and the cold, the wind, and the snow which threaten to engulf the lovers' "five firelit nights" foreshadow the "death" that follows the brief but passionate blaze of their love. "Simplicities of Summer", by contrast, quietly celebrates a relationship that is almost at peace with itself:

My peace is in this: that each nightfall must bring you back,
and the lamplight, under my eyes, die warm on your face,
that your voice must be the last sound I hear before sleeping,
and your breath, asleep, be what I hear if I wake.[25]

The genial warmth of a Maltese summer pervades this "most
serene of Stow's love poems",[26] but even here there is separation:
"as we ripen, apart on two boughs of noon". The separate worlds
of summer and winter are juxtaposed in "A Pomegranate in
Winter", which is dedicated to Patrick White, "the author of *A
Fringe of Leaves*".[27] The poem is a haunting recollection of
summer in winter, prompted by the out-of-season fruit:

Bought in a frosty market, with the glaze
of far hot gardens on them; hoarding still

a southern flush ingrained in stubborn rinds.

The myth of Persephone/Proserpina is used again in this poem to
give resonance to the lonely grief of the lover, waiting long
months for the promised seasonal return of the beloved, and also
to the alienation of the goddess, who must forever journey from
one world to another:

O Proserpina.

You who will come, with violets and narcissus,
when blackthorn flowers next year; whose presence is

the scent of woodbine and of meadowsweet,
and drunkenness of bean-fields, death of hay;

you haunt us yet. I see the breeze-whipped gold
about your eyes, in two worlds turned elsewhere.

Now is your fallen season. Now you reign
queen-consort of all darkness . . .

The poem ends with a characteristic blend of contrary emotions
as the poet visualizes Pluto, who has gained and lost Proserpina:

Red-lipped you turned, when he had thought you gone;
and by that red announced the generous fall

which made you his, that grieved one's, loneliest
of all immortals, personed ache of loss.

The poem draws together very skilfully the myth, the White
novel in which Garnet Roxburgh forces his attentions on his

half-willing sister-in-law Ellen, who remembers the passion of their encounter long after she has fled, and the poet's own bitter-sweet memory of a southern summer in the midst of a northern winter.

"Efire" also relies upon its literary context for an important part of its effect. The poem refers to an incident in Camoes's *Lusiads* (Canto IX, stanza 75ff.) in which Venus creates an Isle of Love, complete with nymphs, for Vasco da Gama's men.[28] One nymph, Efire (the Portuguese form of Ephyre), is pursued by Lionardo, a much-disappointed soldier who has "decided that he has no luck in love". She flees at first, but is won over by his pathetic eloquence. The poem is Lionardo's plea to her:

> Look cold, but do not turn.
>
> All I could never win – gleam, echo – mingle.
> Slake my sight only, lifting one leaf-flecked arm,
>
> thrust back your hair, and stare, uncomprehending,
> at this rough thing the luck of winds set down.

Lionardo has learned from bitter experience to expect and to ask for little, and he already imagines Efire as no more than a memory, a foreshadowed nostalgia, who watches indifferently as his boat pulls away from her shore. He does not expect to find love, and like Endymion seems almost to prefer his lover to be unresponsive: "Eyes morning-calm . . . blank as that sea to which they gaze away". His tone is one of subdued yearning mingled with despair, and the two-line units are rhythmically hesitant and redolent of melancholy.

In "Enkidu" the grief is keener, and the elegiac lament of Gilgamesh is bitter and unreconciled, though the memories of Enkidu are happier ones.[29] The poem refers to *The Epic of Gilgamesh*, but does not rely as heavily on its literary context as "Efire". In the first twelve lines of the poem, which is again written in the extended two-line unit that Stow prefers, Gilgamesh recalls his first meeting with the gazelle-like Enkidu:

> Enkidu: when you came through the gates of the city
> with the heart of a deer, with the eyes of your brothers, the deer,
>
> when you fought me, young tyrant of Uruk, and wrestled me down,
> you seeded yourself in my heart. Then the land grew green.

The anapaestic rhythm of the lines expresses both the lingering joy of Gilgamesh's memories, and, in the second half of the poem, the starker grief of his lament: "Enkidu: all our lives we were dying together". The poem employs a good deal of sexual imagery,[30] and the sense of loss is as fiercely physical as in "Persephone" or "Western Wind When Will Thou Blow".

The grief of love is again the theme in "Orphans Betrothed", which takes its title from Rimbaud's "Ouvriers".[31] Stow here extends his long, loose line into a sentence or two of prose-poetry, and the two young lovers speak, or rather think, alternately. Their thoughts are not shared, however, and the gap between them emphasizes the isolation that even in love remains unbreached:

> "A gale that night flung the gaslight about our room.
> He did not see it; in sleep he is alone. I pretended he
> was at sea, and cried, for the fears and homecomings.
> For the simpler grievings not of orphans betrothed."

Love is not all grief, however, and as "Incubus to Virgin" indicates, it has its lighter moments:

> Lady, I had no thought; never was, to my knowledge,
> once in your room where all those treasures lie
> mummy-wrapped for their licensed tame *huaquero*.
> Somebody came, but truly, it was not I.
>
> And the threat in my glance that so tossed about your bolsters
> must have been on its way somewhere else when you stopped it in
>   flight.
> Honestly, darling, I never considered you that way.
> But now that you've raised it, God knows how I'll spend tonight.[32]

This poem, with its arch, teasing tone, recalls the Elizabethan and Jacobean love lyrics Stow admires, and serves as a reminder of the recurring humour that lightens the lonely austerity of much of his work.

Stow has written two groups of poems as libretti for works of Music Theatre on which he has collaborated with the composer Peter Maxwell Davies. Music Theatre derives from Schönberg's *Pierrot Lunaire* (1912), and has developed greatly in the last two decades, with Peter Maxwell Davies as its most distinguished exponent.[33] Davies has a strong interest in the medieval period, and he likes to overlay the work of earlier periods on the contemporary, as Stow does in *The Girl Green as Elderflower*.[34] They are both interested in people "in extremis",[35] and the works for which Stow wrote the lyrics, *Eight Songs for a Mad King* (1969) and *Miss Donnithorne's Maggot* (1974), are concerned, like *Pierrot Lunaire*, with madness. Stow sees the two works as connected, like *Visitants* and *The Girl Green as Elderflower*: "I wrote the Libretti of *Eight Songs for a Mad King* and *Miss Donnithorne's Maggot* to be complementary. The Mad King is desperately tragic, and Peter Maxwell Davies's music often mocks the King, and one can't help laughing, and myself I find that distressing. So I wrote *Miss Donnithorne* as a companion piece, at which one could laugh with a clear conscience."[36] The two works have been performed together, as well as separately, with great success.[37]

In his "Note on the Text", Stow has described the original inspiration for *Eight Songs for a Mad King*:

> The poems forming the text of this work were suggested by a miniature mechanical organ playing eight tunes, once the property of George III . . . One imagined the King, in his purple flannel dressing-gown and ermine night-cap, struggling to teach birds to make the music which he could so rarely torture out of his flute and harp-sichord. Or trying to sing with them, in that ravaged voice, made almost inhuman by day-long soliloquies . . . The songs are to be understood as the King's monologue while listening to his birds perform, and incorporate some sentences actually spoken by George III.[38]

In performance the voice is certainly ravaged – it requires a virtuoso performer – and the torture the King endures, which includes the eighteenth-century propensity to "laugh and jeer" at madness,[39] is agonizingly recreated. The composer has said of the music:

> The sounds made by human beings under extreme duress, physical and mental, will be at least in part familiar. With Roy Hart's extended vocal range, and his capacity for producing chords with his voice (like the clarinet and flute in this work), these poems represent a unique opportunity to categorize and exploit these techniques *to explore certain extreme regions of experience*, already opened up in my *Revelation and Fall*, a setting of a German expressionist poem by Trakl.

And the dramatic component of the work on stage may be gauged from the further comment: "The climax of the work is the end of No. 7, where the King snatches the violin through the bars of the player's cage and breaks it. This is not just the killing of a bullfinch – it is a giving-in to insanity, and a ritual murder by the King of a part of himself, after which, at the beginning of No. 8, he can announce his own death."[40] The eight poems are relatively unstructured – as befits mad monologues – and they change direction abruptly with the King's wild swings of mood:

7. Country Dance
Scotch Bonnett
Comfort ye, comfort ye, my people
with singing and with dancing,
with milk and with apples.
The landlord at the Three Tuns
makes the best purl in Windsor.
Sin! Sin! Sin!
black vice, intolerable vileness
in lanes, by ricks, at Courts. It is night on the world.
Even I, your King, have contemplated evil.
I shall rule with a rod of iron.
Comfort ye

The echo of Lear's madness here matches the musical echoes of the score. Like Cawdor in *Visitants*, who also kills himself for fear of an invading madness, the King is unable to bring together the warring elements of his nature, to find some harmony between his inner turmoil and his kingly role. His songs are characterized by a jumbling together of starkly surreal images, and by a deep pathos which nonetheless borders on the ridiculous:

Who has stolen my key? Ach! my Kingdom is
snakes and dancing, my Kingdom is locks and
slithering. Make room!
Pity me, pity me, pity me. Child,
child, whose son are you?
. . . .
Dear elms, oaks, beeches, strangling ivy,
green snakes of ivy, pythons. God guard trees.
Blue-yellow-green is the world like a chained
man's bruise.
I think of God. God is also a King.

The King has lost his liberty, his role as ruler, his people, his Queen, and his health. In the last poem he imagines the ultimate loss of his life:

The King is dead.
A good-hearted gentleman, a humble servant of God,
a loving husband, an affectionate sire.
Poor fellow, he went mad.
He talked with trees, attacked his eldest son,
disowned his wife, to make a ghost his Queen.[41]

The fracture of the personality here, and, in the earlier poems, the boiling over of images normally contained in the sub- conscious, bear testimony to the King's plight, the most telling image of which is his desperately ridiculous attempt to teach birds to sing like instruments.

Miss Donnithorne's Maggot is concerned with a different kind of madness, what Burton calls "Maids' Melancholy". Miss Don- nithorne is thought to be one of the models for Dickens's Miss Havisham in *Great Expectations*, as Stow explains in his Program Note:

> It seems likely that there were at least three models for Miss Havisham of Satis House. One was a woman known to Dickens's friend James Payn. Another was a long remembered London appari- tion, the White Woman of Berners Street, described in Dickens's sketch "Where We Stopped Growing". And the chiefest of them, we can say from the weight of circumstantial evidence, was Miss Eliza Emily Donnithorne, of Cambridge Hall, Newtown, New South Wales.[42]

Miss Donnithorne's husband-to-be, a naval officer, failed to appear for their wedding, and was never heard of again. Miss Donnithorne never recovered from the shock and humiliation, remaining within doors for more than thirty years, and wearing her bridal dress to the day of her death. Her wedding breakfast was left on the dining-room table, mouldering away, because she would not allow it to be touched.

The four poems which tell her story are less tortured than the King's songs, and formally more regular. The comedy of the situation is more emphasized, and while there is still pathos, it is lightened by humour:

> She danced like a candle. "Ah who would not be me?
> To keep her bed all the day, embowered in a tree
> that springs from the cellars, all flushed with wedding wine
> and drops its white dew on me, at dawn when I dine."
>
> The palm by her bedside, it stooped through the bars,
> more gentle than whiskers, more sweet than cigars,
> till full like a spider's egg grew her lovely moony face
> and happy little spiders chased all up and down the place.

The cheerful rhythm here belies Miss Donnithorne's plight, and the discrepancy between the two indicates that her life is divided between a spider-haunted present, and a romantic dream of the past. Her world is made up of bitterness and decay, romantic fantasy, wedding dreams, a pitiable madness, and a crude sexuality:

> But behind my shutters, at my door open on the chain,
> I listen to the voices among my darkening trees.
>   Billy is innocent and Joey is a villain. Joey shouted at my window:
> "Fifty-five and never been ******!"
>   He said to Billy: "They go mad if they don't get it.
> They need ******," he said, "to keep them right."

But still she dreams that her golden-haired officer will come to claim his bride:

> I come! I come. O Heart, I am faithful as you are.
> I am perilous as pear-flower that falls at a touch,
> I am virgin. O chevalier,
> I come.[43]

Her madness is a lingering melancholy that borders on, and occasionally crosses over into delusion, rather than the compulsive, howling misery of King George. Both have lost the things they most cherish, and in the ensuing grief a part of their reason has also been lost. The two works need to be seen and heard in performance, but even as unaccompanied poems they are arresting evocations of that painful country that lies between sanity and madness.

The last three works in *A Counterfeit Silence*, "Stations", "Thailand Railway" and "*From* The Testament of Tourmaline", are also sequences of poems. Covering the range of Stow's interest, and with the richness and intensity of his best work, they form a fitting culmination to the book. "Thailand Railway", which is related to the prisoner-of-war scenes of *The Merry-go-Round in the Sea*, is a series of ten separate but related scenes from the life-in-death of prisoners forced into slave labour on the infamous Burma-Siam railway during the Second World War. Stow recreates the experience with sharply visual clarity, as he does in the novel:

> These skeletons ribbed and tanned like droughtstruck sheep,
> these monkey-faces, hooding their hot sunk eyeballs
> — these are young men.
>
> Limbs that the surf washed, lips that the girls farewelled.

The hatred of the prisoners for their captors gives meaning to their lives:

> My enemy: my passion. At dead of night,
> licking my wounds, I begin to think I love you.
>
> Certainly none were ever so bound in love
> as we are bound in hate: O my ideal!
>
> One sight of you, and life grows meaningful.
> One blow: new strength to every slave who watches;
>
> . . . .
>
> Lover: I mean to take you like a sponge,
> and wring your blood out on Hiroshima.

But there is also, at times, a contradictory forgiveness:

> But I watch the children canter through clumps of gums,
> and shrill galahs take wing in a silver blizzard,
>
> and suddenly all my store of hate runs low,
> runs out; and their simple health annuls my bitterness.
>
> For, in the end, what charge is there to lay
> but this: Be children still, in peace, for ever?

And, as always in Stow, there are the memories:

> Voices in the night: strong voices; young
> voices where none is young, one would have said.
> Voices in unison; voices from the dead,
> telling, though much has died since songs were sung,
> much, much remains: a long, long trail a-winding.
>
> (*CS*, 66-70)

"Thailand Railway" is an extraordinary feat of imaginative sympathy, created from the memories of others,[44] and celebrating a legendary Australian experience with great compassion and insight.

"Stations: Suite for Three Voices and Three Generations" develops themes begun in "Endymion", "The Land's Meaning" and "Ruins of the City of Hay", and it relates directly to the settlement in Australia of Stow's own family, which, he says, "has a rather extraordinary record of having been British colonists since the reign of James I, in Virginia, Newfoundland, South Australia and South Africa".[45] The poem portrays the restlessness that drives colonists to leave home in the first place, and then to be uneasy when they settle in the Eden of their dreams:

> It is the Western destiny to father
> further and further virginal Utopias
> past ever wider, ever-asperging seas.

> . . . .

> Here then, in this most bare, most spare, least haunted,
> least furnished of all lands, we are to foster
> greenly the dream, the philadelphic idyll,
> and in good faith and in good heart dream on.
>
> (*CS*, 61)

As the poem demonstrates, however, it is not easy to dream on. Life is hard, and often violent. And the unquiet sleep of the settlers is disturbed by their guilt at the dispossession of the native people, and the despoliation of the annexed country. Markets collapse, crops fail, and the outside world − in the form of an ageing Europe, or an unacknowledged Asia − refuses to be left behind.

"The Woman", the first of the three voices, begins and ends the poem with these lines:

> *Across the uncleared hills of the nameless country*
> *I write in blood my blood's abiding name.*
>
> (*CS*, 57, 63)

Her three other sections are concerned with the rape of the land, her hopes for her family, and the grief of war. In the first she is troubled by the white usurpation:

> I have robbed from the starving women, I have gone down
>
> to the pool of children and stolen, I have conceived
> a tall blond son, and the pool and the land are his.
>
> (*CS*, 58)

But by the third she is unrepentant:

> War blacks out the land,
> that knew before us neither hearth nor lamplight,
> only the last lost tremor of nomad fires.

> I will not think the justice of our tenure
> questioned by that old guilt.
>
> (*CS*, 62)

"The Man", the second of the voices, who comes as a free settler, not a convict, to the new country, finds that he is also sentenced "forever to remain", imprisoned more subtly and more effectively than any convict:

> *Forever to remain* – the condemnation
> pronounced on graver felons – was for our fathers,
> coming in freedom, a discipline, a promise,
> always retractable.
>
> That is not our case,
> the sons: who ran as children wild
> in an unfenced, new-named inheritance.
> Boys of a greedy spring, horizon drunk,
> peacocked its gold, its streams, declared their stations
> casually by fair water, changed, were changed,
> learning at last that country claims its station
> as men do theirs, and skylines lock around us
> surer than walls: *forever to remain*
>
> (CS, 59-60)

The irony of this reflection on penal colonies and its circularity are both characteristic of Stow, as are the flashes of descriptive colour like gold in a fossicker's pan, and the tone of muted bitterness at being a prisoner of landscape and history.

"The Youth", the third of the voices, is uneasy with his birthright, having inherited along with his stations the restless, searching spirit that drove his forbears to journey from the old world to the new:

> My father has faltered in nothing: his hearth is established,
> his sons are grown; we shall reap the predicted harvests.
> Only I, riding the flat-topped hills alone,
> feel in the inland wind the sing of desert,
> and under alien skin the surge, the stirring,
> a wisdom and a violence, the land's dark blood.
>
> (CS, 59)

It is a short step from this unease to the journey of self-discovery into the desert that we find in *To the Islands* and "The Land's Meaning", and that step is taken in "*From* The Testament of Tourmaline".

If "Stations" is about the complex fate of being an Australian, "*From* The Testament of Tourmaline", like the *Tao Teh Ching*, from which it is derived, is about achieving wisdom and inner harmony by shedding the concerns that dominate the speakers in "Stations", and most of us most of the time:

This is the ideal: to embrace with the whole soul
  the One, and never, never again to quit it.
To husband by will the essence of light and darkness,
  to grow passive and unselfknowing, as if newborn.
Till the doors of perception are cleansed and without distortion,
and knowledge, motive, power become curious noises,
a total wisdom being paid for a total yielding.

                                          (*CS*, 73)

A Counterfeit Silence thus ends, like *Outrider*, with a poem that questions the possibility of communicating at all, and particularly in poetry. Stow has described his recent poems as "mostly private letters" which try "to counterfeit the communication of those who communicate by silence",[46] an aim reflected in the title of his last book, in its Thornton Wilder epigraph – "Even speech was for them a debased form of silence; how much more futile is poetry, which is a debased form of speech" – and in this last poem:

If my words have had power to move, forget my words.
If anything here has seemed new to you, distrust it.

I shall distrust it, knowing my words have failed.

                                          (*CS*, 75)

There is a part of Stow which, curiously perhaps for a poet, distrusts the whole business of writing, with its rhetoric, its strategies and its manipulations. He is drawn instead to reticence, to silence, to a Taoist abandoning of the talkative personality. But since there is also a passionate and articulate poet inside him as well, he has not ceased to write, though there have been some long pauses between publications, most notably between 1969 (*A Counterfeit Silence*) and 1979 (*Visitants*) when he published no books. The tension between speech and silence is evident in the two novels which broke that silence. Even in *Visitants*, with its strong, exciting narrative, and climax of tragic intensity, there is the silence of Cawdor at the centre of the turmoil. And *The Girl Green as Elderflower* is an altogether quieter book, indirect and reticent in approach, from which the reader must tease out the meaning, as the reader of Stow's poetry must when he is in his reticent vein. But the rewards are generous: a haunting music penetrates the silence, and brilliant images rise out of the austere and lonely landscape that Stow has made his own.

6   Circling Days

The Merry-go-Round in the Sea

My mare turns back her ears
and hears the land she leaves
as grievous music.

"Outrider", Stow

The nostalgia of permanence and the fiend of motion fought inside
the boy.

The Tree of Man, Patrick White

In *The Merry-go-Round in the Sea* (1965), a semi-autobiographical
account of growing up in Geraldton in the forties, Stow bids hail
and farewell to the Australia of his childhood. Autobiographies
of childhood are more commonly attempted at the beginning or
the end of a writer's career than in the middle, and they are often
under-distanced, sentimental or self-indulgent.[1] Stow, however,
avoids a too intense involvement in his remembered experience,
and the book, which is beautifully spare and functional beneath
its rich surface of lovingly remembered detail, is a triumph of
artifice and control. The autobiography of childhood is "situated
at a midway point between fact and fiction, between prose and
poetry, between imagination and experience",[2] and *The Merry-
go-Round in the Sea* effortlessly straddles these polarities. While
Stow has adhered to fact ("there is nothing in it that didn't happen
in life"[3]), he has so transformed his raw material that it becomes
more than the story of a single child and his family – so much so
that Australian readers of Stow's generation find that the book
recalls their own childhood experience with extraordinary
vividness. The subtlety of the book, however, lies less in its subject than in its "grievous music", the variations it works on the
emotions of childhood and growing up. Memory, nostalgia,
bitterness and love are skilfully interwoven to evoke a lost,
cherished, bitter-sweet world of quintessential experience.
Nothing later in life is ever quite so intense, so keenly felt, so un-
complicatedly moving; and if there are areas of human experience that are unknown to a child, they are met, when they come,

with emotional responses rooted in childhood. *The Merry-go-Round in the Sea*, Stow's elegy to that unforgotten experience, is one of the finest Australian novels to appear since the Second World War.

It is a less speculative work than *Tourmaline*, and more emotionally compelling. There is not the same struggle to express experience that of its nature resists easy expression, and that draws on a religious vision unfamiliar to most readers. But the books are alike in their deliberate structures. Stow admires the "Victorian ingenuity" of Dickens and Conrad when they plan their novels, and prefers it to what he calls "the easy path" of Jane Austen who writes "a novel rather as if it were one's own diary".[4] *The Merry-go-Round in the Sea* is certainly not diary-like, and Stow has planned it as carefully as *Tourmaline*.[5]

The pattern in *The Merry-go-Round in the Sea* is binary. The titles of the two parts, "Rick Away: 1941–1945" and "Rick Home: 1945–1949", reflect the central importance of the Rob/Rick connection/separation. The parts are symmetrically juxtaposed, each covering four years, and each consisting of ten chapters. In the first part Rick goes away to war, and then comes home. In the second he is at home, and then goes away. The intensity of the war years is succeeded by the bland boredom of peace, which creates in Rick a restlessness unknown in the terrible days of slave labour. While the war is on, and Rick is away, Rob's world is relatively stable, though threatened by external forces. When the war is over, and Rick comes home, that world begins to disintegrate, riven by internal forces of growth and decay as well as by the changes brought about in Rick by the war. Rob's days circle, like the merry-go-rounds and the windmills, but time also moves on, and both Rob's world, and his perception of it, change. He learns, like Rick, that there is no going back to the known nations, except in memory and nostalgia, which crystallize into art. The novel then is as carefully wrought as a sonnet, its two parts interwoven and interconnected, and yet strikingly contrasted. The first part, in which Rick returns home, points towards closure. The second, in which he chooses to go away, points towards openness. Together they maintain a fine tension between the contrary emotions that dominate the book, and that lead Rob to realize, with "agreeable sadness", that time and death will inevitably "stain the bright day" of childhood.[6]

The two-part structure of the book is echoed in its dual protagonists and its double point of view. Rob and Rick are separate characters, but they share so much of each other's experience and consciousness that they often seem almost to be two halves of the same person. Rob is so accustomed to being told that he looks like Rick that when Jane Wexford tells Rob that she thinks Rick is "good-looking" and "terrific" (167), Rob takes it as a compliment to himself as well. More significantly, while Rick is a prisoner-of-war crucial moments of his consciousness are transferred to Rob, and so into the novel, by a process which the Celts in the family are happy to believe is a kind of mental telepathy. And at the end of the book, when the Maplestead clan is discussing Rick's failure to grow up, Margaret Coram suggests Rob may be the only one of them who understands him: "He seems to be trying to turn himself into a carbon copy of Rick" (260). Rick's alleged "immaturity" parallels Rob's adolescence here, and the *doppelgänger motiv* is used throughout by Stow to juxtapose Rick and Rob facing essentially similar experiences of alienation from the safe, clannish world they both love and find themselves compelled to leave. Stow telescopes Rob's childhood and Rick's "maturity" so that primal childhood feelings extend into adult life with remarkably little modification. And this in turn suggests that the complications and sophistications of adult life overlay but do not alter fundamentally the outlines sketched in the life of a child.

Rob's experience of death, for example, though not directly connected with Rick – who encounters death in far-away prisoner-of-war camps – has this double quality: "One of the boys from school who played around the wharf was killed by a ship, crushed against the piles as the ship drifted gently in. It meant nothing to the other boys. The dead boy had simply ceased to come to school. Life beneath the wharf went on" (206). In an earlier adult parallel, Janet Cooper finds it difficult to connect the account of her husband's death given to her by a returned comrade with the Peter to whom she had said goodbye two years before: "He was racking his memory for every detail he could think of concerning Peter, and what he remembered seemed to have no bearing on her husband. He remembered some other Peter, some other Rick. They were people she had never known or seen" (118). While the grief of a wife is certainly not the same as the unconcern of schoolmates, the sense of unreality which so quickly overtakes the memory of the dead in the minds of the living is very similar. Rob knows only indirectly of his aunt's grief – which is described by the adult narrator – but in the scene which immediately precedes this description

Rob discovers the only photograph of Aunt Kay, with its pencill-
ed inscription: *"Fare well is just two little words, but they hold a deal
of sorrow"* (115). Rob is thus brought to share the grief, and the
sense of loss, that time and war bring to the adults of his family.

Stow uses double characters in *Tourmaline* (Kestrel/Random)
and in *Visitants* and *The Girl Green as Elderflower* (Cawdor/Clare),
as well as in *The Merry-go-Round in the Sea*; but his most striking
use of the *doppelgänger* is in the poem "Him", in which the other
self of the poet becomes his lover in a dream:

> And nightlong, lifelong, through all the dreams shifting landscapes
> we clove together, childlike, and yet, like warriors, grave
> till an instant before the dawn. And then I wept, and reached out,
> knowing such grief as a child bereft knows forever,
> watching my only lover, my own self, walking away.[7]

At the end of *The Merry-go-Round in the Sea* Rob wakes from the
dream of childhood as he watches Rick ride away: "He stared at
the blue patch of Rick, feeling bitter, uncryable tears. Rick was
going, although everyone had loved him . . . The world the boy
had believed in did not, after all, exist. The world and the clan
and Australia had been a myth of his mind, and he had been, all
the time, an individual" (283). Rob's grief here is as much for the
loss of a self, personified by Rick, as for the loss of a group and
national identity, and for the loss of his own past. At the very
moment that he begins to become an adult, Rob loses Rick — the
model adult self he would most like to become. The dream of
childhood is over, and Rob is left to find a way towards maturity
on his own.

The book's preoccupation with doubleness is further evident in
its narrative method. In the opening scene a boy asks his mother
to give him a ride on the merry-go-round. The narrator who
presents the scene is aware of the thoughts and feelings of the
six-year-old Rob, but is also a good deal older. He moves into the
boy's mind, seeing things as he sees them, and then moves out,
seeing things with the eyes of a mature man, a poet, who lingers
over details and gives them special significance. This double
perspective is apparent in the third paragraph of the book:

> Beyond the merry-go-round was the sea. The colour of the sea should
> have astounded, but the boy was seldom astounded. It was simply
> the sea, dark and glowing blue, bisected by seagull-grey timbers of
> the rotting jetty, which dwindled away in the distance until it seemed

to come to an end in the flat-topped hills to the north. He did not think about the sea, or about the purple bougainvillaea that glowed against it, propped on a sagging shed. These existed only as the familiar backdrop of the merry-go-round. Nevertheless, the colours had entered into him, printing a brilliant memory. (11–12)

There are three different elements in this vivid description: the scene itself; the six-year-old boy's unthinking acceptance and recording of it; and the poet's perception both of the scene, and of the boy's perception of the scene. The third point of view includes the other two without absorbing them. It remembers what it was like to be a boy, seeing everything, and noticing nothing. Because the book is written by the adult, however, the detail is not incidental, it is not mere background; it has been selected and shaped into adult significance. But the constant shifting of the point of view means that the detail which is significant for the adult has no particular importance for the boy. The book is built on this double perspective, which gives a haunting resonance to the boy's everyday experience. What we encounter then is not only memories of childhood, recalled in all their original freshness, but those memories seen through the elegiac perspective of an adult. The adult knows that childhood is passing, and that it includes within itself in embryonic form those bitter experiences of the adult world which sentimental adults like to think children know, and should know, nothing about.

The choice of the third person – "the boy" – distances the child from the man he has fathered, and emphasizes the generational gap between the writer's selves before and after growing up. Its function is not only to shift the book from autobiography to semi-autobiography, but to suggest that semi-autobiography is all that the divided writer can honestly attempt, in writing of a boy who is and is not he.[8]

The Merry-go-Round in the Sea is also dominated by two images, Australia and the merry-go-round, which are related, like Rob and Rick, and are in a sense the same, as well as being distinct. In Stow's note (Dope for Blurbwriter), included in the manuscript sent to his publishers, he emphasizes the connection between the two: "The aim was, by exploring an Australian clan, a smallish town and the country around it, to awaken a sense of the identity of Australia, its history and fate. The merry-go-round is both the boy's life and Australia's life, and the sea is both

Time and the world beyond Australia."[9] While this is something that Stow had been attempting in various forms from the beginning of his career, *The Merry-go-Round in the Sea* is his most ambitious and considered reading of his native country to date.[10]

The result is a remarkably comprehensive account of Australia. Rob's intense awareness of his Australian nationality and heritage spans the book from beginning to end. As early as the second page we find him reflecting on the country:

> The boy was not aware of living in a young country. He knew that he lived in a very old town, full of empty shops with dirty windows and houses with falling fences. He knew that he lived in an old, haunted land, where big stone flour-mills and small stone farmhouses stood windowless and staring among twisted trees. The land had been young once, like the Sleeping Beauty, but it had been stricken, like the Sleeping Beauty, with a curse, called sometimes the Depression and sometimes the Duration, which would never end, which he would never wish to end, because what was was what should be, and safe. (12)

It is a young/old country with a double history like Rob/Rick. It has had no period of maturity between its old youth, when the oldest of continents was new, and its new youth, which began with European settlement. In *To the Islands* Stow mirrors this discontinuity, and its accompanying sense of absence and emptiness, in the failure of relations between the black people of the first age and the white people of the second. For Rob, Australia is what was, and therefore safe, until it is rejected, along with his other images of safety, in the penultimate paragraph. Between the two crucial discoveries of Rob that mark the beginning and the end of the book — that of time and that of individuality — is crammed an almost encyclopaedic account of the country, its poetry, its flora and fauna, its manners and customs, and above all, the claims it makes on those who live within its boundaries. Of course it never reads like an encyclopaedia, because Rob's experience of Australia is unselfconscious, and therefore seemingly random. It is no more than his boyhood background; but it is nonetheless surprisingly complete. Almost every phase of the country's history is included: from the first sightings of the West Coast, the Costa Branca, by the Portuguese and the Dutch; and the more ancient presence of the Aborigines, evidenced in the Hand Cave; through the convict days of building in stone, and the pioneering days of shearing-sheds with slits in the wall for rifles; to life in a placid country town, and eventually the comparative sophistication of metropolitan Perth. The mixture of races which has made this history is also represented: Aboriginal, Anglo-Saxon, Celt, Southern and Northern European; and so too is the complex cultural heritage derived from these many sources.

The poems Rob hears as a child reflect this complex heritage. They range from nursery rhymes and hillbilly songs, which seem able to cross barriers of time and place remarkably easily, to local, nationalistic works like "My Country", and the various contestants for the title of unofficial national anthem, like "Advance Australia Fair" and "Waltzing Matilda", which Rob is taught at school.[11] It is indicative of his multiple citizenship that while he listens in class to a girl recite "My Country", he is copying out:

> What have I done for you,
> England, my England? (89)

He learns "Lord Randall" at Aunt Kay's knee, along with "tales of glamourie and darkness" (273) and allegiance to Bonny Prince Charlie. Rick at one point calls him: "Gaelic through and through. Just a fey old Highlander" (217), and he is fascinated by the preacher from the Hebrides at Aunt Kay's Kirk, who speaks of "a magical island in the river of time" (113). He learns the poetry of *The Last Post* and *Anzac*:

> They shall grow not old, as we that are left grow old:
> Age shall not weary them, nor the years condemn. (97)[12]

And on Christmas Eve he hears Lisa singing "O Tannenbaum" in German, her voice going "out high and true into the hot summer night" (229). Most striking of all, however, is his simultaneous discovery of the poetry of Australia and his own alienation:

> Now that he had no Aunt Kay to read to him the boy was discovering Australia. He would not let his mother read the poems Aunt Kay used to read, because he could not tolerate the slightest departure from Aunt Kay's manner of reading, and so his mother was free to choose the poems that she liked. And the poems she liked were poems about Australia, about sad farewells at the slip-rail and death in the far dry distance, where the pelican builds its nest. Gradually Australia formed itself for the boy: bare, melancholy, littered with gallant bones. He had a clear idea where Australia began. Its border with his world was somewhere near his Uncle Paul's farm, in the dry red country. Once past the boundary fence, the bones would start. He built in his mind a vision of Australia, brave and sad, which was both what soldiers went away to die for and the mood in which they died. Deep inside him he yearned towards Australia: but he did not expect ever to go there.

Only Harry and the soldiers could go to Australia. He would say
the poems, thinking of Harry and the soldiers.
    Tall and freckled and sandy,
    Face of a country lout,
    That was the picture of Andy,
    Middleton's rouseabout.
He did not know what a "lout" was. But Andy had the face of Harry
and all the soldiers. (78–79)[13]

Of all the alienations that Stow writes about, this sense of Rob's
that he lives outside Australia, and will never go there, is
perhaps the most poignant. That a fifth-generation Australian
should feel, at the age of seven, so complete a separation from
his country is indicative of the intense loneliness that Stow sees
as the lot of European settlers in Western Australia.

Not only does Rob feel divided from Australia, but he senses
that Australia is itself divided: "his world was not one world, but
had in it camps of the dispossessed" (66). The dispossessed are
the "blackniggers" who haunt the fringes of Rob's world without
ever being satisfactorily accounted for:

> Rob did not mind the blackniggers, some of the older ones he rather
> admired. But his mother was furious because Nan was sitting next to
> a blacknigger in school. "They're dirty," said his mother. "They all
> have bugs in their hair."
>
> It was funny about blackniggers. They were Australian. They were
> more Australian than Rob was, and he was fifth generation. And yet
> somehow they were not Australian. His world was not one world.
> (89)

Rob sees with childlike clarity the difficulty of deciding who is
"Australian" and who is not, and it makes him uneasy in his identification with the peoples of his land. And when he searches his
family history, and becomes fascinated with "blood", his friend
Mike Ashcroft reminds him that there are class as well as race
divisions in his world. Mike dislikes Rob's "Pommy" accent (224),
and is unimpressed by Rob's antecedents:

> "It's got to be something in your blood," Rob said. It was his view
> now that all history was a matter of blood.
>
> "That's a lot of bulldust," Mike said. "Hell, Australia was built by
> people who didn't know who their grandparents were. You can be
> anything you want to be, and you ought to be what you want to be,
> not what your grandpa was."

But having voiced these unexceptionably egalitarian sentiments,
Mike promptly lapses into the depressive *alter ego* of the
Australian character:

"Well, what are you going to be?" Rob demanded.
"A drunk," said Mike. "I haven't got any talents." (216)

Rick is later to complain of the "smug wild-boyos in the bars" with their chorus of: "Relax, mate, relax, don't make the pace too hot. Relax, you bastard, before you get clobbered" (281), while Rob has learned quite early in his life that: "nobody wanted anybody else to be good at anything" (64). Even the "Australian Heroes" reflect this embracing of failure: "They're all so sad . . . They always die in the desert or shoot themselves or something" (250). This is particularly true of Rob's personal heroes, the "Poets", like Adam Lindsay Gordon and Byron, who can ride and swim rather than write poetry: "it would not have mattered if they had never written anything at all" (102). Australia, he thinks, "was a good country for Poets" (103), being sad – the emotion Rob associates with poems and songs throughout the book – and littered with bones. Heriot reflects on: "the idolatry of death, the god least despised in this country of suicides",[14] and Rob admires Gordon, who shot himself, and Barcroft Boake, who hanged himself with his stockwhip: "He supposed that their bones were still out there, with Leichhardt's, bleaching in hot tragic Australia" (103).[15] In Rob's melancholy view Australia's divided people find it an easier country to die in, or to die for, than to live in.

The theme of alienation, of the separation of the writer from simple identification with the country of his birth, has been a major theme of twentieth-century literature, and in particular of postcolonial literature.[16] In Australia, which is largely a country of immigrants, and where special factors of distance and cultural isolation have operated, this theme has taken on distinctively local meanings.[17] No one has explored those meanings for the postwar generation more searchingly than Stow, who has defined what is local and unique in that alienation, and related it to the broader and more universal alienation that all post-Wordsworthian men experience as they grow from the organic security of the unified world of childhood towards the complex and fragmented world of adulthood. The attacks on the secure world of childhood come both from inside and outside that world. The attack from inside is an inevitable consequence of the passage of time, the growth of maturity, the beginnings of adolescence and sexual awareness. The attack from without comes for Rob/Rick in the form of the war, which takes Rick away, and permanently separates him from the country he left behind.

The book begins and ends with the merry-go-round, and it appears at crucial stages throughout, becoming a powerful and complex image which embodies the major themes, yet without so obtruding itself as to interrupt the naturalistic contexts in which it appears. In the scene which opens the novel it is specifically connected both to the circular movement, which Rob covets, and to the linear movement, in which he has already realized, at six years old, that he is trapped: "The merry-go-round revolved. The world turned about him. The Library, the car, the old store, the courthouse. Sunflowers, Moreton Bay figtrees, the jetty, the sea. Purple bougainvillaea against the sea" (13). Rob covets the security of the known world, wheeling slowly before him. While it remains reassuringly familiar, his own position within it may remain unquestioned. Time and again in the pages which follow he seeks to place the familiar objects of his world in a fixed position which he can view from the central revolving vantage point of the merry-go-round, as when he deplores the postwar development of Geraldton, or regrets the onset of adolescence.

At the same time he is already aware that he is in love with what is passing:

> He was thinking of time and change, of how, one morning when he must have been quite small, he had discovered time, lying in the grass with his eyes closed against the sun. He was counting to himself. He counted up to sixty, and thought: That is a minute. Then he thought: It will never be that minute again. It will never be today again. Never.
>
> He would not, in all his life, make another discovery so shattering. (14)

This is the first, traumatic breach in the charmed circle of childhood innocence. No other circle that Rob inhabits will ever recreate the serenity that existed in the timeless present before that shattering realization, which Stow recalls again in "Jimmy Woodsers", a bitter poem of exile: "On a morning in March I said goodday to time".[18] One morning, like any other morning, the child realizes that life is finite, that he is perilously rooted in the sea of time, and that he has already begun to die. Rob is destined to create further circles of safety and insularity, to try to maintain a still point in his turning world; and these circles are destined, like the first, to be breached by time and change. Rob fights this inevitable process with the power of nostalgia, the emotion which dominates the book:

In the boy's memory his own past took on the enchantment of poems, so that already his uncle Paul's bleak farm at Dartmoor was transformed, was a poem, was a piercing nostalgia. Anything might bring it back to him: the smell of yeast or of a certain soap, a smell of petals like the big New Guinea beanflowers sweetly wilting. He remembered a century, a whole era that he had spent with Aunt Molly, teasing wool, picking burrs from wool and teasing it for a quilt. He remembered the *ark-ark* of the crows from the ringbarked trees, the kangaroo dog he used to ride, the savage turkey gobbler he had humiliated and tamed by stripping it of a tailfeather. The farm was a smell of chaff, a taste of saltbush, a sound of water swishing in square tanks on the back of a truck. The farm was summed up in one perfect image, like a poem: a morning of mist, himself at the door, saying: "What, look at what?" and then seeing, and sighing: "Oh." Sighing: "Dawn's got a foal. Oh." (47)

This superbly evocative passage is typical of the method of the novel. Beneath a surface redolent with sensuous detail, and selected, it seems, almost at random, is in fact a carefully structured pattern of meaning.[19] In addition to describing the texture of Rob's memories of Dartmoor, it illustrates the nature of his response to them, thereby increasing our understanding of the power nostalgia has over his imagination. This latter leads directly to the novel's thematic concern with the conflict between the continuing process of life and the desire to contemplate the perfect circle of the past, its safe, hermetic world fixed by the transforming power of nostalgia. And this in turn becomes an image for the creative process which produced the novel, Stow's own poem for his lost unforgettable childhood.

The merry-go-round image is particularly prominent in the first chapter, which is something of a set-piece proem like the first chapter of *Tourmaline*, and which begins and ends with the merry-go-round. At the end it is the other merry-go-round, the one in the sea, that Rob has created in his imagination, and that he yearns after with the intense longing of a child denied:

He thought how he would swim far out into the deep water, past all the fences, so far that looking back he would see the world transformed, as it had been from the dinghy. He would swim miles and miles, until at last the merry-go-round would tower above him, black, glistening, perfect, rooted in the sea. The merry-go-round would turn by itself, just a little above the green water. The world would revolve around him, and nothing would ever change. He would bring Rick to the merry-go-round, and Aunt Kay, and they would stay there always, spinning and diving and dangling their feet in the water, and it would be today forever. (25)

In this poignant attempt to regain, by an act of imaginative will, the paradise that Rob has just realized he is losing, there is a skilful and sensitive blending of the two narrating voices. While the childlike tone, and the simple clarity of vision and expression are entirely authentic, the adult poet has shaped both the image and the chapter to give emotional depth to the boy's imagining. A double response is thus evoked from the reader, who recalls his own childhood desire for permanence in all its original freshness, while at the same time seeing it through an adult perspective of unillusioned but feeling sympathy. Stow harmonizes the two responses into a passionate, moving nostalgia.

The forces that threaten the closed world that Rob covets are already apparent in this opening chapter. The violent history of his young/old country haunts its uncertain present. In *The Road to Gundagai*, published in the same year as *The Merry-go-Round in the Sea* (1965), Graham McInnes wrote of his boyhood in Tasmania in terms very similar to Stow's: "This overpowering sense of exile, this feeling of the hostility of a strange land, this insensate brutality of the early convict days lay like a cloak of Nessus over the Tasmania of my boyhood, and I reacted to it strongly."[20] Rob, as we have seen, is intensely conscious of history. On a visit to the Shot Tower of Geraldine, for example, he hears Rick reflect on the past: " 'What miserable bloody beginnings this country had,' Rick said, 'when you think of it. First, half-starved abos, then marooned mutineers, then lead-mining convicts. And at last, respectable folks like us Maplesteads' " (246). Rob has not of course absorbed all of this by the age of six, but he is already conscious of the curse – the Depression – with which the land has been stricken, and which has at least the virtue of halting change. The war, of which he is already aware, threatens to end that stasis: "the one danger he really feared, which was made up of time and change and fragmentary talk of war" (22). Rob wants the circle of his world to remain secure, familiar, unchanging. It is a feeling that is strong in childhood, and threats to it are resisted. In *Myself When Young* Henry Handel Richardson describes "the new and bitter realisation that to live meant to change. No matter how fast one clung, how jealously one tried to stem the flow, in time all things changed and passed."[21] Rob would also hold back the tide if he could, and he does indeed try, though he also comes to realize that temporary, partial victories are all that he can hope for.

The merry-go-round image reappears at the beginning of

chapter three, immediately after Rick has gone away to the war. Rob's life turns, a circle of simple rituals:

> The boy's life had no progression, his days led nowhere. He woke in the morning in his room, and at night he slept: the wheel turning full circle, the merry-go-round of his life revolving. There had been a jolt, with Rick's going, but the grief faded, as if, when he was riding the merry-go-round, another child had climbed aboard and the merry-go-round had bumped, jolting a little on its iron stays, and then grown steady again and gone on turning. (44)

In the long, clear days of the summer holidays, progression seems to have halted, and Rob's life is again circular, unchanging, and safe. But Rick's departure has affected Rob more than he realizes, and his memories of Rick, and questions about him, trouble the adults of his family during the four years Rick is away. When Rick returns, at the end of the first part of the book, he writes the last two lines of Donne's "A Valediction: forbidding Mourning" in Rob's autograph book:

> Thy firmness makes my circle just,
> And makes me end, where I begun.
> Richard Maplestead
> 1945
> (158)

At the time Rob does not understand the meaning of these lines, which indicate that Rob and the family have been to Rick what the merry-go-round in the sea was to Rob in the first chapter: "It was remembering you for three and a half years that kept me circling" (278). Rick wanted to come back to the circles of home, family and country, and the writing of the lines in Rob's book expresses his belief that he has come back, spiritually as well as physically. But "dreams are awful glamourizing things" (278), and Rick's return is destined to fail despite his passionate belief in it for three and a half years, just as Rob's dream of reaching the merry-go-round in the sea is far from realized when he eventually gets there. The circle appears charmed from a distance, but on close inspection it turns out to be only another moment of stasis in the restless onward movement of life.

The twelve-year-old Rob is made aware of how far his life has moved forward when he notices the merry-go-round he used to play on when he was six:

> It seemed that he had not noticed the merry-go-round for years. The broken seat had vanished long ago, and the bent stays drooped down against the iron centre post. It looked curiously forlorn.

"I was mad about that," he said, "when I was a little kid."

Perhaps he would do something about the merry-go-round when he was grown-up and rich. Perhaps he would restore the merry-go-round, and put a plate on it, like the people who had given the town the horse-troughs. He would build the merry-go-round again, and put on it a plate saying:

Presented
to
The Children of Geraldton
by
The Hon. Sir Robert Coram Esqre
D.S.O., M.L.A., LL.D.,
A.D. 2000

And since a merry-go-round was something that people ought to think about, like a sundial, he would put a thoughtful motto on it, like a sundial. And he knew what he would write on the merry-go-round . . . It would be the lines that Rick had written in his book on the night he came home from the war. (228)

When Rob finds his image of timelessness has decayed with time, he imagines building another to replace it, as his father has earlier converted an old windmill-head into a merry-go-round for Rob and Nan to play on in their own backyard. All things fall and are built again, and at this point in the story Rob does not seem unhappy that it is so. His desire to add a motto to his merry-go-round shows that Rick's motto has stayed in his mind, though he still does not understand it fully. For the reader, the passage links the merry-go-round image and the lines from Donne even more closely together. The *Merry-go-Round in the Sea* might be seen as Stow's gift to the children of Geraldton, and Australia, and its motto – something to think about – is the Donne passage, which Stow thought of using as an epigraph for the book.[22]

Rob himself continues to think about it, and it is only at the end of the book, when Rick tells him that he is going away, overseas, that he realizes the full extent of its meaning: "Rick was going, although the boy loved him, and he had taken back the lines that he had written in the boy's book at the end of the war. The world the boy had believed in did not, after all, exist. The world and the clan and Australia had been a myth of his mind, and he had been, all the time, an individual" (283). The realization of his separation from Rick, and from the safe circles of his childhood world, makes Rob bitter here, as we have seen, but it is worth remembering that the lines from Donne belong to a poem entitled "A Valediction", that it is a farewell poem which asserts that the separation of people who love one another need not diminish their love. Rick may already have realized this when he chose the passage, from a farewell poem, to mark a ·homecoming.

Rick's eventual decision to reverse this homecoming and to leave the family again comes to seem as inevitable as Rob's growing up. Both find their interests changing, despite the piercing nostalgia they feel for the past. As soon as the war ends, Hughie knows that the fierce intimacy of his mateship with Rick will change, and will decrease, as they return to their separate civilian worlds in Australia. Rick fights this change as Rob fights the changes that follow on his growing up, but the changes continue for all that. Similarly Rick and Jane Wexford fight the change in their relationship, while both recognize that it has irrevocably taken place. Being an individual means that separation from another, loved individual is as inevitable as separation from the close circles of childhood. In Patrick White's *The Aunt's Story*, Theodora leaves her niece Lou, whom she loves, to go overseas, just as Rick leaves Rob: "Theodora looked down through the distances that separate, even in love. If I could put out my hand, she said, but I cannot. And already the moment, the moments, the disappearing afternoon, had increased the distance that separates. There is no lifeline to other lives."23 There is the same inevitability here, the same isolation, the same sense of time irrevocably passing and changing the closest of relations, that pervades Stow's novel. By the end of the book, Rob has learned this essential lesson. With adult life comes the understanding that that is the way it is, and that, while the bitterness that Rob feels is never entirely overcome, the pleasures of childhood may be recalled, and even recaptured, in memory. Stow does not go as far as Proust, who suggests in *Remembrance of Things Past* that the loving recreation of experience in retrospect is superior to the original experience. But he does want to build a merry-go-round for other children to play on, and other adults to remember, and the ultimately is what his book is.

Towards the end of the book Rick says that Australia "was a good country to be a child in. It's a childish country" (250). He uses the past tense to indicate his realization that it is impossible to go back to childhood, however much he might have wanted to when he came back from the war. It is not necessary to experience the violence of war, as Rick did, to become separated from childhood. Time and growing up are enough, as Rob discovers. Rick finds his life boring and frustrating after the war.

It is irksome being an adult in what he regards as a childish country. Rob, and others in the family, suggest that the fault may be with Rick, who is constantly described as immature, but Stow seems to agree with Rick. There are no adults in the book whose experience matches the intensity of Rob's, except for those "adults", like Rick and Aunt Kay, who share the pleasures of the child's world. Even the adult perspective in the novel is curiously restricted in that its gaze is firmly fixed on Rob's experiences of childhood. It adds an elegiac lament to those experiences, but not an adult explanation. The adult perspective is not extended to the lives of the adults in Rob's world. These are seen, almost entirely, as a child would see them, and not as an adult looking back on his childhood would understand them. Rob's parents, for example, are clearly outlined, but they are not subjected to the searching, unforgiving scrutiny of Hal Porter in *The Watcher on the Cast-Iron Balcony* or Patrick White in *Flaws in the Glass*. Stow has said of his book that "when I write about people I know, as here, I don't go into the people at all; they are a kind of wallpaper for me".[24] *The Merry-go-Round in the Sea* is a lyric, not a dramatic work, and adult characterization is not at a premium.

Nor are adult explanations of social change, as is evident in the description of the postwar boom in Geraldton: "So he walked the streets, and then rode his bicycle through the streets, and at last drove his car through the streets, asking himself how a country town on the sea had become a provincial seaport, how a world so congruent, so close-knit by history and blood and old acquaintance, had become fragmented into a mere municipality. But he knew the answer, by that time" (223). If the adult Rob knows the answer, he does not pass it on to the reader. We may assume that the mature Rob, like Randolph Stow, has become aware of a larger, less congruent, and more fragmented world outside the Geraldton he remembers from childhood, just as Rick experiences the horrible realities of war in the book, and cannot subsequently re-enter the clannish world he left, with its simple loyalties and restricted vision. We are given some brief glimpses of Rick as a prisoner-of-war, but his life in "legendary Europe" (213), like Rob's life after fourteen, is outside the scope of the book, and is not described.

While a clear distinction is maintained between Rob's own view of his childhood and the adult view which parallels and accompanies it, the two are also closely connected. The experiences related in *The Merry-go-Round in the Sea* include war, death, loss and separation, and if children understand these less completely than adults, they feel them just as intensely, if not more so. Rob's experience is not just that of a child; it is also that of a man recalling his earlier experience with the understanding of an adult, and the two combine to form a perspective of wide-ranging human sympathy. When children grow up they both change and stay the same, and this ambivalence is acutely rendered by Stow. Time is forever moving on, and the circle of experience inevitably widens; but later experience never quite matches the intensity of those early years, which live on in the memory, and shape the adult's life.

At the end of the novel Rob is fourteen, troubled by the onset of adolescence and sexuality, and looking back to the safe circle of his childhood life. "I wish I was a kid again" he says twice in the final scene with Rick (278, 280). He is being forced out of the charmed circle of family, town, and known world by his imminent departure for boarding school in Perth. The scene is a bitter one, not only a severing of ties with the known and loved for each of the characters individually, but also a severing of the ties between them – the closest personal relationship in the novel. The novel concludes in a painfully open-ended manner, which contrasts deliberately with the closed ending of the first part, where the lines from Donne reinforce the merry-go-round image of a firmly-centred world with which the novel opens. The second part ends with the dismantling of the merry-go-round, and of the childhood imagination which had fostered it: "The boy stared at the blue blur that was Rick. Over Rick's head a rusty windmill whirled and whirled. He thought of a windmill that had become a merry-go-round in a back yard, a merry-go-round that had been a substitute for another, now ruined merry-go-round, which had been itself a crude promise of another merry-go-round most perilously rooted in the sea" (283). The precise interlocking of related images here mirrors the intricate structure on which the book is built. Part one ends with the assertion of permanence and circularity, part two with the assertion of transience and linear movement. In part one memory and nostalgia triumph over mutability, in part two that triumph is swept away. But something remains in the form of the novel itself – a reaffirmation in the enduring form of art that the transient can achieve a kind of permanence.

Rick's view of Australia as "a good country to be a child in . . . a childish country" (250) catches the contradictory, bitter-sweet feelings of the author as he looks back on a golden childhood with fierce nostalgic longing, and at the same time sees it not only as transient, but also, which is worse because less forgivable, incapacitating when it comes to making an effective accommodation with mature experience. Australians, like Americans, are sometimes exhorted to love their country or to leave it. Stow shows that one must do both and that one cannot do either, using his double protagonist with great skill to focus these contradictory and impossible demands. For Rob, at least until the last scene of the book, it has been a good country to be a child in. No other Australian memoir or autobiography from Henry Handel Richardson to Patrick White can match the evocation of childhood in *The Merry-go-Round in the Sea*, with its intensely vivid recreation of Geraldton and its hinterland in the forties, seen through the expanding mind of a boy. As Rick says of *The Young Desire It*, "it feels young. He was young" (256).[25] Stow has given us the definitive account of what it was to be young in that Australia.

The portrayal of Rick, however, and in particular of the bitterness felt by everyone close to him on his eventual repudiation of Rob and Jane, family and country, is a necessary balance to the lyricism of the portrayal of Rob's childhood. Without this balance, the nostalgia might have teetered over into sentimentality. As it is, the book is not sentimental, despite the obvious temptations of such a subject. A good example of how finely Stow balances the warmth of nostalgia and the bleakness of ongoing experience is the development of the Rick-Hughie relationship. This begins as the archetypal mateship, forged, in classic manner, in the crucible of war and the terrible isolation of slave labour for the Japanese. But, as Hughie predicts, it begins to end as soon as the war ends, and though there are some gallant attempts to recapture its fierce, binding loyalties, particularly in Hughie's extended visit to the Maplesteads, it moves inexorably towards the petty squabble about Hughie's taste that marks its virtual end.[26]

Rick's relationship with Jane also ends in bitterness. He wants someone to love him, but is himself "frozen" (220). All that remains of him after his wartime experience is, as S.A. Ramsey observes, "a hollowed-out shell".[27] Despite her awareness of this, Jane drifts into the engagement with him, against her better judgment, and is repaid with a half-hearted, self-indulgent attachment instead of a mature commitment. Rick and Jane play at being lovers like overgrown children: Rick is less than responsible towards Jane, and she responds with the schoolgirl gesture of attempted suicide when they separate. They can neither love nor leave one another.[28]

The Merry-go-Round in the Sea then is dominated, like *The Girl Green as Elderflower*, by the emotions of love and grief, and by the contraries of change and stasis. These abiding concerns of Stow are summed up in "At Sandalwood", the finest of his poems recalling childhood:

"The love of time, and the grief of time: the harmony
of life and life in change. – In the hardest season,
praise to all three; and the crow's uniting voice
in the empty hall of the summer."

Dead eyes have loved and changed this land I walk
in the grief of time, watching the skins of children
harden under its sun. – My sad-coloured country,
bitterly admired.

I hide, from time and the sun, on the wide veranda.
My great-grandfather's house. Out there, on the straw-brown
    sandplain,
the christmastrees and the blackboy, tougher than ancestors,
bloom in a fume of bees.

"Love time. Love time, love lives on the grief of time.
Change defines changelessness. Hourly, on your journey,
you will turn to speak, you will find your companions altered.
    Such love, such grief cannot tire."

And the crow's voice in the empty hall of the summer
joins sun and rain, joins dust and bees; proclaiming
crows are eternal, white cockatoos are eternal:
the old names go on.[29]

Rob too goes on at the end of the book, loving, grieving, living in Australia, while Rick leaves for Europe and another kind of life. The country in which Rob is left to grow up alone lies on the edge of Asia, an alien continent which produced the war that took Rick away for the first time, and never really allowed him to return. Rob, left alone, looks out towards his merry-go-round, "perilously rooted in the sea", as generations of Australians used to look out to an image of Britain beyond the sea, a fixed point and a homing beacon in the flux of antipodean existence. This image of another, truer home – nourished by successive waves of migration to and from what was seen as the cultural life source – contributed to the restlessness of a people that could not live content in either home. Heriot's final choice of the islands, of the Aboriginal way in preference to the European, has not yet been followed by many of his countrymen, many of whom remain estranged from the land they inhabit. Rob seems destined to share, like Rick, this restless inability to settle, to take possession, once and for all, of the country, the soul of Australia, and to live in it as a native son and not as a visitant.

7 Bushranging

Midnite and Stories

The Governor's son has got the pip,
The Governor's got the measles.
But Moondyne Joe has give 'em the slip.
Pop goes the weasel.

One of Rob's boyish enthusiasms in *The Merry-go-Round in the Sea* is a passionate interest in his family's history, and he is particularly impressed by the story that "Great-grandmother Maplestead hid Moondyne Joe under her bed".[1] Bushrangers are now revered folk-heroes in Australia, where Ned Kelly and Ben Hall are names to conjure with, and Rob wants to feel that the family connection with Moondyne Joe is a personal link with the roaring days of robbery under arms.[2] But Western Australia saw little of the wild colonial boys who boldly defied authority and made fools of the hated police. And Rick is not much impressed with the bushranging prowess of the local Moondyne Joe:

> "You're not getting starry-eyed about poor silly old Moondyne, are you?"
> "Why not?" the boy asked, rather forlornly. "He's the only bushranger we ever had."
> "Some bushranger. Bush-burglar's more like it. Just a house-breaker and a horsethief who liked to hole up in a romantic cave in Great-grandfather Maplestead's back paddocks."
> "Well, if he wasn't a bushranger," Rob said, "he was a sort of what-d'you-call-it, a Houdini. Heck, the governor built a special cell for him at Fremantle gaol and bet him that he couldn't get out of it, and he got out with a spoon."
> "He was a pathetic nut," Rick said, "and he ended his career peddling aphrodisiacs." (218)

Eastern bushrangers died game, tragically cut down in their prime by the traps; they did not end up peddling aphrodisiacs, or living to a quiet old age.[3] Rob therefore has reason to feel aggrieved at this debunking of the family's pet bushranger, who should have been a legendary figure from Australia's glamorous past.

When Stow came to write a bushranging story for children, he not unnaturally chose the story of Moondyne Joe as one of his models. Moondyne, or Joseph Bolitho Johns, was a mild-mannered minor thief: "his robberies were mostly trifling and he rarely resorted to violence".[4] Stow's Captain Midnite is even less formidable than Moondyne Joe − a simple, orphaned boy of seventeen, he is as unlikely a desperado as one might find. The mock-heroic manner in which he is presented humanizes the bushranging myth for young readers − Khat tells Midnite "clean your teeth and go to bed"[5] − while offering the pleasures of parody to more experienced readers. Stow has said that he envisaged a double audience for the book:

> It can be read by children, but it isn't meant exclusively for children. I suppose it came as a kind of sequel to *Merry-go-Round*, and should be read in the same spirit as when Rick reads to Rob there. When Rick reads the story of the Vinegars to Rob, he gets more out of it than the child does ... it's not to be segregated as children's literature, but children do read it, in a number of languages.[6]

Some reviewers doubted the wisdom of aiming the book at both simple and sophisticated readers.[7] Very few children, if any, will have read *Voss*, for example, though if they live in Australia they may have heard the story of Leichhardt and they will have read some bushranging tales. On the other hand children like a little iconoclasm, and they are able to enjoy books with an adult dimension, like *Gulliver's Travels*, if the narrative grips their imagination. *Midnite* has in fact proved popular with young readers, and it was highly commended by the judges of the Australian Children's Book Council in 1968, running second to Ivan Southall's *To the Wild Sky*, which was chosen as book of the year.

The story opens more like a European than an Australian fairytale "in a cottage in a forest", though the forest is in Western Australia "a hundred years ago" (9). Midnite has been orphaned by the death of his father, and "left all alone in the world with his five animals" (10), who promptly begin to speak to ease his loneliness. Khat, the Siamese cat, decides to organize the six into a bushranging gang, though it is clear that he is working with unpromising material:

> This is the place to tell you some things about Midnite that make him different from most heroes in books. One of these things you may have guessed already. It is that Midnite was not very clever. In fact, he was rather stupid, though even Khat forgave him this, because he

was so good-natured. Another thing is that he was not very handsome, not nearly so handsome as Khat or Major or Red Ned, and he
always needed a haircut. But he had nice blue eyes, white teeth, and a
brown smiling face. (11)

The language here is simple enough for quite young children,
who can readily identify with an anti-hero in a world which is
free of adults. The self-conscious, ironic manner of the narrator,
however, who assures the reader that "this is a true book" (10), is
more likely to appeal to adults who have encountered such narrators before in Fielding and Thackeray. The simple and the
sophisticated are brought together in the narrator's personal
appearance at the end of his first chapter:

> "I think I see somebody, a hundred years from today, sitting at a
> typewriter, making up a book called *Midnite*."
> "What is a typewriter?" asked Midnite.
> "It is a machine for writing books," said Khat. "People living a
> hundred years from today will be preposterously lazy." (20).

It is clear that the desire for immortality in art is shared by lazy
authors, Siamese cats and boy bushrangers.

Midnite's opponent throughout the book is Trooper O'Grady, a
good-humoured pickpocket who has turned policeman because
"a young man who had already learned bad habits might feel
safer if he became a policeman" (22). Trooper O'Grady, whose
real name is Murphy, seems genuinely fond of Midnite, though
his sense of professional duty obliges him to imprison his friend
in the great grey gaol by the sea at frequent intervals. Midnite for
his part regards O'Grady as his "best human friend" (56) despite
his bitter disillusionment when O'Grady picks his pockets.
Beneath this camaraderie of cops and robbers is the clear suggestion that the police, never much liked in Australia since convict
days, have profited a good deal more from crime than the
criminals have. When, for example, it becomes evident at
Midnite's first trial that O'Grady has stolen Judge Pepper's watch
and money from Midnite, and is obliged to return them in court,
he remains unpunished, while Midnite is sentenced to twenty-
five years in gaol "for laughing" (56). Such a wild miscarriage of
justice seems all too plausible in the fantasy world of the book,
and has satiric implications for the outside world as well.

With the help of his animal gang Midnite proves as difficult to
incarcerate as Moondyne Joe, who was more accomplished as an
escapologist than as a bushranger.[8] While this irritates the
Governor, and Queen Victoria, it keeps Trooper O'Grady in

gainful employment, and it enables Midnite to enjoy a series of adventures of the kind expected of bushrangers. He spends a night under Mrs Chiffle's bed, for example, fulfilling her lifelong ambition to hide a bushranger there, and quite as agreeably remarks in her Visitor's Book that: "the underneath of Mrs. Chiffle's bed is remarkably free from dust & fluffy stuff" (33). He also attends a dinner party at Mrs Chiffle's to which only ladies have been invited, because "most of the ladies in the Colony were in love with Midnite", while "most of the men in the Colony wanted to put him in gaol" (42). It is there that he meets the passion of his life, Miss Laura Wellborn, whom the author, like Sterne, declines to describe, leaving the reader free to imagine for himself "the most beautiful young lady in the world" (43). Miss Wellborn proves, however, to be as mixed a blessing as Trooper O'Grady. She finds Midnite's Secret Hideout, and is delighted when told that she cannot return home: "But how romantic! . . . I shall be your Maid Marian, and we shall go bushranging together, and we shall be the talk and terror of Australia" (78). Upon closer acquaintance, however, she finds her enforced imprisonment tedious, and her captor a great disappointment: " 'You are not handsome at all', sobbed Miss Laura, 'and your hair needs cutting, and you are only a Boy' " (79), and she makes Midnite's life so miserable that he takes her back from the Hideout to the Zamia Creek Hotel, where she promptly betrays him to the authorities. She also invents a less than accurate account of her imprisonment: " 'Miss Laura Wellborn', said O'Grady, 'states that she was kidnapped in a desperate and fascinating manner by the prisoner, and chained up in a cave, and that the prisoner made a slave of her, and that he was always trying to kiss her, and that she has never had such a romantic adventure in her whole life' " (91). The fact that the last part of this story is the only part that is true unfortunately escapes the notice of Judge Pepper, and Midnite goes back to gaol, indeed, like Moondyne Joe, to a cell constructed especially for him, and intended to be escape-proof.

While he waits for Khat to release him, Midnite writes his lifestory for the newspapers, and publicly swears off Wine, Woman and Song. When he escapes the gang decides to head for the Never Never Desert, "where all the poets and explorers go to die" (85), and it is there that they encounter "Johann Ludwig Ulrich von Leichhardt zu Voss" (who in Australia called himself Mr Smith), and his two bad-tempered camels Sturm and Drang (107). Barcroft Boake's poem "Where the Dead Men Lie"[9] comes in for its share of parody, along with Leichhardt and Voss, before Midnite strikes gold, and becomes Mr Daybrake, millionaire. The entire sequence is replete with satirical variations on the legends of outback Australia in the nineteenth century, which Stow combines so deftly with his brisk and fanciful narrative that, as in *Gulliver's Travels*, the satire does not seem out of place.

Stow's sense of humour is evident throughout his work. His earliest novels include laconic Australians like Fred in *The Bystander* and Rusty in *To the Islands*, while his latest novel *The Suburbs of Hell* sparkles with dry East Anglian dialogue. But it is in *Midnite* that his sense of humour really comes into its own. When Midnite is robbing Judge Pepper on his first bushranging adventure, the coach driver, with disarming affability, offers to help:

> The driver, meanwhile, had been counting the loose change that he kept in his trousers pocket, and he said to the bushranger: "Four and twopence. Is that any use to you, mate?"
>
> "Oh, no," said the bushranger, embarrassed. "No, you keep it."
>
> "You can have it, mate," said the driver, "if you need it."
>
> "Oh no, please," said the bushranger, "you have it. I've got rather a lot of money, as a matter of fact."
>
> "I wouldn't want to leave you short," said the driver. (25–26)

The juxtaposition here of the egalitarian mateship ethic and the Robin Hood philosophy of helping yourself at the expense of the rich sets up a sharply-observed comedy of manners. And Mr Daybrake's later interview with Queen Victoria demonstrates how the rich are encouraged from above, if not from below. The Poet Laureate recites his work "ON THE OPENING OF THE EXHIBITION OF ANGLO-SAXON MILLIONAIRES (1869)":

> Money to right of them,
> Money to left of them,
> Money in front of them
> – Borrowed or plundered?
> Where did they get the stuff?
> Had they played clean or rough?
> When would they have enough?
> – So we all wondered. (119)

Midnite is subsequently promised a (colonial) knighthood, to encourage richness, but his membership of the heavy brigade is short-lived. On his journey back home to marry Miss Wellborn (at the Queen's instruction), he is bushranged of sixteen million pounds by Trooper O'Grady:

"It's not fair," said Midnite, with tears of bitterness in his eyes. "I have worked very hard for three years to get all this money, and now you are going to bushrange it from me."

"Such is life," said O'Grady, which was a famous saying amongst bushrangers. (124)

This ironic misapplication of Ned Kelly's famous last words caps a series of easy-come easy-go role reversals, the satiric import of which is balanced by the sense of fun with which they are contrived.

Not the least surprising reversal is Miss Wellborn's decision to marry Midnite after all. While Mrs Chiffle encourages both parties, and urges them to observe all the niceties of romantic fiction, it is Khat who actually persuades the lady with hard, pragmatic argument:

"*I* don't want a stupid husband," said Miss Laura.

"Don't you?" said Khat. "Most ladies do. He would give you no trouble, and would always do exactly as you told him. He is also extremely rich . . . And the Queen is going to make him a Knight. Just think: if you were Lady Daybrake, with a rich, stupid, good-natured and almost handsome husband, every lady in the world would be jealous of you."

"That is true," said Miss Laura, thoughtfully. (130–31)

So Miss Wellborn declines into a wife, and Captain Midnite's gang lives happily ever after.

Midnite remains one of Stow's own favourites among his novels. Completed on a return visit to Perth in 1966, it was comparatively easy and enjoyable to write. He has described it as "an experiment in Victorian structure as against the cinematic structure of the earlier books",[10] and the narrative is certainly linear, moving straightforwardly to an expected ending in familiar, fairytale manner. The reader is drawn in by the lively invention and the sense of fun, and attacked by the pseudo-naive tone which is alternately funny and cynical. As *The Merry-go-Round in the Sea* so amply demonstrates, Stow remembers his own childhood with extraordinary clarity, and he writes for other children with an engaging sense of what will amuse a young reader – or a jaded adult. The passionate concern with defining Australia, so important a part of *The Merry-go-Round in the Sea*, is sardonically up-ended in *Midnite*, which demonstrates instead a very Australian scepticism about national myths. And the elegiac note is replaced by a light-hearted acceptance of the turnings of fate's wheel. "Such is Life" cries Midnite on the last page, and so it is in the fictional world of childhood.

Stow published no novels between *Midnite* (1967) and *Visitants* (1979), and his only book in that period was *A Counterfeit Silence* (1969), a selection of new and previously published poems. He did, however, publish two short stories in the years before and after *Midnite*, "Magic" (1966) and "Dokonikan" (1968), which are versions of Trobriand Island myths, and which point the way forward from *Midnite* to the grimmer world of *Visitants*.[11] The stories deal with incest and cannibalism, and the fate of those who violate taboos. Stow has drawn on myth a good deal in his more recent work, in poems like "A Pomegranate in Winter" and in *The Girl Green as Elderflower*; and the cargo cult myth of the brothers Kulua'ibu and Dovana lies at the heart of *Visitants*,[12] as Daniel Evans's account of the Umbali massacre lies at the heart of *To the Islands*. "Magic" and "Dokonikan" come from the same world as *Visitants*, and they share the theme of alienation and a desperate search for psychic and sexual companionship. The writing, which reflects the original language of Biga-Kiriwina in its language and syntax, is spare and taut. And the stories have the resonance that Stow admires, reaching outside the culture from which they spring, and finding an echo in alien worlds.

"Magic" is an expanded version of the first half of the *sulum-woya* myth which Stow found recorded in Malinowski's *The Sexual Life of Savages*, and which was also told to him in "an almost identical version" in the same village in 1959.[13] The myth describes the transfer of love magic from the island of Kiriwina to the island of Iwa, and testifies to its efficiency in breaking down even the most powerful of inhibitions – those concerning brother-sister incest. Stow omits the second part of the myth, which documents rather tediously the transmission of the magic, and adapts the narrative of the first part into an intense and vivid account of the temptations and the consequences of taboo sexuality.[14] In his version it is clear that Lalami and Soulava are troubled by their reluctant and half-suppressed desire for one another before any magic is used. He has dreamed erotically of her, but denies the suggestion that she has used magic to make him dream. When the magic pot of coconut oil "accidentally" spills over Soulava, however, she is convinced that she is under a spell, blinded by an irresistible passion, like Tristram and Iseult's. Taking the initiative she pursues her brother, who flees from her to begin with, but who eventually accepts the inevitable consummation of love that is also death. The story, which has parallels in many cultures, explores the blindness of sexual passion and the lure of the forbidden. Both Soulava and

Lalami, who is a future headman of the village, have alternative, socially-approved partners available to them. They know that the shame and disgrace of incest is such that they must die if they pursue their desires. The constraints of custom and fear are indeed so strong that they resort to "magic" to escape into a brief, doomed idyll of wish-fulfilment.

"Dokonikan" is also a story of magic, love and death. Dokonikan grows up ugly, with rows of teeth like a shark. Since none of the girls will love him, he takes to eating people. Unfortunately this attempt to ease his loneliness by absorbing other people has the reverse effect: his loneliness increases as his feasting depopulates his village and then his island. Finally his sister, who alone has understood and remained with him, goes off to another island where she can eat sago instead of people. The last two people left on Dokonikan's island then conspire to kill him. Bulutukwa arms her son Tudava with a magic that blinds Dokonikan with love, and allows Tudava to kill him.[15] It is ironic that Dokonikan, who has tried unsuccessfully to use magic to bring him a lover, ultimately dies in the happy, mistaken belief that he is at last beloved. Perhaps because it lacks something of the European horror of cannibalism, "Dokonikan" is less intense than "Magic" – it is difficult to take too seriously a story in which eating the people one covets is regarded as antisocial rather than taboo.[16] But the loneliness of the malformed Dokonikan is poignantly caught. Like Kailusa in *Visitants* he must live alone, and death is the only end to his isolation. The linking of love and death in both the myths belies the view that the Trobriands are paradisal islands where sexual despairs are unknown. And Stow's choice of the myths reflects his concern with the failure of love. He sees ultimately only the frailest of links between one life and another.

The setting for Stow's only other short story is the more familiar Western Australian landscape. "The Arrival at the Homestead: A Mind-Film" (1979–80) is again concerned with love and death, but the narration owes more to the elliptical ciné-novels of Claude Simon and Alain Robbe-Grillet than to primitive mythology or conventional fiction.[17] The return to a run-down homestead recalls the beginning of *A Haunted Land*, but the nature of the man returning, and his involvement in the action, are more enigmatic. The ten brief sequences shed fragmentary light on "A BUSH TRAGEDY" and "SEQUEL TO A TRAGEDY", two newspaper headlines which lack their accompanying stories – stories which thus become a subtext that the reader must reinvent. In the seventh sequence a man remembers reading these newspaper accounts as a boy, and also seeing the accompanying pictures – studio portraits "retouched .to the point of inhumanity" – of "a man in Australian Army uniform, and a woman in her best hat of World War II" (166). The other sequences suggest a grim tale of illicit love and violence. In the first a woman reluctantly awaits the arrival of her lover/husband/death. In the fourth her lover arrives and finds her passionate. In the sixth he (or another man) arrives and finds her murdered and decomposed in bed, like Homer Barron in Faulkner's "A Rose for Emily".[18] In the eighth a man/her husband/her killer, who has been living alone (except for her body) in the house, finds and reads a letter, and then shoots himself. The abrupt changes and the compulsive repetitions of the sequences suggest an agonized obsession with a childhood tale that has taken on an unbearable adult reality. And this in turn connects "The Arrival at the Homestead" with the Trobriand stories, and with the classical myths and medieval legends that Stow has adapted in his recent poetry and fiction. In all of these cases he has creatively reworked stories that have stayed in his mind, and that have gradually gathered the parallels and correspondences that give them their final, multilayered texture.

Powerful and suggestive though they are, Stow's short stories, like many of his poems, are haunting fragments that need to be viewed in the wider context of his *oeuvre* if they are to yield up their full significance. His real *métier* is the short novel, which is long enough to create its own context, and short enough to retain that unity of conception and imagistic patterning that characterizes his best work. No such work appeared in the decade that followed *Midnite* and *A Counterfeit Silence*, but the books that eventually broke that long silence were well worth waiting for. *Visitants, The Girl Green as Elderflower* and *The Suburbs of Hell* are the work of a fully mature talent, and command respect as major novels.

8 Going Troppo

Visitants

*Sur trop de couches désertées fut mon âme livrée
au cancer du silence.*

"Exil", St-John Perse

I kept, like Asian monarchs, from their sight.

"Epistle to Dr Arbuthnot", Pope

Visitants (1979) is the first of Stow's novels to be set outside his native Western Australia. The setting, a tropical colonial outpost reminiscent of Conrad, is the Trobriand Islands, best known from the work of the distinguished anthropologist Malinowski, who describes the island culture in a number of his books.[1] Stow worked in the islands, off the east coast of Papua, as an anthropologist and cadet patrol officer in 1959, the year in which the book is set, and the white characters in his novel occupy a position of uneasy colonial authority over a Melanesian people only a few years away from independence.[2] As early as in *To the Islands* Stow had portrayed the conflicts inevitable in such a colonial relationship with perception and sensitivity. In *Visitants* he returns to the theme, and treats it with a maturity and a sureness of touch that the earlier novel did not always command. Like Heriot, Alistair Cawdor crosses the boundary between black and white, becoming ultimately "a black man true", though only in death.[3] The tragic course of his alienation and suicide is depicted in *Visitants* with a stark intensity and a richness of resonance that set this novel alongside *The Merry-go-Round in the Sea* as the finest that Stow has written to date.

It was a difficult novel to complete. Though he had written the first three sections, and composed the fourth, by early 1970, Stow did not write down the ending until he had written the sequel, *The Girl Green as Elderflower*, at the beginning of 1979. Only when Cawdor had been resurrected as Crispin Clare could Stow bring himself to describe his death, which looked "so black, so pessimistic, that I wanted to finish *The Girl Green as Elderflower* first, a novel about recuperation, in order to put myself into the mood for putting the final touches to this other novel about disintegration".⁴ The two books are closely interdependent, as the history of their writing indicates, and they need to be read and assessed in terms of one another. Stow has always been fond of juxtaposing contraries, but this is the first time that he has written a pair of books, each hardly more than novella length in itself, which complement one another so symmetrically.⁵ While *Visitants*, like *The Merry-go-Round in the Sea*, is a story of alienation, *The Girl Green as Elderflower* is, less equivocally than *To the Islands*, a story of the journey back from alienation, of the finding of a home.⁶ Grief and shame are the dominant emotions in *Visitants*, grief and love the dominant emotions in *The Girl Green as Elderflower*, and when the two are viewed together, the result – a combination of Stow's most harrowing account of the anguish of alienation with his most hopeful account of the recovery of love – is a powerful and compelling vision of the divided human heart.

Visitants opens hauntingly and enigmatically. The two epigraphs from *The Tempest* and *The Broken Heart* suggest a magic island peopled supernaturally, and a royal tragedy of silent grief.⁷ The Prologue describes without comment the appearance of visitants – four human figures in a disc-shaped craft – in the sky above Boianai in Papua in June 1959. These visitants are observed by the Reverend William Booth Gill, "himself a visitant of thirteen years standing" (1), and thirty-seven Papuans.⁸ After a Dramatis Personae headed "Witnesses at the Inquiry" (3), the reader, his curiosity thoroughly aroused, encounters a sequence of mini-narratives ascribed to the five witnesses and the presiding officer. These tell what emerges as a consecutive story about the visits of a government patrol to the island of Kailuana, off the northeast coast of Papua, and while the story becomes progressively recognizable, and indeed compulsively readable, the mystery remains. The opening paragraph, for example, echoes the death of Cawdor, and cannot be understood until the book has been completed, but it makes an ineradicable impression on the reader: "And he screamed: The house is bleeding. There is nobody inside, he said. But I said: No, *des'*, it could not be like that. A house is strong, I said, and has its own time. You will see, I said; you will see how a house endures" (7). This first segment of the narrative, which is the island girl Saliba's, consists of memories about houses, about MacDonnell's house where she lives and where the inquiry is taking place, and Cawdor's house, which is both his bleeding, untenanted body, and the resthouse at Vilakota where his blood drips through the floor on to his houseboy Kailusa. As evidence it is cryptic but crucial, plunging the reader into the midst of things, both narrative and imagistic, without explanation. The reader has to pick up information as he goes along, though the sequential narrative and the judicious choice of the witness best able to describe each sequence ensure that, as in Faulkner's *As I Lay Dying*, the reader is able to follow the story progressively and gradually to piece together its significance. He does not, however, eventually find any segment from the central character which illuminates Cawdor as fully as Addie Bundren's segment illuminates her. The author of *Visitants* is privileged, but not omniscient, as he indicates in his final "Note": "Like William of Newburgh, recording a strange aerial apparition over Dunstable in 1189, 'I design to be the simple narrator, not the prophetic interpreter; for what the Divinity wished to signify by this I do not know' " (191). Cawdor remains ultimately enigmatic, like Michael Random, a visitant who never quite becomes one of us.

As the reader navigates the complex of opening passages, and as the witnesses follow one another, it becomes apparent that two separate inquiries are being conducted: the official, government inquiry, and the real, novelistic inquiry. Like the narrator at the inquiry in *Lord Jim*,[9] MacDonnell, the island planter at whose house much of the action takes place, has no faith in officialdom:

> The futility.
> But they must know, they say, where it began, for the sake of their files. Just a formality, to have it in black and white. And then it will be there forever, lying on a shelf, turning grey.
> It is ended. That was the point. (8)

The black and white of the coroner's file is a lie and turns grey. The novelist's file, on the other hand, will try to tell the truth, to capture the shadings, to explain what really happened. But the fact that he chooses the form of an official inquiry suggests that Stow is aware that he too ultimately reduces experience to a limited black and white record. What he records are the witnesses' "inner monologues . . . their responses to what other people are saying out loud about recent events",[10] and only a novelist can give us access to such private memories and reflections. It quickly becomes apparent that Stow has also exercised the novelist's privilege to pattern his narrative. Even more than *The Merry-go-Round in the Sea*, *Visitants* is as tightly-written, as singly-imagined as a sonnet. Every image has its echo, every theme its variation, and nothing is extraneous. Despite this patterning, however, and despite our privileged access to the inner monologues of the characters, the mystery of Cawdor remains, ringed by facts and impressions, like the Boianai sightings, but ultimately inexplicable.

The retrospective narrative begins with the arrival at MacDonnell's house on Kailuana of a patrol headed by Cawdor and his cadet assistant Tim Dalwood, a principal witness. The curiosity which greets them on arrival is as intense as if they were visitants from another planet and not just from an alien, ruling culture. If they come to observe, they also come to be observed, and their every action is scrutinized, even through cracks in the shower floor, with fascinated attention.[11] There are three native witnesses, Saliba, Osana and Benoni, whose evidence and commentary reveal, among other things, this relentless observation, and some of the reasons for it. Saliba, a boisterous, buoyant, "giggle-powered rocket" (34) of a girl, is fascinated by Dalwood's size and in particular, according to MacDonnell, the size of his organ, "like the long yam" (12). Benoni, heir apparent to the Paramount Chief Dipapa, seeks Cawdor's friendship and support in his bid to succeed his uncle, who is plotting with Metusela to disinherit him. Osana watches Cawdor for mistakes he can use against him.

The comparatively sophisticated Osana is a hostile witness. The official translator for the patrol, he has been made largely redundant by Cawdor's command of the Biga-Kiriwina language, and he resents it. According to MacDonnell he enjoys: "daunting the maries with his high office and his keyhole-glimpses of Dimdim life" (77), but the presence of Cawdor devalues his position, as Cawdor explains to MacDonnell: "His prestige is falling. For six months now he's been trying to drive me out, and he's still waiting for the moment when I overhear something that goes just a bit too far, and turn round and paste him. Then I'll probably be finished here, and he'll be back where he was: Prime Minister of Osiwa, the man the Paramount Chief comes to for favours" (80). It is hardly surprising to find that this motivation does not surface in Osana's own segments, but we do see him watching Cawdor with fascinated hatred. He sees, for example, and resents, the thoughtless contempt with which Cawdor treats his own devoted houseboy Kailusa while criticizing Dalwood for humiliating his boy Biyu:

> The idiot Kailusa . . . There was nothing in his mind but Mister
> Cawdor who never saw him. On the table where Mister Cawdor and
> Mister Dalwood sat that night was a wooden bowl, that went
> everywhere with Kailusa. In the bowl were the best flowers Kailusa
> could find. It was like a piece of Mister Cawdor's home, that travelled
> with him, whether he noticed or not. So Mister Cawdor dropped his
> cigarette butts among the flowers, because that was his custom,
> whether he noticed or not. (103–4)

The resentment Osana feels at such slights reflects both his
contempt for "ignorant" natives and his distaste for his own
subservient position. In response he treats Cawdor with a
nagging insolence calculated to provoke him – as it finally does
– to enraged retaliation.

Osana has the advantage of understanding all the conversations he overhears, and he is able to use Cawdor's own
knowledge of the native language against him. Wherever the
patrol goes he spreads the news that Cawdor's wife – his
sinabada – has deserted him. The effectiveness of this tactic is
demonstrated when the patrol visits the remote island of Kaga.
The natives murmur the rumoured news almost like a chant,
till finally Dalwood, who does not understand the language,
picks up and repeats to Cawdor the sentence he is constantly
hearing: "*La kwava i paek'* " (60). He is appalled when Cawdor
translates:

> He dropped his voice, though no one within earshot could have
> understood the English. "You said: 'His wife refused.' "
> The quietness seemed to hit me in the head and in the gut, like a
> rush of blood brought on by fear or shame . . .
> "I didn't know," I said . . . "How do they know?"
> "Osana tells them. Or Sayam, or Biyu. Everybody's interested. A
> great old Dimdim comedy."
> "*Why* should it matter so much? It's happened to plenty of other
> people, plenty of *them*."
> "Oh, yes, but," he said, "I'm a Dimdim, and you don't often see a
> Dimdim so – at such a disadvantage. And they have theories . . .
> She'd be amazed. I'm amazed." (61)

The passage is replete with ironies. Cawdor has just humiliated
the Kaga men, albeit unintentionally, by asking them about the
outbreak of cargo cult – Vailala madness – that took place on
the island seventeen years before, during the war with Japan.
Cawdor's interest is impersonal, anthropological; but the men
are deeply shamed and refuse to answer his questions. They
humiliate him in return by their curiosity about his wife's deser-

tion. Cawdor recognizes, and ruefully exploits the irony when he translates the rest of the native murmur for Dalwood:

> " 'His shame, I think, must be very great.' "
> "It's mad," I said. "Their idea of shame − "
> "Of course it is," he said. "But that's just them. Our custom is different." (62)

Osana knows that Cawdor feels the humiliation acutely, and that the Dimdim and island cultures are not unalike in judging a wife's desertion. MacDonnell has also observed the effect on Cawdor: "I remember thinking, as he walked away, that when a man has been humiliated too often . . . the place where it shows itself is in the shoulders" (80). This follows their discussion of Osana's attempts to provoke Cawdor by spreading the gossip wherever they go. MacDonnell's suggestion of an accident with a revolver leads to another humiliating confession by Cawdor, that his "friends", who fear that he will use it on himself, have confiscated his revolver. Osana eventually wins his struggle with Cawdor, and in his last segment he triumphantly blames Cawdor for the uprising and its accompanying deaths. Throughout his segments, which characterize him as well as Cawdor, we see the action through the eyes of an educated native uneasily poised between one culture and another. Like other observers in that uncomfortable position, he has a sharp eye for the shortcomings of both.

Saliba, the second of the native witnesses, works in MacDonnell's house. She bears the Dimdims no malice, but is naturally curious about them, curious enough to accept Dalwood as a sexual partner on one occasion (73). When MacDonnell subsequently protests, rather hypocritically, to Cawdor: "I'm responsible for that girl", Cawdor replies bluntly:

> "No, you're not," he said. "She's been responsible for herself a good four years now."
> "That's all very well," I said, "but what if there's a child? What if she's in love with him?"
> "You know there's never a child," he said. "And never much love, either. All there is is curiosity, and that doesn't leave any complications." (79)

Dalwood is left with claw-marks down his back − a small but telling image of relations between the races − and Saliba, her curiosity satisfied, is left, as Cawdor predicts, with a fondness for Dalwood that causes her no discomfort. Of all the witnesses Saliba is the least involved with Cawdor, but the testimony she gives to the inquiry is valuable, partly because its sympathy balances Osana's hostility, and partly because she too occupies a dual vantage-ground, in her own society and in MacDonnell's house. She can thus describe the outbreak of cargo cult that occurs on Kailuana as a native participant, and the domestic behaviour of the Dimdims as it appears to an outside observer who lives among them. It is no small part of Stow's achievement that she is engaging and thoroughly convincing in both roles.

The man Saliba is really interested in is Benoni, heir to the island chief Dipapa and the third of the native witnesses. Benoni, like Osana, has seen more of the Dimdims and their government than the occasional patrol: he has lived on Manus Island and speaks pidgin and some English. He values Cawdor's friendship, recognizing that he is knowledgeable about the islanders' customs, sympathetic towards them, and a skilful handler of delicate situations. Benoni asks Cawdor to explain the star-machine, and he seeks his support in claiming his rightful inheritance, a claim Dipapa is trying to thwart by adopting the wild-eyed visitant Metusela as his heir. The whites like Benoni, who is their idea of a chief, as they fear Dipapa (and his lieutenant Metusela) who is the natives' idea of a chief. When the crisis comes, however, Benoni demonstrates his own adroit political ruthlessness, persuading his would-be lover Saliba to murder Metusela for him, and conniving (at least) in the poisoning of Dipapa by his former lover Senubeta. Cawdor is peripheral to these events, and largely ignorant of them, though he tries to ascertain the truth, since they take place within his patrol area. The first time he arrives on Kailuana he is already ill and pre-occupied enough to overlook Benoni, who is waiting on the beach to greet him (29). And early in "Visitants", the second part of the novel, Cawdor is wearily uninterested in Benoni's requests (85), though he is later wildly excited by his account of the star-machine (105–7). Benoni's account serves to document, from an uncomprehending point of view, the strange and passionate enthusiasm for the star-people and their "landing-ground", the circle of stones called Ukula'osi, that fills Cawdor's last weeks.

The evidence of the three native witnesses combines to realize the setting in which Cawdor's tragedy is enacted, and to ensure that it is not impenetrable, like Conrad's Heart of Darkness, to a white observer. There is mystery, but no mystification in *Visitants*. Dipapa's much-feared sorcery does not save him, the star-people do not come, and the cargo shed near the ring of stones remains empty. Cawdor's suicide, on the other hand, is real, and mysterious. And it is particularly important, in a book where this central inner landscape remains largely uncharted, that the outer landscape which reflects it should be clearly and credibly realized. For this to happen the three native witnesses must be convincing and convincingly native, and here Stow has been remarkably successful, at least to Dimdim eyes, because of his skilful use of language.[12] Though the book is written in English — with a few native words which are unobtrusively translated in context — it conveys the impression of being multi-lingual with extraordinary effectiveness. Stow has described his method of composition: "I just needed to be able to suggest when people were speaking English and when they weren't, so I did that by translating more or less literally what they would have said in their own language, then putting it into an English which was flavoured by their syntax and their idiom."[13] The success of this method may be illustrated with a passage of dialogue from one of Saliba's first segments:

> "Taubada?" said Naibusi.
> "Ki, Naibus'!" said Misa Makadoneli. "You have shaved your head."
> "E, taubada," said Naibusi. "It is mourning."
> "Truly," said Misa Makadoneli. "Then who has died?"
> "Bakalu'osi, taubada."
> "Ah, my grief for him," said Misa Makadoneli, shaking his head.
> "He was my friend, that old man." (10)

The names, the forms of address, the phrasing, the syntax, and the few native words here combine to shift the language away from English and towards Biga-Kiriwina. While it is notoriously difficult to convey the feel of one language in another,[14] Stow succeeds, I think, and the speech of his native characters is neither wooden nor stagy. Osana's first words, for example, are strikingly vivid: "Mister Dalwood's clothes are always white. He is clean like a hospital. He looks as if they painted him, like the boat. I would not like to have blue eyes. They are not natural. I would not like to have big white teeth. They are like shells" (13). At its best, in passages like these, Stow's version of the native language has the spare clarity and depth of his other writing, and as a result the human context of Cawdor's story comes as alive as its brilliantly-coloured tropical setting. Stow also uses the native idioms "my grief for you", and "your shame" as motifs throughout the book, emphasizing the crucial, and parallel, roles that the emotions of grief and shame have in the lives of both the islanders and the whites.[15]

The witness who is closest to Cawdor, and whose evidence is

therefore central to the inquiry, is Tim Dalwood. He has a boyish enthusiasm for his job at the beginning, and a boyish admiration – untempered by understanding – for his boss Cawdor, which is best expressed by the analogy he uses of Batman and his "boy-apprentice" Robin. But if the relationship begins on a comic-strip level it soon develops, and in the process Dalwood matures rapidly, ultimately crossing the shadow line when he takes command of the patrol from the "troppo" Cawdor. It is not a relationship that develops into intimacy. Dalwood tries to be close to Cawdor, but soon realizes that he is no older brother and that he fights off any close approach. Puzzled by this separateness, he calls Cawdor "a Martian":

> "You were talking Martian because you are a Martian. That's what I always thought. That's why the excitement over the saucer. It's got your people on board. People like you," I said, laughing at the idea, and yet it wasn't a joke, but something I'd seriously imagined, just before, in the dark. "Your folks," I said, thinking of his wife and what it must have been like for her, trying to talk to that, to love that, that visitant. (131)

The Dalwood who had earlier found it hard to understand how Cawdor's wife could have deserted "such a hell of a good bloke" (22) can now sympathize with her finding him too alone to live with. He also remembers Cawdor's excited response to Benoni's account of the star-machine:

> It was very extraordinary to see Misa Kodo's face. What was in his face was like joy.
> His voice was strange too, with joy, or excitement. (105)

And when Benoni completed his story, Cawdor asked to be told if the star-machine reappeared: "If it comes again, run to me, tell me. I want to speak with those people. It is my very strong desire. If I talk with those people, my joy will be great, very great" (107). When Dalwood later protests: "I don't understand you, that's all. Whose side are you on – the Martians?", Cawdor tries to explain his enthusiasm to his bewildered companion: " 'We're not alone,' he shouted. 'Ah, you thick lump, can't you see it? We're not alone' " (112). Paradoxically, however, his joy at the prospect of a peopled universe emphasizes his isolation from his own kind.

Dalwood's most striking view of Cawdor comes at the structural centre of the book. "Visitants" is the title of the second of the book's four parts, as well as of the book as a whole, and at the end of the "Visitants" section, that is at the centre of the book,

Dalwood sees Cawdor at the Vilakota resthouse, the centre of his world, the place where he feels most at home, and the place where he is to die:

> Slowly I turned to face him, and suddenly it struck me how extraordinary it was, that geometrical arrangement that put him at the centre of the world.
>
> Between me and the resthouse was a semi-circle of people, their brown backs towards me. Behind the resthouse was an equal semi-circle of houses, rain-stained grey-brown. The houses followed the contour of the crescent of grey cliff, which was outlined against the sky with a crescent of forest.
>
> The resthouse stood on stilts at an equal distance from two seas. On the right the water was dark and swelling, on the left flat and green. The open veranda of the resthouse was square, and was covered exactly with matting. At the centre of the matting Misa Kodo sat, cross-legged in white clothes, looking out.
>
> I thought: Yes, that is what a king would look like. Not like Mak. Not like Dipapa, even. But remote like that. Alien like that. Now he looks like he must feel. (137)

In this unforgettable vision of Cawdor he is "looking out" from the centre of a Taoist emblem of the square Earth surrounded by the circle of Heaven,[16] but his gaze is unseeing. Encompassed and observed by people, he remains entirely alone, immobile as an icon or a Buddha, rapt in self-contemplation. Stow had in mind, he has said, the Buddhist kings of Siam who received their first Western visitants on a raised stage, in a hieratic attitude, remaining absolutely im.nobile throughout the "audience".[17] Though not immobile in other parts of the book, Cawdor is certainly silent, and a ruler who does not speak is doomed to a life-sapping isolation. This may extend to his people, as a silent epigraph to *Visitants*, which Stow had in mind, but did not use, suggests: "*Sic Amyclas dum tacerunt perdidit silentium*".[18] The author is himself silent at this point in the narrative, and his preference for suggestive visual effects rather than psychic analysis is nowhere more apparent than in this eerie overlay of man-made geometric symmetries on the softer and more random contours of nature.

Though Dalwood learns a good deal about Cawdor in the short time they are together he remains far from understanding him. He relates much of what Cawdor said and did, and adds observations of his own, like the one just quoted, which are imaginatively apt if uncomprehending. He also develops as a character himself, learning from such scenes, and from Cawdor's fate, the value of stereotyped roles: "I thought: I will be different now. See nothing by accident. Hear nothing by accident. Say nothing by accident. Move through the villages like royalty, like a wooden figurehead" (186). To this point in the book Dalwood – who is young, optimistic, and able to relate to other people – has acted as a contrast to the broodingly introspective Cawdor, who knows the value of royal ceremonial, but cannot maintain its impersonality. If Dalwood learns to move through the villages like royalty it may make him a better kiap, but it may also impose personal strains of the kind which contribute to Cawdor's collapse. Calantha in *The Broken Heart* continues to dance with royal decorum as she hears of the death of those closest to her; but she later pays a bitter price for this alienation of natural feeling.

In addition to their memories, observations and opinions, the witnesses report something of Cawdor's history, and some of his rare and brief self-descriptions. Late in the book, for example, Dalwood recounts the bald facts of Cawdor's family history. He was born on Guadalcanal in the Solomon Islands, the son of a Christian missionary. His mother seems to have died early, perhaps murdered by the Japanese. His first language was not English. He was educated at boarding schools, presumably in Australia. One of his two comments about his father comes when Dalwood calls him "crazy" because he is "in love with that star-machine". "My father," he replies, "believes that Jesus Christ was the son of God. Boy, is he crazy, but no one says so" (131). While this comment does not tell us very much about Cawdor's feelings towards his father, and the only other one (71) is even more neutral, it is clear that he is deeply shaken by the news of his father's death.

Cawdor's self-descriptions are also infrequent, but one of them at least, though brief, is fairly explicit. At the end of "Sinabada", the first part of the book, he tells MacDonnell something of his marriage:

"In my second stint up here," he said, "I was twelve months alone on a patrol post. I never saw anyone to talk to, it was just me and the locals. Everyone said how can you stand it? I thought I stood it pretty well, I thought I was happy, I guess I was. But when I went South on leave, first of all I couldn't stop talking, it was like a disease, but there was no one to talk to. So I shut up, and then I couldn't talk at all. I couldn't talk and I couldn't know anybody. I went South to have a good time, spend my money, but I couldn't know anybody. So I went to ground in my father's house in Sydney, because of that – because I knew him, more or less. Then this girl, this woman, started coming.

He asked her to come, I think. And I could talk to her, and she talked to me. So I asked her to marry me. You won't understand this, but it was *that* that I wanted, to be married. So we did marry and came to Osiwa and it didn't work and she went and it's finished. Now you know. It's going to be my leave again soon, but this time I won't take it. I'm not going to take any leave again. I'm going to stay here, in these islands, and if they transfer me I'll resign and be a trader or something, but I'm not leaving. I can't know anybody. I only ever knew her, and she never had any idea what she wanted, and she wouldn't try. (71)

Cawdor repents this confession, partly rum-inspired, almost as soon as he makes it. It reveals how few and how frail his personal relations have been, how reluctant he is to talk about them, and how intense his aloneness has been both before his marriage and since his wife's desertion. His year alone on the patrol post seems to have damaged what ability he had to communicate normally, leaving him able to talk only non-stop or not at all.[19] His wife, whom he married, ironically, because he "could talk to her" may well have found the alternation unbearable. The frantic edge to Cawdor's "I couldn't know anybody . . . I can't know anybody" indicates not so much self-pity as a desperate realization that he has ceased to relate to other people, that the cancer of silence has taken hold, and that he has lost the ability to reverse his condition.

Cawdor's story and the events on Kailuana are interwoven in such a way that they echo one another. The two juxtaposed epigraphs from *The Tempest* and *The Broken Heart* first suggest parallels between the public story of the island and its visitants and Cawdor's private tragedy. This is reinforced by the four-part, almost symphonic pattern of the book, in which the first and last parts are mainly concerned with Cawdor, and the second and third with the public events on the island, though there is of course considerable interweaving. And while the focus does to some extent shift away from the protagonist in the two central parts, it is I think clear that the public events parallel and reflect Cawdor's inner turmoil, so that character and context remain inextricably linked.

When for example Dalwood sees the church at Wayouyo, he finds a building taken over for alien purposes. Cawdor at the time is struggling with an alien personality that he feels has invaded his "house". The Wayouyo church is decorated with: "shapes in wood, beautifully carved, brightly painted. Hearts, clubs, diamonds and spades" (93), as well as with a cross. Inside this bizarre church/casino is another cross:

The earth floor was bare, but at the end where an altar might have been in the God-times, a huge black plane, another ebony one, hung upright from a rope. As I came near a puff of wind hit the wings and twisted it round, and I was looking into eyes.

Cowrie-shell eyes, the underside of the shell, like puckered white lids with no eyeballs behind them. They stared back at me, out of an ebony face. It was a pilot, there could be no doubt about his being a pilot: he was wearing all his gear, I made out the straps of his parachute and the goggles, pushed up on his helmet. He hung there by the neck, with his arms stretched out, crucified on his plane. (93)

Before he has time to take in this black parody, Dalwood is confronted by Metusela:

"You see?" he called. "You see this fellow?"
"Yes." I said. "Very good."
"This Jesus," he said. "Black man Jesus. No white man Jesus. Jesus black . . . You hear," he said more quietly. "One time you kill black man Jesus. Another time, no. Another time, no more." (94-95)

Dalwood is the ideal narrator for this frightening scene, being white, a stranger to the island, and reticent enough to let it reverberate in the reader's imagination without obstructive explanation. Cawdor would have seen it before, and no doubt described it coolly in his patrol diary. What frightens him is internal, and we get only the most fleeting glimpse of his two conflicting personalities, related yet alien, at the end of the book; but Dalwood's experience at Wayouyo acts as an objective correlative for that conflict and the terror it creates.

The same may be said of the entire third part of the book from which Cawdor and the other whites are largely absent. Saliba and Benoni alternate as narrators to describe the outbreak of cargo cult which begins in the village of Olumata and spreads to Wayouyo and Obomatu.[20] It is through their eyes that we see the initial conflict between the villages, the rush of painted men chanting that the star-people will come (149), the wild destruction of fruit-trees, houses and animals, the ceremony in which Metusela, metamorphosed into "man of the stars" Taudoga (157), retells the cargo myth and incites the islanders: "Burn your houses. Burn your food. Burn your skirts and yavis and ramis. Go hungry till we come. Go naked till we come. Dance, sing, make love. We are very near. We may come tomorrow. We are coming with trucks and shotguns and bombs. We are bringing the children of Kulua'ibu their cargo" (158). Benoni sees this bizarre ceremony, and the orgy of destruction which accompanies it, as engineered by Dipapa to deprive him of his inheritance, and with the help of the younger men, Saliba, and Naibusi he puts an end to it. Metusela disappears, quietly killed by Saliba. The islanders return to their burned-out villages. Not long after Dipapa dies, poisoned it seems by his wife Senubeta, who was once Benoni's lover, and Benoni inherits the chieftainship. All of which might seem far removed from Cawdor's difficulties, except in an administrative sense, if we were not reminded of him by five excerpts from his patrol diary inserted at intervals into the narrative. These serve partly to continue the narrative, partly to distance the reader from an otherwise too intense involvement in an engrossing story, and partly to heighten by contrast the excitement it generates. Cawdor's dry, clinical tone is that of an investigating officer engaged on an official inquiry – not unlike the inquiry into his own death. His curiosity is tempered with an anthropological detachment, and his speculation is restrained by a judicial concern for hard evidence. One effect of this is to remind the reader that truth is elusive, and that explanations serve rather to reassure the inquirer than to disclose what actually happened.

Interspersed as these extracts are through the narrative, detached in tone, observing not participating, printed in italics to separate them from the surrounding text, they offer, or seem to offer, some insight into the dead man's mind. In the remainder of the novel there are only two such extracts – for the most part Cawdor appears only as he is seen by others, not as he sees himself. But the reader turning to the diary to discover the real, inner Cawdor finds himself as much puzzled as enlightened. There are almost no personal comments. The impression is rather of an unemotional observer, conscientiously gathering and recording what information he can. Since we know from other sources that Cawdor is physically ill at the time, and in a state of emotional turmoil close to breakdown, the tone of the diary suggests an almost schizophrenic dissociation between his mental and emotional lives. The very absence of emotion in the diary points to this condition. Like Ford's Calantha, Cawdor clings determinedly to his public role as the only sure point in a disintegrating world:

> *It's a comforting institution, that scheme of things. When the Japs dropped a bomb on the MacDonnell's copra shed, Kailuana laughed. Not that they wanted to see the MacDonnell done out of anything, but a copra shed exploding, that was funny. No one said: "What about me?"*
>
> *Keep thinking about time, vast stretches of time, so as not to think: "What about me?" Where was I when the mountains came out of the sea.*

Seize hold of that moment, concentrate on it, meditate on it. Then I know
where I stand with time and it doesn't matter. It doesn't matter. Alistair,
Alistair, she said, it doesn't matter. Don't think about it, it doesn't matter.
(31–32)

Cawdor's obsession with time is very like that of Faulkner's
Quentin Compson on the day he commits suicide. Quentin also
seeks to escape from an intolerable present into the larger
dimension of history.

In the final section of the book, entitled with some irony
"Troppo", Cawdor returns to the centre of the stage for the last
act of his tragedy. By this point it is clear that the condition from
which he is suffering is not one restricted to lonely bearers of the
white man's burden in the tropics. Dalwood will not go troppo,
we come to realize, and MacDonnell has survived, in a fashion,
his long life on Kailuana. For his part Cawdor feels more at home
in the islands than in Australia, and strongly resists the suggestion that a period of leave "back home" would help him to
recover. Cawdor is no Kurtz. He does not find a darkness in the
islands which releases a corresponding darkness in himself, one
that he cannot control without the constraints of civilization. The
turmoil on the island reflects Cawdor's inner turmoil, but it does
not cause it, or even release it. His disease, which is activated by
the desertion or death of the people close to him, and which is
exacerbated by his physical illness, is his isolation, his
aloneness, his inability to draw together the fragments of his personality, to relate them to one another, and so to relate himself as
a coherent person to others. He carries this sense of alienation
with him, and no change of environment will take it away.
Indeed the only environment on which he has a hold, albeit
tenuous, is that of the islands where he was born and where he
now works. As the patrol diary indicates, he clings to his work,
with its scientific detachment, with the rational part of his mind,
while excitedly hoping that the star-people exist, and will save
him by bringing the contact – the cargo – that he needs to
alleviate his condition.

In this fourth part of the book we see Cawdor's few lifelines to
other lives being cut. Early in "Troppo" Dalwood tells
MacDonnell that Cawdor's father has died: "When we got back to
Osiwa last time, there was a telegram to say his father had died. I
think he felt that more than he expected" (171). By this point
Dalwood recognizes – as Naibusi and MacDonnell had foreseen
some time earlier – that Cawdor is past the point of no return:

"Mak, it can't last much longer."
"No," I said. "I'm very sorry for both of you, but it can't. I saw that in his eyes." (172)

Cawdor then allows himself finally to be provoked by Osana's malice into losing his temper and rushing at him with a bushknife: "Osana was terrified. Misa Kodo meant to cut off his head" (175). Dalwood disarms him, however, and takes over the patrol. While this is a necessary precaution it deprives Cawdor of the work which gives him his only hold on the world outside his mind. He turns inward, withdrawing into himself. Dalwood finds him at the stone circle, and the diary extract which immediately follows indicates that he is preoccupied with the star-machine. Finally Cawdor hears on MacDonnell's radio that his friend Jack Manson, with whom he had intended to stay for a time, has disappeared, presumably taken by a shark.

The different reactions of the three men to the brief news item are characteristic. Dalwood, concerned about Cawdor's deterioration, thinks of the possible effect the news may have: "I wondered whether Alistair had heard it, and whether it had given him any more crazy ideas about flying saucers". MacDonnell is suspicious and cynical: "I can't help thinking, a bit fishy. At least, people will say so, and think so. The clothes left on the beach – we've all heard that one before. Sad, anyway, for his wife. Of course he can't be presumed dead for seven years". Cawdor vividly imagines the ugly scene: " 'He'd probably had a row with Sheila, and stormed out of the house for a while . . . It's the watch I can't get over,' Alistair said. 'The watch ticking away on the beach, when Jack was – all in bits' " (181). Cawdor's intense imaginative sympathy cannot focus itself any longer on other people, since the people to whom it is most naturally directed are gone. It therefore turns inwards seeking some reconciliation with himself.

That reconciliation is attempted in his suicide which, like everything else about Cawdor, is ambiguous. It is an act both of despair and of joy, as even the comparatively phlegmatic Dalwood realizes: "My first thought, when Keroni's torch burst into the room, was that it had been done in frenzy, with exultation. I thought that it must have been with a sort of joy that he did it" (185). And the final message that he leaves for Dalwood, and that is to become his epitaph, is certainly not despairing, though it is curiously and yet typically encoded in Biga-Kiriwina, a language Dalwood does not read, and incorporates a quotation he is unlikely to recognize:

"Timi, my younger brother Timi:
Do not be sorry. Everything will be good, yes,
everything will be good, yes, every kind of
thing will be good." (188)[21]

Cawdor's last spoken words, recalling the visit to the cave of the
dead at Budibudi, are also hopeful: "I saw. Timi, I saw. Down the
tunnel. My body. Atoms. Stars" (185). These assertions are,
however, shrouded in pathos, since the reader knows enough of
Cawdor's despair to recognize the courage of desperation. Much
of the force of the very moving climax of the story comes from
the ironies and juxtapositions with which it is presented. The
moment of death, for example, includes a similar assertion by
Cawdor which is mocked by its context: "He reached out his
useless left hand and laid it on my arm. He said: 'I can never die.'
Then he died" (186). Talking to Dalwood earlier in the novel,
Cawdor had foreshadowed his own death, and regeneration:

"Have you ever heard a piece of music marked *troppo agitato?*"
   "I don't think it's possible," I said.
   "I think it is. I want to hear it. At the end, all the instruments would
be in bits."
   "I'll bet it's been done," I said.
   "Ah, but this would be tropical," he said. "I can see it," he said. "The
glue would melt in the heat, and the wood would warp, and the
strings would rot away with damp and snap, one after another. The
brass would turn green, and mildew would be growing on the wood-
winds. When it was finished, the instruments would be thrown in a
heap, and they'd begin to sprout and turn into the trees they were
made from. And reeds and vines, and the wind would blow through
them and the birds would come. That part I'd mark *finito*, or *troppo
troppo*." (48)

There is a similar linking of death and rebirth through the
physical universe in the poem "A Feast", in which "an old dark
man in Mwatawa village" builds a living house to die in. And
Cawdor is to be "reborn" as Crispin Clare in *The Girl Green as
Elderflower*. Stow's own comments on Cawdor's suicide are
illuminating:

I think that there's a mixture of − I don't know, one could say reconciliation and also alarm. His last words before this are that he's had a
vision of himself as a sort of − he says a tunnel. He's had a vision of
himself as being made out of atoms, stars. The atoms *are* stars. This
body that he's killing is a universe. Therefore it cannot die, it can only
re-form. So that when he says: "I can never die", this is not simple
irony − well, it's not irony at all − it is a statement of an illumination

which he's had. And when in his last note he says: "everything will be good" – which is written, of course, before he's had this illumination – he's saying something along the same lines: that it doesn't matter if his physical body dies, the elements will re-form, and all will be well, as Dame Julian of Norwich says: "Sin is behovely; but all shall be well, and all shall be well, and all manner of thing shall be well."[22]

Cawdor's alarm at the alien invasion of his body is stilled by his suicide, which "kills" the invader and prevents further disintegration. At the same time his suicide is a seeking for salvation, for reconciliation, like the Kailuanans' cargo cult uprising. The islanders are oppressed by an alien culture, which threatens the life of their own. The self-destructive elements of the uprising – the destroying of their physical being in the form of food and houses – are prompted by the grief and shame they feel because their culture is inferior to the Dimdims'. They destroy their own life supports in the irrational hope that they can arrest the invasion, and receive the cargo of Dimdim. Cawdor's motives are similarly contradictory. He seeks both an escape and a reconciliation in death: he dies so that he may not die, and so that all shall be well.

If Cawdor finds some reconciliation in death, it is not shared by those who are left behind. The desperate grief of Kailusa, Cawdor's hunch-backed houseboy, who kills himself in a symbolic act akin to suttee, is set beside the official regret of Mr Browne's preliminary report: "The illness and death of Mr Alistair Cawdor, PO Osiwa, has distressed people throughout the islands. Though his irrational mental state in the last weeks of his life has contributed to our difficulties, we remember him as a tireless worker, and a remarkable diplomat. It could perhaps be said that he came on the scene a little too early in the Territory's history" (187). This detached, if not unsympathetic account contains some of the truth about Cawdor, though in looking only at his public career it ignores much of the real life of the man. Osana's penultimate section offers a further contrast. His catechism, which sums up the issues of the inquiry as he sees them from his hostile point of view, blames "Mister Cawdor" for the cargo cult outbreak, and the accompanying deaths of Teava, Metusela and Dipapa. His last, strange question is not "Why did Mr Cawdor die?" – Osana is glad he is dead and the cause does not concern him – but the unanswered and unanswerable "What caused Mister Cawdor?" (188). In stark contrast again is the final speech of the novel, moved out of sequence for effect, in which Osana translates Naibusi's account of Cawdor's last words to her before he left Kailuana:

"O Naibusi, my mind is very heavy." He said: "I am sick." He said: "I think I am going to die. I want to die. I do not want to be mad. I am mad now, Naibusi, and I will not be better. It is like somebody inside me, like a visitor. It is like my body is a house, and some visitor has come, and attacked the person who lived there." He said: "O Naibus'. O my mother. My house is echoing with the footsteps of the visitor, and the person who lived there before is dying. That person is bleeding. My house is bleeding to death." (189)

There can be no question that despair and terror predominate in this harrowing description of a spirit divided against itself, and that these were crucial motives for the suicide which followed.[23]

Visitants, then, is a fuller account of the psychodrama of Cawdor's last weeks than the official inquiry it parallels. The information we are given to help us penetrate the enigma of Cawdor includes not only the silent evidence of the witnesses, and the extracts from his diary, but the accompanying events of the novel.[24] The outbreak of cargo cult, for example, with its irrational destructiveness, its breaking of taboos,[25] its releasing of murderous aggressions, its frenzied belief in the arrival of cargo from the stars, all punctuated by detached excerpts from Cawdor's diary, is both an account of actual events on Kailuana, and an image, an echo, of the turmoil inside Cawdor. As the villagers destroy their food and their houses, expecting cargo to come from Dimdim, so Cawdor destroys his house – his body – while hoping, like a religious mystic, for enlightenment and deliverance from the heavens. Cawdor tries to kill Osana as Benoni seeks the murder of Metusela and Dipapa. At the same time part of Cawdor's mind, the part that writes the diary, watches the behaviour of the villagers dispassionately, and would like to believe that their behaviour bears no relation to his own internal conflicts. He is afraid of the visitor who has come and attacked the person who lives in that part of his house. But he knows, finally, that the mortal conflict between occupant and visitant is killing him.

Earlier in the book, however, Cawdor appears almost frenziedly anxious to encounter the star-people, and not in the least afraid of them. In fact he both fears and craves contact with the visitants. He fears it, as we have seen, because it invades and dispossesses his innermost self. He also craves it because he is afraid that, despite tantalizing clues that we may not be alone, the universe is as empty as the cave of the dead at Budibudi. When explored, that cave did not lead down to an underworld like Virgil's which, however bleak, was at least peopled. It was simply a black hole leading nowhere. If there is no life after death, and if there is no quasi-divine extraterrestrial life either, then there is no relief from Cawdor's existential isolation except perhaps in death. Since Cawdor cannot accept either of these alternatives death seems the only way. His suicide is an ultimate exploration of the psychic and cosmic unknowns that lie beyond death, a last desperate attempt to make contact with a being like himself.

The star-people observed by the Reverend Gill were friendly enough to wave back when waved to, and curious enough to come "quite close towards the ground" when signalled with a flashlight, but they "showed on the whole no interest in anything but their machine", and they did not land after all, leaving the witnesses "very disappointed" (1–2). A wartime Spitfire did once crash on Kailuana, but when the islanders tried to cook on the ammunition it carried, "their cargo went bang in their faces" (87). Cawdor's marriage – his attempt to talk, to make personal contact – had much the same effect. He has come closer to the witnesses at the inquiry than the star-people did to the witnesses at Boianai, but he remains aloof. Though "his silent presence", as S.A. Ramsey says, "dominates . . . the action of the novel and the inquest which takes place after his death",[26] and though we sense his grief and shame, he remains ultimately a visitant, not one of us as Hamlet or Lord Jim is one of us. Stow has not documented Cawdor from the inside, as Dostoevsky might have done. Though there is no lack of imaginative sympathy, there is no psychiatrist's file for us to read, only the evidence of his associates in his last weeks, some fragments of his diary, and a pattern of events which seems to reflect his struggle. T.A.G. Hungerford, to whom the book is dedicated, suggests that its final statement is "exactly the same word from all of us – black, white or brown – to all of us. I am as distant from you as the stardwellers. We may visit, and perhaps hover, and even exchange certain friendly signals. But in the end you will never know about me more than I care to reveal".[27] The final block in Cawdor's case is, however, not so much that he does not care to reveal himself, as that he cannot. He tells Dalwood that he learned the island language only to discover that there was nothing to talk about but "sex and yams" (109). For reasons that he himself does not understand, this accomplished linguist has failed to master the language of those who are close to him, and so they remain estranged. It is his silence that destroys him.

9   Seely Suffolk

The Girl Green as Elderflower

Sin is behovely, but all shall be well.

Julian of Norwich

The sharp compassion of the healer's art
Resolving the enigma of the fever chart.

"East Coker", T.S. Eliot

The Girl Green as Elderflower (1980) is both a companion volume
to *Visitants* and a long-meditated statement of the author's vision,
marking a period in his life. As *The Merry-go-Round in the Sea*
was the fictional summation of his twenty-five years in
Australia, so *The Girl Green as Elderflower* reflects the years in
England which followed. The books then are completed, complementary chapters in the spiritual autobiography of the
author: *The Merry-go-Round in the Sea* celebrating Geraldton, and
the death of childhood; *The Girl Green as Elderflower* celebrating
Suffolk, and rebirth into maturity. Some of the contrasts that
emerge between the two are anticipated in the early poem "Child
Portraits, With Background", in which the poet contrasts a girl's
childhood, "In Southern Forest", where "all the year was green"
and "life is safe and endless", with a boy's childhood "On Northern Downs", where "the year was eternal summer . . . life . . . a
white bird . . . not to be held" and "the crows cried continually of
death".[1] The poem outlines many of the contraries which recur
in Stow, and in particular it juxtaposes the two homes to which
he, and other Australians of his and preceding generations, felt
contradictory allegiances. The restless Richard Mahony could
settle in neither, and Martin Boyd's families move from one to
the other with a poignant, lingering regret that neither can
satisfy them, except, like Proust's Florence and Venice, in an-
ticipation. Stow, however, seems to have found the way home
that eluded Mahony. *The Girl Green as Elderflower* celebrates
Suffolk with quiet, abiding pleasure, and without the fierce,
nostalgic sense of loss that embitters the celebration of Western
Australia in *The Merry-go-Round in the Sea*.

The connections with *Visitants* are, however, more immediate than the connections with the earlier work. *The Girl Green as Elderflower* is a sequel to *Visitants*, and is, as Stow says: "the optimistic side of the very black story of Cawdor".² Crispin Clare is the version of Cawdor who might have survived being "bowled over by tropical diseases, some way from a doctor". He was, he tells Jim Maunoir, "a very raw anthropologist, working for one of the colonial governments", before he came to grief and eventually resigned.³ As the story unfolds, the similarities between his experience and Cawdor's become apparent. But though they overlap in this way, the characters, and their stories, remain distinct. The echoes are deliberate, but the two remain apart. The book is in fact built on echoes, parallels and overlappings, not only of Cawdor and Clare, but also of Clare in twentieth-century Suffolk and *The Lord Abbott's Tales*, three twelfth-century Suffolk legends which Clare translates and reworks during his convalescence. Suffolk is a haunted land, and Clare is haunted by its legends; but the spirits turn out to be friendly, and their stories have a therapeutic effect. He is able to project his own suffering on to the protagonists of the legends, "in their plight to see an image of my own" (136). When his own experience becomes a story, a history, he is able to shed it, to put it into the past, and so to begin his life again. The emblem of his return from death to life is the Tarot card of the Hanged Man which Amabel uses to tell his fortune, and which Matthew Perry sends him from Iran, with its inscription: *"Your card = Resurrection"*. When Clare, who has tried to hang himself, sees the front of the card, "he felt a horror of it" (108), but when he turns it over and reads the paradoxical inscription, the horror recedes into the past, where it belongs.⁴

Clare's Suffolk is not only green and pleasant, and benignly legendary, it is also a peopled place, with all the complex texture of an old civilization. Generations of his ancestors have lived there, and one of them, also named Crispin Clare of The Hole Farm, is buried in Swainstead churchyard. Sharing his name and living in his house, Clare has a sense of belonging to a family and a tradition stretching comfortably back into the Middle Ages. There is a family in the present as well, Clare's recently widowed cousin Alicia and her three children, who enjoy having a newly-returned relative as a neighbour, and who draw him enthusiastically into their family life, and urge him to stay. There are also old friends, like Matthew Perry, who turns up unexpectedly and helps Clare through a memory-haunted night. And there are new friends, like Jim Maunoir, a temporarily retired Jesuit, who helps Clare's recovery more than the priests and psychotherapists who have treated him in an official capacity. This feeling of presence, of warmth, of being surrounded by people is starkly absent from the Australia of Stow's early novels, a land almost as vacant as the empty planet of "Endymion". Behind a mere four generations of European settlement in Geraldton stretches a vast emptiness – an image of the cosmic emptiness that terrifies Heriot and Cawdor – lit only by the nomad fires of another, alien people.[5] This loneliness in the face of the silent bush and the seemingly empty continent ran as a major theme through much of Australian literature, particularly in its early days.[6] And the people of Australia , the most urban-ized on earth, still congregate in coastal cities, seeking relief in propinquity from the emptiness of the interior of their country. As *The Merry-go-Round in the Sea* movingly demonstrates, however, that relief may not survive childhood, and dispossess-ed adults like Rick are more inclined to look across the sea to the Jamesian richness of Europe, than to explore like Voss or Heriot the "great subtlety" of their own country.[7] A descendant of the Australian poets "who died of landscape",[8] Cawdor dies of aliena-tion. Clare, by contrast, is able to make the journey back from alienation, but only in the healing landscape of Suffolk, which has accommodated aliens for eight hundred years.

The visitants that Cawdor is so anxious to meet in the hope that they will relieve his isolation do not come to his rescue. Heriot finds no islands, except those of his own vision, Random finds no water in the desert, only golden cargo, and Dalwood and Cawdor find no souls in the cave of the dead at Budibudi. The star people, if they exist, are shy of human contact, and whether through reluctance or indifference, they offer only enigmatic evidence that the cosmos is peopled. The visitants in *The Girl Green as Elderflower*, however, though strange, are human enough, and local. They come from the past, from under the earth or the sea, not out of the sky, and, as Robyn Wallace observes, they bring life: "the underworld, or otherworld, whether it is the country under the sea or the country under the earth or the country under the conscious self, is finally the source of life, and of a life which can accommodate death".[9] They show Clare the way back from death to life, teaching him to accept death, as Malkin promises to go "hand in hand, to the gate" (51) with Osbern Bradwell.

The seasonal progression of the book echoes Clare's psychic

regeneration. *The Girl Green as Elderflower* is more explicitly a seasonal book than any of Stow's novels since *A Haunted Land*. Clare's story does not follow the full cyclic pattern of the year, with its emphasis on repetition, but only that half of it which moves from January to June in the northern hemisphere, though the full seasonal range is represented in the inner stories. The change for Clare in the frame story is from midwinter to midsummer, from cold to warmth, from death to new life, from the white of snow to the green of growth, and from the green of the elderbud to the white of the elderflower. As this last reversal of colour patterning suggests, however, the book is not simply a celebration of new life. While Clare's story is one of recovery, the legends that he translates are heartrending stories of loneliness, loss and alienation. The victims are displaced from their native surroundings by accident, cruelty or violence, and they can neither live at peace in the worlds into which they are thrust, nor return in peace to the lives they yearn for and remember. It is this common fate in the stories that Clare responds to, since it echoes his own. Even a close and settled society like Suffolk has its visitants. And even high summer carries with it the memory of the winter which preceded it, and which will follow: "the insistent note of the countryside was white embowered in green" (107). It is the knowledge of death which gives life its mystery, its shape, and its poignancy.

Like so much of Stow's work, *The Girl Green as Elderflower* depicts psychic divisions and conflicts in search of an elusive reconciliation. What is unusual in this book is its acceptance of conflict and irresolution as part of a divine dispensation. This is evident in Jacques Maunoir's final, moving statement to the green girl as she lies dying:

> "In love is grief," he said, "in grief is love. As your grief for him is love, so is my grief for you. Pity my grief. Let my grief teach you to love mankind.
>
> "Truly there is in the world nothing so strange, so fathomless as love. Our home is not here, it is in Heaven; our time is not now, it is eternity; we are here as shipwrecked mariners on an island, moving among strangers, darkly. Why should we love these shadows, which will be gone at the first light? It is because in exile we grieve for one another, it is because we remember the same home, it is because we remember the same father, that there is love in our island.
>
> "In the garden of God are regions of darkness, waste heaths and wan waters, gulfs of mystery, where the bewildered soul may wander aghast. Do not think to rest in your village, in your church, in your land always secure. For God is wider than middle earth, vaster

than time, and as His love is infinite, so also is His strangeness. For His love we love Him, and for His strangeness we ought to fear Him, lest to chastise us He bring us into those dark and humbling places.

"I, even I, have known a prodigy and a marvel, and I have wept for two children, and feared in their plight to see an image of my own. Nevertheless I did not despair, for them or for myself, knowing that even in their wandering they rested still in reach of God's hand. For no man is lost, no man goes astray in God's garden; which is here, which is now, which is tomorrow, which is always, time and time again."

Mirabel's eyes, which had been closed, slowly fluttered open. Into them there seemed to come the paradox of a green flush as she died.

"This I believe and must," said Jacques Maunoir. "I believe, and must." (135–36)

The intense conviction of this powerful credo, with its echo of Dante's *Purgatorio*,[10] represents a significant development from Stow's earlier work. The images of island and garden, of land and sea recur, as do the contrasts of home and exile, the love of mankind and the estrangement of each man from his fellows, and the emotions of love and grief seen against a background of time and eternity. But the emphasis is different, and more hopeful. If God is strange, and human life is bitter, there is nonetheless a home with God to which man may find his way. On his journey to that home he will encounter the Green Man, who presides over the cycle of growth and decay, and who "is neither cruel nor merciful, but dances for joy at the variousness of everything that is" (127). The face of the Green Man haunts Clare from his first, midwinter dream to the end of the book. He represents, as Helen Watson-Williams says: "an affirmation of the beauty, the diversity and the inexhaustibility of the natural world".[11] His garden is literal and natural, and it is all too possible to go astray in it, as the green girl does, before she finds a home with Matthew Pedlar, and later, perhaps, with God. In the world of *The Girl Green as Elderflower*, divided as it is between these two deities, contraries remain, and continue to evade reconciliation. But there is a greater emphasis than before on the Christian virtues of faith and hope. And charity, the love of man, is no longer "a weed of the waste places",[12] but a natural growth in the human heart.

The Girl Green as Elderflower is the first of Stow's novels to use one of his own poems as epigraph:

Even such midnight years
must ebb; bequeathing this:
a dim low English room,
one window on the fields.

Cloddish ancestral ghosts
plod in a drowning mist.
Black coral elms play host
to hosts of shrill black fish.

My mare turns back her ears
and hears the land she leaves
as grievous music.

These first two stanzas and the refrain from "Outrider", the title
poem of Stow's second collection of poetry, capture the moment
of waking from feverish nightmare into the unfamiliar, almost
surrealistic, and yet strangely soothing surroundings of "a dim
low English room,/one window on the fields". Australia recedes,
still heard as grievous, fading music, the memory of which will
run in the brain, and in the nerves and the blood as well. The
poem is a very personal one, and its use as an epigraph suggests
that the novel will also be unusually personal and self-
referential.

This book is also the first in which Stow has a writer as protagonist, and we are given some insight into the complex process
by which his personal experience and his reading are blended
and transformed in his art. Stow has made extensive use of myth
in his recent poetry, juxtaposing ancient myth and modern experience so that each echoes the other and a resonance is set up
between them. *The Girl Green as Elderflower* uses the same
technique, though it is a good deal more complex than
"Persephone" or "Penelope", since there are three separate sets of
legends which parallel Clare's experience in the novel. Stow has
cited a parallel in Janacek's *The Excursions of Mr Brouček* for the
adventurous structure that he chooses:

This is an opera about a drunken innkeeper, I think he is, who in his
cups has one vision where he goes to the moon, and meets all kinds of
strange people; and in another one he finds himself back in the
middle ages. And some of the people, I think most of the people, that
he sees in these episodes are people that he knows in his ordinary,
everyday life – we've already seen them on the stage. I was already
intending to do *Elderflower* like this, but I was just a bit uncertain as
to what people would make of it – if they could understand the
device that I intended to use. After seeing that Janacek brought it off

with no trouble I was confirmed in thinking that was the way to do it. So I went ahead.

The difficulties are greater in a novel, since the author cannot rely on the reader recognizing the faces of the doubled characters: "The structure would be less surprising if it had been a film, if one could *see* the faces of the characters from the framing story who take part in the inserted stories. It is rather a cinematic way of doing things".[13] Stow is nonetheless extraordinarily successful in moving the characters of the novel in and out of the frame story and the inserted stories in such a way that multiple resonances are created in an unpretentious and seemingly effortless manner.[14] The personal narrative of Clare is set against the medieval legends he rewrites, peopling them with the family and friends who assist in his recovery. In merging the two, Clare is able to project the burden of his own illness on to the victims of the legends, and so to begin to reify that illness as something past and separate, like the legends.

The book opens with a plan for therapy evolving in Clare's mind: "Quite how to go about doing it Clare could still not see, but the impression was strong with him that the doing would be important, might even be the rebeginning of his health. That idea of health was all but novel to him, he had sunk so deep, and it presented itself with an urgent attractiveness in the new year's astonishing first white light" (3).[15] Like Heriot at the beginning of *To the Islands* and Diana Ravirs at the beginning of *The Bystander*, Clare has just woken from sleep, and like the poet of "Outrider", he has been dreaming of "that planet (ah, Christ) of black ice" which he compulsively revisits in dreams. Rewriting the legends which haunt his conscious mind may help to draw the memory of his own experience out of the subconscious, nightmare world of sleep, and into the conscious part of his mind, thereby rendering it manageable. The beginning of the book is a prescient one, like the opening of *Visitants*, and anticipates what is to follow: Stow does not write one sentence, like Tristram Shandy, and trust to Almighty God for the next. Rather, like Henry James, he is conscious of the essential business of his narrative.[16]

Clare is brought back into contact with his daytime self by a telephone call from Mikey, inviting him to Martlets to receive a message from the ouija board. Walking from the Hole Farm to Martlets, Clare surveys the country, the place to which he has returned in search of recovery. It is the home of his ancestors, and though he has lived there only briefly, and without enthusiasm, as a child, he now finds its permanence comforting:

> There was a twinkling weatherfastness about Swainstead in the snow. Since the late Middle Ages, when it had prospered on the trade in woollens, it had been a substantial village, almost a town, and its substantial houses suggested no want of anything comfortable, ever. After the Clares had left the soil for the law and other professions, a solicitor among them who had thrived announced the fact by buying the house he most admired in his native place. Martlets was not grand, but it had about it the weight and confidence of money, with another quality which money could buy, a high-handed stance towards time. (8)

Not only is the snow-covered countryside in striking contrast to the heat-soaked aridity of Western Australia, or the tropical lux- uriance of the Trobriands, but the foursquare solidity of the village and the house is antithetical to the crumbling Malin, or to the teetering Rotten Wood of *Visitants*. In "A Feast" the poet prefers the "burgeoning and perennial house" of an old man in Mwatawa village to the stately Burleigh House,[17] but in *The Girl Green as Elderflower* it is clear that the comfortable substance of Martlets and Swainstead gives to Clare a reassuring sense of con- tinuity after a lifetime of wandering from one colonial outpost to another, watching the Empire disintegrate. If he does not share the passionate enthusiasm of Martin Boyd's returning Australians for the English country house, he does have a strong and more enduring feeling of having found his permanent home. Like Gardencourt in *The Portrait of a Lady*, Martlets has the mellow glow, the reassuring patina of age.

It also offers Clare a ready-made family which, like his own, is recovering from trauma:

> Last year . . . because his wandering convalescent's freedom was beginning to seem like being lost in space, he had called again at Martlets, and had found Alicia newly widowed, Marco a fraught adolescent half rebellious and half obsessed with duty, the two younger children in different ways disturbed. And somehow he had stayed, tied by threads of old association and new habit. "Oh, don't go away," Alicia said once, down-to-earth as a factory foreman; "I should be sad." "You int so much in demand, booy," said Marco, "that you can't spare some time for us." "I *love* Crispin," Mikey would enthuse, rubbing his cheek against the cousinly bristles; while Lucy, less ex- trovert, would sometimes beg: "Crispin, do please take Mummy out for a drink, she's being just awful." (9)

Clare finds Suffolk all of a piece, seeing parallels between the characters in the legends and Alicia's family and their friends. The unearthly fairy-child Amabel, for instance, startles him when he first arrives by telling his fortune, with aplomb, from a pack of Tarot cards: " 'You made a mistake,' said Amabel, 'and there's going to be trouble, but you'll get out of it and be very happy. But you will need to be much bolder in love' " (11). He is even more unnerved later by the messages that come to him via Amabel from the ouija board. Malkin, the fantastic sprite whose story he has been reading, addresses him in Latin. She then introduces a spirit who is an *alter ego* of Clare's, and who addresses him in Biga-Kiriwina: "It said its name was Kulisapini. That's my name. It said: 'You'll never escape.' It said: 'I'm still here.' It means I died there" (18). The abrupt intrusion of this voice from the past brings back Clare's fever, and he passes out. Discussing the experience later with Alicia, he concludes that Amabel and the ouija board were able to tap his thoughts without his knowledge:

> "It was you, of course, who were writing the Latin."
> "I think that's true," he said, "but I don't understand. I didn't fake it. Nor did Amabel. She was somehow getting messages from me." (21)[18]

Clare's mind, like Cawdor's, has been divided against itself, and it is the self-destructive half that transmits the message. His recovery requires that he learn to accept that part of himself, and the "death" that it brought, as the Clares at Martlets have accepted the death of their husband and father. While they grieve, and the children are disturbed, they also accept it in a way that Cawdor cannot accept the death of his father and Jack Manson, and Heriot cannot accept the killing that human life entails. Clare is eventually able to accept the Alsatian's devouring of his pet cock-pheasant as "the way of the green god" (68), and he learns from his cousins the way back from despair.

He also learns from Jim Maunoir, whom he meets in the Shoulder of Mutton pub. As we have seen, Clare is suspicious of mental and spiritual health professionals, and when he divines that Maunoir is a priest he is initially hostile. Maunoir is quick to reassure him:

> "Listen," Maunoir said. "No, look at me, Crispin." His shadowed eyes were offered like a vow. "No one will be sent to you in this country. And I am not a priest."
> "No?" said Clare, doubting. "Would you lie to me, Jim?"
> "I was a Jesuit," Maunoir said. "I'm not one now."
> Clare put his head down, and breathed deep. He looked at the toes of his Wellingtons among the fag-ends. He started to laugh.
> "What's the joke?" Maunoir asked.
> "I'm paranoid," Clare said, still laughing. "Paranoid. It *is* a joke."
> Maunoir said genially: "It wouldn't take much to convince me you

were psychic. *Non psycho sed psychico*. A fatherly funny. Here comes
the beer from your cousin. Sit up straight now and drink it like a
man."

Clare pushed aside his emptied pot and looked at the circles on
circles stamped in drying beer over the shining wood of the bar. So
inside atoms. So in all space. The everlasting terror of a process
without term.

"How did you know?" asked Maunoir, his glass at his mouth.

"I notice things. I'm a trained voyeur. Like you, Jim."

"Try again," invited Maunoir. "That hardly got through my hair
shirt."

Saluting Mark, drinking Mark's beer, Clare thought to ask: "What
does it feel like, for you?"

"Maybe you know," said Maunoir. "It feels like being lost in the
woods."

"Yes," Clare said. "Yes, I do know." He thought of his dream, of how
he had looked up out of his hole, his pit, his wolf-pit, and seen the
foreign leaves, which had formed themselves into a face, invulnerably amused.

Jim Maunoir had grown remote, gazing beyond Clare's shoulder.
His eyes were clouded over. He had the mouth of a good little boy,
the priest's favourite.

Clare thought of Alicia's voice. He said: "Don't go away, Jim; I
should be sad." (32)

Cawdor can talk to no one like this, once his wife *has* gone away,
and so he turns inward to the dialogue with himself, becoming
preoccupied with atoms and space, "the everlasting terror of a
process without term". Heriot's world is also almost empty:
Justin accompanies him loyally, but cannot share the burden of
his inner journey. The loneliness of the Law is similarly intense.
Though he lives in the community of Tourmaline, he can
address his real thoughts only to the putative reader (if any
exists) of his testament. Clare, on the other hand, can share his
experience with Maunoir almost without talking, because
Maunoir knows what it feels like "being lost in the woods": as a
wounded physician he is qualified to heal.

When he returns home on the night he meets Maunoir, Clare
begins work on his version of *Concerning a fantastic sprite*, the
first of the legends he adapts from collections like Ralph of
Coggeshall's *Chronicon Anglicanum*. The original, which Stow
translates from the medieval Latin into English in his appendix
(145–46), is the story of Malkin, whisked away while her mother
is working in the fields, and transformed into an invisible sprite.
Longing to return to live with mankind, she becomes a familiar
and friendly visitor to the house and family of Master Osbern

Bradwell. Clare reworks this one-and-a-half page story into a twenty-two page narrative. Osbern Bradwell's house becomes Martlets, and Malkin first plays her tricks when the Clare children and their friend Amabel are playing Monopoly, while their father, attended by a tall priest (Father Maunoir), awaits his death in an upstairs room. The children are frightened at first, but they quickly come to cherish Malkin, who has a mischievous sense of fun, and who likes to escape from her spirit world to play with human children.

Her history, when it is told, is a piteous one. The child of an incestuous rape, she has been wished to the devil when only one year old by her fifteen-year-old mother, who resents the burden of her unwanted child, and the lost opportunities that the child represents. When she is approached by the priest, who tells her a series of related stories of children wished to the devil, the mother is unrepentant, and refuses absolutely his plea that she summon her daughter back to the world of men. Malkin is therefore doomed to remain forever a spirit, cut off from her own kind. As such she represents all those psychic victims who are locked into perpetual childhood by parental cruelties. Denied a family, and even an identity, her development has been arrested at the point of final rejection by her mother. Only her mother can free her to grow into a human person, but her mother, also the victim of parental cruelty, will not release her.

Clare finds in her terrible isolation, her process without term, an image of his own alienation and despair: " 'Malkin,' he said, 'we're birds of a feather, gal' " (35). We know little of his own childhood, and one reviewer has gone so far as to suggest that the little that he tells Maunoir about it is false, and should not be believed by the reader.[19] We do know that he felt "lost in space" (9) before coming to Suffolk, and that in the dream from which he wakes at the beginning of the book "he had looked up out of his hole, his pit, his wolf-pit, and seen the foreign leaves, which had formed themselves into a face, invulnerably amused" (32). While this dream aligns him more directly with the green children of the third legend than with Malkin, it certainly suggests that he has personal experience of alienation, and that this has led him to attach himself to the family at Martlets as Malkin attaches herself to Osbern Bradwell's family. As we have seen in *Visitants*, it is not Stow's practice to seek exact analogies, but rather to parallel stories that echo one another at a distance, creating a complex fugue of similarity and difference. Whatever his previous experience, the Clare who broke down in the

tropics has sought like a child a refuge of security and affection
in which to recover, remembering only too vividly what it is like
to be outside the human community, like Malkin, and to be
rendered psychic by affliction. Because of her mother's refusal to
withdraw her curse, Malkin can never be released from her
plight. Clare, by contrast, can learn from her story something of
his own way back to the world of men.

The second part of the book is set in the spring month of April,
Eliot's cruellest month. Like Rob Coram, Clare exults in his
senses:

> The cuckoo had for Clare of all touches the most magicianly, the
> most transforming. When he lay in his bed in the early mornings,
> looking out from his pillow over the clearing of the old fishponds, the
> cuckoo with its frail assertiveness expanded everything, till the wood
> grew huge as the ancient man-scaring forest of High Suffolk, and the
> sound was a tender green.
>   At the edge of each window the apple tree, agitated by bullfinches,
> intruded branches of tight flushed buds. In the nearest field the
> combed bay earth was lined with the first spears of barley, and the
> poplars on the horizon had about them now a copper-coloured mist.
>   He thought on one such morning, listening to the cuckoo, that his
> provisional happiness had put down roots, that the fact of it would
> endure. (65)

If there is cruelty in all this new life – John's Alsatian eats Clare's
pet pheasant – there is also the kindness of Matthew Perry, a
former school friend of Clare's who comes to visit him from
London. Perry has heard the story of Clare's suicide attempt
from "a man on leave from out where you were" (74), and he
comes to offer support. He persuades the reluctant Clare to retell
the story, and the experience is cathartic, comforting them both.
Clare is helped by telling the story while Perry, who reveals that
he is a Jew, is helped by helping Clare: " 'I do *you* good?' said
Clare, and laughed in his surprise. But he knew what Perry
meant. In his weakness, without forethought, he had found a
way to comfort a man made lonely by strength" (78). Perry
claims the Tarot card of The Fool, which Clare finds in his
pocket, as his own:

> "The Fool is the Wild Man. Therefore me."
>   And he could be, too, thought Clare, surveying him. A wild man's
> smile. A wild man's elsewhere-looking eyes. (72)

And when Perry returns to London, Clare's mind naturally turns to the story *Concerning a wild man caught in the sea*, which he begins to adapt that night.

Once again the original legend is considerably enlarged, from one page to twenty, though the outline is retained. And there is again an eerie mixture of twelfth and twentieth-century details, which animates the original while at the same time retaining its strangeness. The setting is autumnal – in contrast to Clare's spring – and the Clare family reappear as the Constable's family, though their role is a relatively minor one. The centre of the story is the friendship which develops between the wild man from the sea and John, his keeper. Like Cawdor, the merman is silent, unable to speak, though he listens to John's transistor radio with fascination. Like Perry he is an outsider, a man of lonely strength. After escaping through the three lines of nets in the haven, he returns voluntarily, because of his affection for his friend John, to the Constable's castle, where he has been sadistically tortured by the racist Corporal Snart. When John is flogged for being absent without leave, his friend takes him away to his kingdom under the sea:

> The merman stood with his friend in his arms, and looked down sharp-eyed through the gloom. John's eyes had closed, and he burrowed into the merman's shoulder, muttering, almost asleep. A slight white smile divided the merman's beard. He leaped into the sea.
>
> The merman entered into his own kingdom, with its vales and hills, its woods and fields, its orchards bearing acorn-shaped fruits. Among the trees rose his palace, its walls and turrets white as coral, its roofs agleam with copper and gilded vanes.
>
> The great hall of the palace welcomed him silently as master. His grey gaze took in with a quiet joy the familiar things of his life: the Egyptian gold, the Grecian marbles, the complexities of Celtic bronze.
>
> With a gentle movement of his shoulder he shifted the head of his human guest to lie in the crook of his arm. The merman smiled. John's mouth was slightly open, his round blue eyes were wide.
>
> The merman bent his head and lightly, almost timidly, kissed the parted lips, the staring eyes. But John was drowned. The merman threw back his head and howled, in a great bubble of soundless grief. (102)

This abruptly tragic ending is not in Ralph of Coggeshall's account, and Clare perhaps derives it from the ending of "Annis and the Merman", a Danish ballad he incorporates into his version, in which the human wife Annis deserts her merman husband and – like Malkin's mother – her children under the sea. It contrasts sharply with the hopeful conclusion of the Clare-Perry meeting in the frame story, against which it is set. The story of Cawdor/Clare, like John Fowles's *The French Lieutenant's Woman*, has alternative endings. Cawdor's suicide is successful, if that is the word, while Clare has been pirated back to life; and it is, ironically, the same lack of privacy which tormented Cawdor that saves Clare: " 'There's no privacy there. Never, at any hour of the day. I was followed. Daibuna − a friend of mine − he'd never heard of such a thing, never seen a sight like it. But he knew what to do. He cut me down with this bushknife' " (75). Perry has, in a sense, saved Clare, as Daibuna did. The merman, by contrast, kills John trying to save him, and his grief is as desperate as Kailusa's when his master Cawdor dies. Clare is aware of the fine line separating one conclusion from the other. In "Kàpisim! O Kiriwina" the prayers of "an old dark woman . . . in the village church" pirate the dying poet back to a life of "fear and trembling" from which he was escaping with "tears of joy".[20] The two novels and the poem all display a profound ambivalence about dying and returning to life, and this is reflected in *The Girl Green as Elderflower* − the most hopeful of the three − in the discontinuity between the frame story of recovery and the enclosed stories of death and separation. Like Malkin, the merman is trapped in his otherness. Neither can satisfy the longing to relate naturally to the ordinary human world. Cawdor's silence, Clare's alienation, and Perry's Jewishness are further illustrations of this fundamental separation of man from his fellows. But if we perish each alone, and if the green god unconcernedly watches us die, we are still within reach of God's hand, and can find some comfort in one another.

The third of the legends also reflects this ambivalence. Of the two green children who emerge from the earth, one, the boy, dies early, while the other, the girl, lives on into old age, marries the Perry-like Pedlar of Lynn, and becomes almost as white as an ordinary human. Stow translates two sources for the story in his appendix, and again he has enlarged considerably on these, while retaining most of their scant detail. The resulting story is more complex and diffuse than its two predecessors. The green girl, for example, gives a number of different accounts of her former life:

> "Mirabel," said the young man, "are you telling me the truth?"
> "Does it matter?" asked the girl, with a shy laugh. "I have so many truths to tell." (134)

It is also an open-ended story in a way that the others are not. The stories of Malkin and John and the merman end, like Cawdor's, in tragedy. The green girl's story, like Clare's, is unfinished, and full of possibilities. As a result the book as a whole also ends in an open-ended manner, and while this is thematically necessary, it denies the reader the pleasures of closure. Life is open, death is closed. And while both must be dealt with if human experience is to be encompassed, it is the sequence that determines the final impression on the reader. *The Girl Green as Elderflower* was completed before the final section of *Visitants* was written, or indeed could be written.[21] Stow's publishers, Secker and Warburg, who received the books in that order, decided to publish them in reverse order. *Visitants* appeared in winter 1979, and *Elderflower* in spring 1980, and the seasonal choice as well as the sequence reflects the author's vision.[22]

The green girl, according to Ralph of Coggeshall, "showed herself very lascivious and wanton" (148), and Clare shows her trying to overcome her isolation through sexual connections with a number of the male characters. One of the stories she tells of her homeland describes the rites of Saint Martin, "begotten of Satan upon a nun", who presides over "magical orgies and obscene discourses" (131). The elusive green-eyed girl in the framing story is clearly related to her, and even allowing for some boastful exaggeration, Robin's account of his meeting with her indicates that she shares the sexual enthusiasm of her twelfth-century predecessor:

> "You ever sin a blonde girl walking about here?"
>
> "Yes," Clare said. "With green eyes?"
>
> "Thass the one," Robin said. "Well, I was out in the van Monday and I see her walking along miles from anywhere and I stop and offer her a lift. Well, one thing lead to another with surprising speed. I never been raped before, and I recommend it."
>
> Clare found himself oddly shocked, his image of the girl violently revised. "You don't mean that?"
>
> "That's how it seem the first time," Robin said. "The other two was quite voluntary."
>
> The boy was grinning widely, and Clare saw in his mouth something innocently feral.
>
> "I hope," he said, not knowing why he should be concerned, "you were kind to her, Robin."
>
> "Well, I warnt unkind," said Robin. "But don't you worry about her. My experience warnt a rare one, by all accounts. They say there's only three things she's interested in, and two of them are round."
>
> Clare wanted to change the subject, but still had a question. "Where does she come from, did she say?"

"No," Robin said. "She don't go in for talking. But she's a stranger of some kind. I'd say Welsh."

He set down his empty mug and scraped back his chair. "Well, to work," he said. Then, with a return of his enigmatic smile: "Given you something to think about, haven't I?"

"Yes, you have," Clare admitted. "Welsh, you think? I'd never have thought of that." (109)

Stow uses dialect here not, as in Shakespeare, to characterize yokels in comic sub-plots, but to localize and to authenticate the setting and the people, as he says:

> The dialect has a high status in the general view. And it seems to be the opposite of exclusive, to be saying, rather, "To hell with this class/status thing, we're all yokels together". I'm glad it doesn't seem diminishing, as many of the characters are based on my friends: it's a way of remembering them in years to come . . . I used to read things in the dialect, such as "Tom Tit Tot", a Suffolk version of Rumpelstiltskin. But the main thing was listening to expressions I heard in shops, pubs and elsewhere and repeating them to myself over and over, often in bed at night.[23]

Stow has a linguist's ear as well as a painter's eye, and his recreation of the Suffolk dialect, like his Englishing of Biga-Kiriwina, is remarkably successful. His books are as precisely located by their rendering of language as by their exact and vivid recreation of physical environment.

The third section of the framing story, of which Robin's story is part, is shorter than the preceding two. Set in May, it contrasts Robin's thoroughly enjoyable sexual experience with Mark's unhappy one, in which there is an echo of Cawdor's failed marriage. Clare comforts Mark as Perry had comforted him. After they drown his sorrows in a bottle of whisky, Clare finds his mind turning to the story of the green children, which is partly a celebration of sexuality, and partly an elegy for two lost children. The green girl's liberality is an expression of her hunger for love, which she pleads for from her partners:

> Afterwards she said, or pleaded: "Roger, you love me?"
> "Love?" said the taciturn man. "Why, gal, that int one of my words. But," he said, giving her a slap on the rump, "I'll say this for you, you int a bad little old poke." (127)

Her first lover Robin is also reluctant to respond to her "strange intensity" (125), and leaves her for Margery, who bathes in milk. But Matthew, the Jew of Lynn, another alien in a hostile world, responds to her hunger and returns her love. They find comfort in one another, and are able to share their lives.

The fourth section of the framing story, set in June, is the shortest of all – the decrease in length of each successive section indicating Clare's returning health and his diminishing self-preoccupation. It includes an amusing letter from Perry, with news of Maunoir, who is returning to the priesthood, and whose own letter is included in the May section. Clare himself has an academic job, like Maunoir, to go to: his life is again on the move, now that his cure is well-advanced. He dozes in the pub, and his brief dream is, in a sense, the internal story of this fourth part of the book. In the dream an advertising poster on the pub wall is transformed into Lady Munby's woods. Walking through these woods Clare sees Amabel, Alicia, and the green girl, who addresses him in Biga-Kiriwina by his name Kulisapini. Each of the three represents an aspect of the partner he seeks, and that partner is both an actual girl/woman, and what Jung calls an anima. Clare has now the potential for a fruitful and fulfilling relationship, and the book ends, not with Maunoir's eloquent, elegiac *credo*, but with Clare's celebratory toast, which he shares with Alicia, to "seely Suffolk".

Clare is able to recover in Suffolk because he finds there what he has lacked, an identity, a role, and a culture. The gravestone in Swainstead churchyard with his name and address inscribed on it gives him a sense of having come home to a life of continuity, and, since it might be him – or his "dead self" – in the grave, it calms his hysteria about death. Alicia and the children offer him a family role, wanting him as the friend and relative they need to help them through their grieving. Perry and Maunoir offer sympathetic understanding of his ordeal, and a fellow-feeling based on their own related experiences. The local legends not only satisfy his anthropologist's curiosity, and stir his creative spirit, they also link him to his own origins, and mirror his experience. Thus the Clare who has lost his sense of himself to the point of attempting suicide finds a self waiting for him in Suffolk, a self he chooses to accept.

It is a settled, peopled, haunted land, and both the people and the spirits come to Clare's aid, breaking in on his loneliness and drawing him back to life. By responding to them, and to their local legends – or myths from the Collective Unconscious – Clare escapes from the terrible isolation of Cawdor, whose star-people never come, and who loses contact with others and ultimately with himself. Cawdor learns only the frigid, life-denying ceremony of Calantha, to move through the villages "like royalty".[24] Clare escapes from that fate to the life-supporting warmth of the village of Swainstead, where he learns again to relate to himself and to other people.

How lasting the optimism of the ending of the book will prove to be is an intriguing question. Australians who return "home" have an indifferent record of settling there contentedly, and Stow, who is an enthusiastic traveller, and who has the restless blood of three centuries of colonists in his veins, is unlikely to remain in the same place, or the same frame of mind, for very long. *The Girl Green as Elderflower* nonetheless indicates that he has moved further towards reconciliation, and even a hard-won serenity of sorts, than could have been predicted from his earlier books, and this is clearly related to the experience of settling in England. He remains, however, as he has always been, intensely aware of the dualities of human experience. The divided, overlaid pattern of the book reflects the divided history of Cawdor/Clare, as well as their antecedents in the earlier books. And even in this last, most hopeful testament Maunoir's determined belief in a caring God confronts the pitiless amusement of the green god, and the gulf between them is only fraily bridged.

10   A Privee Theef

The Suburbs of Hell

Who can take
Death's portrait true? The tyrant never sat.
Night Thoughts, Edward Young

If *The Girl Green as Elderflower* marks the end of a period in Stow's writing, *The Suburbs of Hell* (1984) marks something of a new beginning. Part thriller and part medieval morality, the book is compulsively readable. The writing is tight, there is more vigour and less anguished personal involvement, and the pace is expertly controlled. Stow has described the book as a modern version of *The Pardoner's Tale*,[1] and like that tale it is a good deal more unsettling than the average murder mystery. The web of literary allusion throughout the book attests to the relentlessness with which death pursues life, and to the reckless enthusiasm with which men cooperate by killing themselves and one another, and this dual pattern is echoed in the narrative. Like *The Pardoner's Tale*, *The Suburbs of Hell* is both a rattling good yarn and a searching exploration of the curious mixture of fear, fascination and indifference with which death, especially if it is violent, is commonly perceived. The result is a powerful meditation on this most abiding of human concerns.

Stow has always been an ambitious and adventurous writer, driven to remake conventional forms to accommodate his contrary and divided vision. In his most recent work he combines, like Chaucer, a gripping narrative and a chilling theme, though the greater length and detail of *The Suburbs of Hell* prevent it from imitating closely the profound, uncluttered parable at the centre of Chaucer's tale. Stow's unusual combination of a naturalistic "whodunit" with a moral tale about the visitations of death makes this a particularly *scriptible* book, one which denies the reader the pleasures and the security of a closed form. The greatest contrasts occur at the beginning and the end of the book. At the beginning the bible-laden reflections of Death, precise, world-weary and yet excited, sit uneasily beside the snug, unpretentious cosiness of Harry Ufford at home. And the ending disregards the reader's desire to be told "who done it", a desire normally satisfied in crime fiction, though not so often in the factual world of police investigation. Stow has always avoided tidy endings – his vision of human experience precludes them – and even the death which closes *Visitants* is a beginning as well as an ending. The difficulty this imposes on him when he writes a thriller is that he is bound to disappoint the expectations of his readers, and the challenge he faces is to persuade those readers that their shock of disappointment is also a shock of enlightenment. The denial of closure in *To the Islands, The Merry-go-Round in the Sea, Visitants* and *The Girl Green as Elderflower* expresses powerfully a vision that remains unresolved. In *The Suburbs of Hell* the success is less complete. It is unsettling not to be told the identity of the murderer, and not to be able to deduce who it is from the inconclusive and contradictory evidence provided. If the moral is, as the title suggests, that no man is secure from sudden and inexplicable death, and that we should therefore so live that we are always ready to die, then the "whodunit" clues and suspicions create false expectations in the reader. And the realization that identifying the killer will not slow the march of death, and may only induce a false sense of security, does not entirely compensate for the reader's sense of frustration.

The insinuating first-person reflection with which the book opens unnerves and intrigues the reader partly because, like the openings of other Stow books, it is not quite consonant with what immediately follows. On the first day of winter Death has returned to Old Tornwich, anticipating a spate of killings which will feed his desire to see inside the lives of those who will die. He quotes with approval the biblical descriptions of death as a thief in the night, defining a thief as:

> "a student of people . . . I have stood in a pub and seen a face, heard a voice, and slipped out and entered that man's house, calm in my mastery of all his habits. But then – ah, the thrill then, after my many studies; to find his things, his self, lying opened before me, all his secrets at my fingers' ends. . . . It is the intoxication of inside".[2]

While these might be the thoughts of a human thief, an outsider voyeuristically looking in, coveting the lifestyle of his victims, they might also be the thoughts of a novelist insatiably curious about the secrets of other people. Like the thief, the novelist can invade his characters' privacy, and kill them off violently if he wishes. And if the perfect "whodunit" has the reader as the murderer,[3] then one in which the writer is the murderer is not without its attractions. The reader is thus involved in the roles of killer and victim, and as these metafictional possibilities echo in his mind, Death goes on to other descriptions of his motives: "It is not envy or anything of hatred . . . No; it is never hostility or malice. Simply, it is correction, a chastising" (2). He seems morally to disapprove of his victims for forgetting that they are mortal, that they owe God a death. He identifies the murderer's first victim as the teacher Paul Ramsey. And he ends as he began with the bible: "*Thou fool, this night thy soul shall be required of thee*" (2). This mixed set of motives offers the reader a typically enigmatic insight into the story which follows. Death strikes randomly, without apparent reason, thereby reminding his subjects that they must answer to him, and chastising their forgetfulness. Human killers, however, usually have motives which, while they may be arbitrary and even bizarre, are also understandable.

The flourish of epigraphs and allusions with which the book begins reinforces the metafictional dimension of the first section. The title is taken from *The Duchess of Malfi*, as the half-repentant Bosola prepares to murder Antonio:

> Security some men call the suburbs of hell,
> Only a dead wall between.[4]

and the book's epigraph is from *The White Devil*:

> *Gasparo.*
> You have acted certain murders here in Rome
> Bloody, and full of horror.
> *Lodovico.*
> 'Las, they were flea-bitings.[5]

Stow has used epigraphs from Jacobean drama in many of his books, clearly seeing an affinity between his own work and the grim world of senseless violence depicted by Webster and his contemporaries. The epigraph to the first section of the book is from *Beowulf* and it reinforces the image of death as a Grendel-like monster, seeking whom he may devour:

> But the demon, a black shadow
> of death, prowled long in ambush,
> and plotted against young and old.[6]

Grendel, like the "Nedlands Monster" referred to in the dedication,[7] and like the killer in *The Suburbs of Hell*, is inhuman in his seemingly motiveless thirst for blood. And yet it is paradoxically true that it is both human and inhuman, natural and unnatural to kill, as the bloody history of human affairs, and the long list of those who have gorged death's insatiable appetite, bear eloquent witness.[8]

Tornwich, where *The Suburbs of Hell* is set, is both intensely and recognizably local, and a microcosm of the larger world. Based on Harwich, where Stow now lives, the town and its surroundings are as fully and as lovingly realized as Stow's other landscapes, and the dialect and the voices of East Anglia are familiar from *The Girl Green as Elderflower*. Some of the houses in the port of Old Tornwich date back to the middle ages, and Stow is fascinated by this time-layered urban landscape. As we have seen, the literary context of the book begins with *Beowulf* and moves through Chaucer and Elizabethan and Jacobean drama to the twentieth-century murder mystery. The physical setting of the book is also multidimensional, with the division between Old Tornwich and Victorian New Tornwich the most obvious, but by no means the only division. Many different kinds of people are attracted to a port. There are the native English whose lives are cosily interconnected, and yet separated by abrupt privacies and reticences. Among the English there are the locals like Harry Ufford, and the imported professionals like Paul and Greg Ramsey. There are sea-based and land-based workers, fishermen, ferry crews, businessmen, smugglers and petty crooks. There are the not-so-English outsiders like Sam Boskum, born in Ipswich but with an ancestry going back to the West Indies and Africa. There are the stranded Yugoslav sailors who are suspected – with classic xenophobia – of committing the murders. They all come together in the pubs and the cafes where the communal life of the town is carried on. And this is all so precisely observed and so authentically recreated that it is easy to forget at times that Tornwich is representative as well as local, that Chaucer as well as George Eliot has written its story, that it is the scene of a medieval morality as well as a novel.

The irruptions of the murderer break in on the reader, however, as they break in on the citizens of Tornwich, reminding both that their worlds are not inviolate. Each of the murderer's appearances is preceded by a bloodcurdling epigraph:

Barabas.
As for myself, I walk abroad o' nights,
And kill sick people groaning under walls:
Sometimes I go about and poison wells . . .

Ithamore.
One time I was an hostler at an inn,
And in the night time secretly would I steal
To travellers' chambers, and there cut their throats.[9]

The effect of these epigraphs, and of the switch to first-person narration for the sections which follow them, and which describe Death "at the shoulder of the gunman, looking down the gun-barrel",[10] is to interrupt both the illusion and the narrative method to which the reader has become adjusted. The *frisson* of terror which accompanies the gunman's appearance is thus reinforced by literary devices which extend the fictional world in two directions: back through literary parallels to a medieval tale of death; and out − through Brechtian alienation − into the reader's own, extra-fictional world, which is not allowed to remain as comfortably separate from the fictional mayhem as is usual in the murder mystery genre. Stow also uses other means to blur these boundaries. The only person to report a possible sighting of the murderer, for example, is a boy nicknamed "Killer":

As Harry was coming down Red Lion Street he heard, from the mist, a sort of hoarse shout, muffled, neither male nor female. Then plimsolled feet were running towards him, and a short body hit him amidships.
"Watch where you're gooin, boy," Harry said, irritably. "Whass that you, Killer?"
Killer was a twelve-year-old boy, and looked very tough. But his face, in the mist-muted light of a streetlamp, was not self-confident.
"Sorry, Harry," he muttered, in an unsteady treble. "Harry − "
"Did you sing out just now?" Harry asked. "I thought I hear someone yell."
"It was me," the boy admitted, reluctantly. "I seen something. I seen − I dunno. A thing." (5)

While the main purpose of this early scene is to introduce the Tornwich Monster as dramatically as possible, it also illustrates, through the ironic naming of the witness, the curious mix of fear and fascinated admiration with which killers are condemned and celebrated, both within fiction and outside it. Like his namesake, "Killer" reappears throughout the book, most notably near the end when he talks to Frank De Vere just before his death.

The enigma of the human gunman is not resolved in the later sections of the book. Each of three initial murders he commits is preceded by a short section in which Death reviews the life of the victim and takes pleasure in knowing him or her at the moment of death, when change becomes impossible. But there is no indication why Death's human accomplice chooses the people he does, and this makes the accomplice seem more like an extension of Death itself, and less like a human, motivated killer. Death describes and imagines the victims like an omniscient novelist viewing his characters and able to enter their private worlds: "now I am inside; I know everything" (Paul Ramsey, 20); "now all that she has been is opened to me" (Eddystone Ena, 40). Death thus occupies a fictional dimension separate from the rest of the narrative, and to which the reader has only limited access. We do not get to know him as he gets to know his victims, and see him only as a shadowy figure of mystery and fear.

The central "character" in the novel is Harry Ufford, whom we first see in his middle years, in "the privacy of his own special place" (3), surrounded by the possessions which reflect the man and his interests. Harry is a devotee of real-life murders – as well as ships and horses – and his copy of *The Murderer's Who's Who* is to be instrumental in the death of Frank De Vere at the end of the book. Among his possessions is a photograph of his father:

> a very good one, taken by somebody famous in that line. It had appeared in a book, with the caption: "Suffolk Fisherman". A face lined and spare as driftwood, prickly with a few days of white stubble, the bright eyes among the weather-lines cautious, guarded, yet kind.
> "You weren't such a bad old boy," said Harry Ufford, out of the wisdom of his middle years. (4–5)

Harry, who would clearly fit this description well enough himself, has L-O-V-E and H-A-T-E tattooed on his fingers.[11] But he is not psychically riven as Cawdor and Random are, and he does not contribute to his own destruction, as a number of Stow's earlier protagonists do, though he does let himself go down to death at the point of rescue. Nor do love and hate oppose one another in *The Suburbs of Hell* as starkly as they do in *The Girl Green as Elderflower*. Harry is occasionally pugnacious when provoked, but on the whole he is remarkably even-tempered, tolerant, and comfortable in his middle years, as few of the young/old characters of Stow's earlier books have been comfortable. His death therefore seems arbitrary, tragic in the medieval not the Shakespearian sense. His destiny is not his character. Only two of the epigraphs are from Shakespeare. One comes

from *Richard III*, when the guilty king dreams of his victims on
the eve of the battle of Bosworth Field (151), and Richard is
closer to the butchers of Jacobean drama than to Shakespeare's
tragic heroes. The other is from *Titus Andronicus* (19), an even
gorier Jacobean drama.[12] The death of Harry, and the depreda-
tions of the Tornwich Monster, serve as grim reminders that any
appearance of comfort and security is deceptive. And as the
headlines from *The Tornwich and Stourford Packet* at the end of
the book reveal for those who take it in, the world of the late
twentieth century is little removed from that of *Beowulf*, with its
constant killing and struggle for survival, or from the macabre
dance of death played out so despairingly in Webster's plays.

If Harry Ufford is a new departure for Stow, there are other,
more familiar people in the book. Paul Ramsey, for example, the
killer's first victim, is a youngish teacher who has been deserted
by his wife and whose life has lost its sense of purpose. Greg,
Paul's brother, is closer again to solitaries like Cawdor. An
unemployable Ph.D., Greg arrives to visit Paul and finds him
shot dead. Greg stays on living in the house – a largely derelict
place that Paul and his wife had begun to restore – gradually
becoming more solitary and eventually going mad after accusing
Sam Boskum of murdering Paul. Harry has earlier predicted the
destructive effect that the killings will have on Tornwich. When
the rumours first begin after Paul's death, Harry comments:
"When he was alive he dint do nobody no harm; and now he's
dead, he's goonna tear this place apart" (25). And later he predicts
the fate of Greg: "All I know is, once you start suspectin, you
might not be able to stop in time before you goo mad" (53). The
trouble with death is that it leads directly to madness and further
death, as *The Pardoner's Tale* points out. And the trouble with
seemingly motiveless murder – there is not even "any sex in it"
(48), as Dave Stutton points out – is that everyone is suspect and
no one can be blamed.

The uncertainty and the inexplicability torment Greg in particular. Already a stranger in the town, he gradually withdraws
completely into the house in which his brother was killed, and
into his own increasingly split and disintegrating mind. This self-
imposed exile is interrupted by well-meaning visits from Harry,
which Greg discourages, and by the arrival of Paul's wife Diana,
whom he sees as "his brother's betrayer" (65). Diana's brisk
commonsense galls Greg, who rejects her offer to give him the
house, which she has inherited. His main weapon against her is
silence, to which he clings, like Cawdor, because he fears its op-

posite: "he knew that if he once began to talk he would never be able to stop, just as he knew that if he once began to weep he would break in two" (67). Despite his restraint, however, Greg's sanity is increasingly strained: "He was sure he did not hate her, but whatever it was that watched her through his eyes watched very coldly . . . If he cried, a fault-line would appear between the two tears, and he would crack apart in neat halves" (68). The approach of Greg's madness is evident in the bizarre habit he develops of ringing up Sam in the middle of the night and playing a music-box into the phone. It is typical of Stow's attention to detail, and his liking for allusive echoes, that the message of the song – Mozart's *"Non più andrai"* – that Cherubino's games with the girls are over, and he must set off to the wars, has its appropriateness to Sam's fate. Eventually Greg is so unsettled by the arrival of spring, and his long isolation, that he recreates what he has come to believe was the scene of his brother's murder. The vengeance he plans on Sam, however, turns inward on himself, and the psychic split he has feared takes place, leaving him "a mad child now for ever" (78). It is clear that Paul's death is not the only factor leading to Greg's collapse – he has been alone and alienated for a good many years and there is madness in the family – but his inability to explain, and to come to terms with his brother's death has certainly pushed him over the edge. The epigraph to his final scene is from *The Spanish Tragedy*:

> *Painter*. And is this the end?
> *Hieronimo*. Oh no, there is no end; the end is death and madness.[13]

Greg's planned revenge proves ineffectual because, ironically, there is no revenge against death except further death, as Chaucer's rioters discovered to their cost.

There is, however, a sense in which Greg does effect his revenge by transferring his psychic illness to the innocent Sam, and to Sam's girl Donna. Sam's eventual fate recalls that of other aliens in Stow's fiction. A West Indian born in Ipswich of a "conformist working-class couple" (85), Sam is doubly deracinated, his African origins obscured by the West Indian slave trade, and his colour wrong for his English, Baptist, working-class childhood. He eventually establishes a precarious position for himself in Tornwich with the help of the tycoonlet Ken Heath, who employs him to drive a taxi. A sexual identity is harder to establish, however, and when Donna rejects him he believes that it is partly because of Greg's racist accusations. And when the rumours begin to affect the taxi business as well, Sam decides that he has had enough. Like the green children he has never really been at home in Suffolk, and he has lost whatever other homes he might once have enjoyed. His tenuous links with the locals look like breaking, and he decides to destroy the identity he has never really succeeded in creating. The loss he feels is evident in his bitter response to Donna's suggestion that he go to the Caribbean: "All you Honkies want to make me believe thass where I come from. Well, I don't. I int never been there. I don't believe I should like it. I don't want to be no foreigner. Why do you stop there, anyway, you Honkies: why don't you tell me to piss off back to Africa?" (99). There is nowhere for Sam to go where he will not be a foreigner, except to the country of death.

The other victims are less fully drawn than Harry, Greg and Sam. Eddystone Ena, the killer's second victim, is as harmless and as well-liked as Paul Ramsey. Another of the loners in the book, though more through circumstance than choice, she certainly does not cooperate with death, though she does reflect at one point: "I do find myself hoping, sometimes in the middle of the night, that I don't live to be an old, old lady" (35). The granting of this wish is only one of the ironies surrounding her death. When Harry arrives to see her on the night she is shot he announces himself as "the Tornwich Monster", and when Ena later opens her door to the killer, she thinks it is Harry come back for his tobacco tin. She persuades Harry, who is sought after as a guardian throughout the book, to spend the night with Greg, when she might have asked him to stay with her. Her selection by the killer remains one of the puzzles of the book. While her life has been hard, she is compassionate, cheerful and self-sufficient, and seems beyond envy or desire. The arbitrariness of her death bewilders and frightens those who know her – murder is bad enough, but murder entirely without motive threatens everyone and eludes detection. The fear of random killing spreads like a disease through Tornwich, creating its own havoc and furthering the destruction begun by the killer.

Commander Pryke, the third of the killer's victims, also seems without enemies, though he is "an irritable tippler" who dislikes Frank for disguising his "Bog Irish" origins with the fancy surname De Vere (7). A retired sailor nearing the end of his life, he can find nothing with which to reproach himself except some shortness of temper with his wife. Death, in his novelist's manner, sums the Commander up:

He is always, now, in a ferment of memories. Other climates, other seas. A trick of light will bring back some place half a world away, and changed utterly by years, passed with no record except in his mind.

The stick on which he leans was given him by his wife when he came back to her finally, to stay forever. The gift said to him that he was old, with nothing before him but a little daily walking for his health. She suggested a dog, and he snapped at her. They found that they had never known each other well. (59–60)

The detached sympathy of this passage is at odds with the shooting of Pryke that follows it closely. Death may be indifferent to his victims, but it is less easy to imagine a man – even a madman – killing randomly and without malice. This problem had exercised the Commander himself when he discussed the earlier murders with Greg, insisting there must be a motive: "But dammit, Greg, man is a motivated animal. There must be some reason, some connection that makes sense, even if only to a deranged mind" (45). A few minutes later, however, he is sure it must be "some stranger, some prowler from outside, that is quite obvious" (47). Like the reader, and the other citizens of Tornwich, the Commander can make no sense of what has happened. The killer's first three victims have no reason to suspect that they may be targets, and they are therefore no more afraid than other members of the Tornwich community. Two of them are old and alone, and not entirely averse to dying, while the third, though younger, has contemplated suicide, as Death points out: "He has looked at me, several times, with a shy curiosity. Once I thought he was going to speak" (2); "One night he took out of its case an old cut-throat razor with a bone handle, and stared at it" (20). Unlike these first three victims, however, Harry and Dave, who are killed by other people, and Sam and Frank, who are killed by their own fear and despair, all realize that their lives are threatened. It might be argued that Paul Ramsey, Ena and the Commander are not really victims at all, being already half in love with death. The true victims are those who are killed by themselves and one another, especially those who – as in *The Pardoner's Tale* – attack death because they fear it – *timor mortis conturbat me* – and only succeed in embracing it the sooner.

The second half of *The Suburbs of Hell* is both less disturbing and more exciting than the first. The already hectic pace increases and the suspense is heightened further. The killings in this part of the book have detectable human motives, and the thrill of the chase is added to the mystery of the first half of the book. Sleazy characters like Frank De Vere and Dave Stutton, who make their money from drugs, move into prominence, while the harmless victims like Sam and Greg, who are characterized more fully, disappear. Harry, who has been the centre of interest, and the moral centre of the book, moves into the midst of the action. He tries to rescue Dave, the son of an old friend, from his involvement with drug-peddling. Dave repays this good-natured concern by arranging Harry's "accident". The description of Harry's struggle to survive his drowning is both intensely dramatic and movingly lyrical:

> He sees the commotion of the churning propeller, and suddenly he is in terror. He begins to shout and wave. And perhaps they see him, perhaps they make out his pale hands and pale face, because the barge veers off, the propeller merely tumbles him in its wake . . .
>
> He goes with the tide, swimming breaststroke in the freezing water. Strangely, he does not feel the cold. He only knows that he is very tired.
>
> He feels something more elevated than self-pity. He feels grief; he mourns. It is tragic and pitiful to him that all his life − the rebellious law-breaking boyhood, truculent adolescence and man's life of loving and feuding − has been tending towards this, the death of an unwanted kitten . . .
>
> The current bears him on. His thoughts drift also, far from the river. Now he returns again and again to the disappointments of his life, the satisfactions denied, the pledges not honoured, the vague something, indefinable, sought in bouts of drunkenness or aggression and never found, always withheld from him.
>
> He cannot tell that the lifeboat has seen him, that messages are flying through the air. Taken out of that world, he drifts . . .
>
> He reaches for the ladder, but his fingers will not close on the rung. They open, they slip away. He drifts from the ladder's foot, and closing his eyes, goes down and breathes in his death. (143-45)

The spare narrative here is reminiscent of Conrad, while the sense of an entire life caught in a moment of poignant reflection recalls Virginia Woolf.[14] Stow, like Woolf, is often a poet of death, but nowhere more strikingly than in this powerful climax.

While it is Dave who arranges the accidental drowning, Harry's real opponent is Dave's boss, Frank De Vere. Frank dislikes the likeable Harry from the beginning, for reasons that are never explained, but which may be no more than the inevitable dislike of the bad for the good. The two men share a drink in the Speedwell on the night that Paul Ramsey is shot −

the first night of the book – and their hostility is evident. Frank accuses the genial Harry of being "half-cut":

> When scenting an offence Harry's face took on an odd expression, mild yet grim. Not moving his head, he said: "Psychologically speakin, young Frank, you're a sort of a Peepin Tom. What the Frogs call a *voiture*."
> "*Voyeur*, you tool," Frank murmured.
> "Is that it? Where did I get *voiture* from, then?"
> "Off the car-deck on the *Felix*, I should imagine." (7–8)

If Frank wins the verbal exchange here, Harry wins the moral exchange. And it is apparent that the sparring between them is in earnest, despite Frank's jokey attempt to pass it off. Harry's later comments that Frank's associate Dave has never shown much interest in women, and that he has a surprising amount of money for "a young fella on the dole" (8), are shrewd and prophetic. We later learn that Frank may have supplied his wife Linda with drugs in lieu of sexual satisfaction, and that he is more interested in "firearms and bladed weapons" (42) than women. His relationship with his business associate Dave is hardly one of friendship, but it may be that he prefers to deal with someone who shares his own sexual disinclinations. Frank's nastiness, evident in this early scene, sets Harry thinking about him more deeply than before.

Frank becomes directly involved with the killings when his wife finds a message in lipstick on her sitting-room window:

NOT TONIGHT:
SOON
The Os of the last word had irises and pupils. (43)

If this is a message from the Tornwich Monster – and there is no other explanation for which there is any evidence – then it is the first and only time that he has warned, and so terrorized his victims. And the message raises further questions. Why is there a warning in this case, and is it intended for Linda, or Frank, or both? Is it intended that Linda should misinterpret it as a message from Frank, as she does, at least to begin with? Linda is later shot, though not immediately killed, and Frank is shot at, without being hit. Is the gunman losing his aim or his nerve? The narrations by Death which precede these two unsuccessful attempts to kill are comparatively detached and impersonal – there is, for example, no first-person reference in Linda's – and there is less of the pleasure of getting inside Frank's character, or Linda's room and possessions. Death, it seems, can only get "inside" at the moment of death, and is therefore not so interested in near misses.

The attempt on Frank's life is the last recorded attack by the Tornwich Monster, and it leaves the reader no closer to finding out who the Monster is. Much of the early evidence in the book points to Frank as the murderer. His rifle appears to be the murder weapon – one assumes the police later check it – he dislikes Harry and Harry's friends (the first three victims), and he is nasty and self-interested enough to kill his associate Dave after persuading Dave to kill Harry. But Frank's thoughts in "A Riposte" (153–56) contradict this evidence and indicate that he is himself desperately trying to identify the murderer before it is too late. Frank thinks it must be Dave, who has motive enough to dislike Linda and to hate him. And it would be a nice irony if Dave, who is dubbed the Monster after Frank arranges his "suicide", were indeed guilty. But the scene in which Frank shows Dave the rifle hidden in Harry's backyard (114–22) shows Dave to have been unaware of the rifle's existence, and therefore to be innocent. Dave's puzzlement leads him to advance the theory that someone, "a nut-case", was looking out of an attic or a bathroom window when Frank first hid the rifle, and that this unknown person is the murderer (119). This theory, which is reinforced perhaps by Stow's original title for the book, *Someone Is Mad Among Us*, and by the reference to the Nedlands Monster in the dedication, has at least the virtue that it is not disproved by the evidence – or lack of it – in the book. It would also be ironic if the killer were Killer, but the boy seems genuinely frightened at the beginning of the book, and, unless his hypocrisy is precociously accomplished, his deductions at the end with Frank are genuinely a couple of guesses behind those of Frank and the reader. So the reader is left to share the uncertainty and suspicion which are tearing Tornwich apart. Is it one of the obvious suspects, or is it an inexplicable nobody like Eric Edgar Cooke, the "Nedlands Monster"? The author himself is not saying: "if it stays like *Edwin Drood*, I don't mind . . . the urge to 'solve' it, and so sweep it out of mind, is one which Death, sardonically, would understand very well. That is part of the moral".[15]

Frank's death at the end of the book, which is brought about with an irony reminiscent of *The Pardoner's Tale*, does leave the reader with some satisfaction. Frank's earlier suspicion that Harry is the Monster is too much even for the pliable Dave to believe; but Frank still thinks that Harry was capable of poisoning a birthday bottle of whisky, and his fear that he has in-advertently drunk most of that bottle chokes him to death.[16] The sweetness of the poetic justice does not belie the moral that the fear of death can be lethal, but it does give a partial sense of closure to the end of the narrative. The identifiable villain gets his just deserts. What happens to the Monster is another question.

In its final pages then *The Suburbs of Hell* deconstructs itself as crime fiction. The morality theme remains, however, and it is Death who has the last word:

> How they have annoyed me with their diversions and sidetracks leading to no development; pathological killers of time . . .
>
> How fluid they are, their characters all potential, veering between virtue and vice, charity and atrocity, begetting and laying waste . . .
>
> But I am the end of all potential. Where change is finished, there I am inside. By me these shifting shapes are fixed. After me, they may be judged at last . . .
>
> He stares up into my face.
>
> He sees me in my own likeness, without disguise. For flesh is a disguise.
>
> He cannot speak or breathe. Yet he speaks to me, with his blazing eyes.
>
> I can read his eyes. I have read many.
>
> *So soon?* he says. *Oh, so soon.* (164–65)

Death is thus finally portrayed, in filmic manner, as the Grim Reaper, and his omnipresence is attested to by the catalogue of headlines from *The Tornwich and Stourford Packet* which follows, and which chronicles the violence of death throughout the world. The reader is left to ponder the moral that after death he too, whether killer or victim or observer, may be judged at last. Finally there is the tailpiece: the Tarot Card XIII – Death – and underneath it the thirteenth-century distich:

> All too late, all too late,
> when the bier is at the gate.[17]

The story of Harry Ufford and the Tornwich murders is thus finally embedded in a medieval context, a time when the bier at the gate was an all too familiar summons.

Death belongs to no single time, however, and Stow expands his picture of a small and close-knit community in trauma into a general meditation on the frailty, the impermanence of life. It is a perennial theme of literature, and Stow echoes works as diverse as *Beowulf* and *The French Lieutenant's Woman* as he

creates a book as multilayered as Old Tornwich. As *Tourmaline,
The Merry-go-Round in the Sea, Visitants* and *The Girl Green as
Elderflower* all testify, Stow likes to explore the rich presence of
the past in the communities he portrays. Unlike these books,
however, *The Suburbs of Hell* does not have a major character
especially sensitive to history, and it is therefore the author –
and Death – who take the longer view. The author's voice in this
last book is less personal and more dispassionate. The writing of
The Girl Green as Elderflower seems to have freed Stow from his
intense concern with the personal crises of 1959–60 which form
the basis of that book and *Visitants*. *The Suburbs of Hell* remains
haunted by fear and death, as these books were, but it is more
fully projected into the central narrative of murder and suicide.
The result is both a loss and a gain: there is less anguish; and
there is also less of the fierce intensity which has illuminated
Stow's books from the very beginning. If, like Harry Ufford, he is
becoming a little more comfortable in his middle age, he remains
aware that comfort is illusory, and he still hears clearly behind
him the steps of the Grim Reaper.

Afterword

A study of an author in mid-career can only conclude, like *Rasselas*, with nothing finally concluded. We can expect more books from Stow in the years to come. He has, for example, been interested for many years in the wreck of the *Batavia* on the Abrolhos Islands off the coast of Western Australia in 1629. The voyage, the wreck, the mutiny and the murders, and the return of Captain Pelsart to exact justice, make up an extraordinarily powerful and dramatic story, and one so suited to Stow's particular preoccupations, talents and experience that it seems a perfect match of author and subject. Whatever books he may write in the future, however, Stow has already completed an impressive body of work. *The Merry-go-Round in the Sea* and *Visitants* merit the status of classics, while a number of his other books are only slightly less accomplished.

Stow learned early that "country claims its station/as men do theirs, and skylines lock around us/surer than walls".[1] Like Conrad he travelled much in his earlier years. But the longest and most important of his journeys was that from the Western Australian country that claimed his childhood to the country that claimed his forbears in East Anglia. It was a lonely personal odyssey that helped to make him a poet of silence and solitude. It also helped to make him a novelist of real distinction, one of the finest Australia has produced. His journey, and the writing that grows out of it, are not yet finished.

Abbreviations

ABR	*Australian Book Review*
ACLALS	Association for Commonwealth Literature and Language Studies
ALS	*Australian Literary Studies*
CS	*A Counterfeit Silence*
JCL	*Journal of Commonwealth Literature*
MFS	*Modern Fiction Studies*
NLA	National Library of Australia, Canberra
SMH	*Sydney Morning Herald*
TLS	*Times Literary Supplement*
WLWE	*World Literature Written in English*

Notes to the Text

1   The Landscape of the Soul

1. Cf. Andrew Gurr: "the modern creative writer . . . is a lone traveller in the countries of the mind". *Writers in Exile: The Identity of Home in Modern Literature* (Sussex: Harvester Press, 1981), p. 13.
2. As Les A. Murray observes: "It will be centuries/ before many men are truly at home in this country". "Noonday Axeman", in *The Vernacular Republic: Poems 1961–1981*, rev. ed. (Sydney: Angus & Robertson, 1982), p. 4.
3. Judith Wright, *Preoccupations in Australian Poetry* (Melbourne: Oxford University Press, 1965), p. xi.
4. The fullest fictional treatment of the contrast between the attitudes of Aboriginal and European Australians to their country is Xavier Herbert's *Poor Fellow My Country* (Sydney: Collins, 1975). Cf. also Judith Wright, *The Cry for the Dead* (Melbourne: Oxford University Press, 1981).
5. The Western Australian landscape is sensitively portrayed by E.L. Grant Watson in the series of novels he set there. See Dorothy Green, "The Daimon and the Fringe-Dweller", in *The Music of Love* (Ringwood: Penguin, 1984), pp. 127-47.
6. James McAuley, *Captain Quiros* (Sydney: Angus & Robertson, 1964), p. 5.
7. Randolph Stow, *The Girl Green as Elderflower* (London: Secker & Warburg, 1980), p. 136.
8. When asked whether there were any particular themes or situations which interested him as a novelist, Stow replied: "Well, the colonial situation, and particularly the situation of someone who is not a new colonialist, someone who is growing up and has accepted as familiar the background of a former colony". Xavier Pons and Neil Keeble, "A Colonist with Words: An Interview with Randolph Stow", *Commonwealth: Essays and Studies Mélanges* 2 (1976): 76.
9. Christopher Koch, "Literature and Cultural Identity", *The Tasmanian Review* no. 4 (1980): 3.
10. Andrew Taylor, "Bosom of Nature or Heart of Stone: A Difference in Heritage", in *An Introduction to Australian Literature*, ed. C.D. Narasimhaiah (Brisbane: John Wiley, 1982), pp. 144-56. Perhaps the nearest to an Australian equivalent of Thoreau's *Walden* would be E. J. Banfield's *The Confessions of a Beachcomber* (1908; rpt. Sydney: Angus & Robertson, 1933), but Dunk Island hardly qualifies as a typical Australian landscape.
11. See "A Feast", in Randolph Stow, *A Counterfeit Silence: Selected Poems of Randolph Stow* (Sydney: Angus & Robertson, 1969), p. 51. The classic statement of this absence is Henry James's: "It takes so many things, as Hawthorne must have felt later in life, when he made the acquaintance of the denser, richer, warmer European spectacle – it takes such an accumulation of history and custom, such a complexity of manners and types,

to form a fund of suggestion for a novelist . . . one might enumerate the items of high civilization, as it exists in other countries, which are absent from the texture of American life, until it should become a wonder to know what was left." *Hawthorne* (1879; rpt. London: Macmillan, 1967), p. 55.

12. See "Stations", in Stow, *A Counterfeit Silence*, p. 62.
13. Harry Heseltine, "Australian Fiction Since 1920", in *The Literature of Australia*, ed. Geoffrey Dutton, rev. ed. (Ringwood: Penguin, 1976), p. 227.
14. Randolph Stow, "Raw Material", *Westerly* no. 2 (1961): 3-4.
15. Patrick White, *Voss* (London: Eyre & Spottiswoode, 1957), p. 475.
16. See "Persephone", in Stow, *A Counterfeit Silence*, p. 56.
17. See "The Land's Meaning", in Stow, *A Counterfeit Silence*, p. 36.
18. Jennifer Wightman, "Waste Places, Dry Souls: The Novels of Randolph Stow", *Meanjin* 28 (1969): 239.
19. Randolph Stow, *To the Islands*, rev. ed. (London: Secker & Warburg, 1982), p. 94.
20. Virginia Woolf, *The Voyage Out* (Harmondsworth: Penguin, 1970), p. 218.
21. Patrick White, *Flaws in the Glass* (London: Jonathan Cape, 1981), p. 42.
22. See "*From* The Testament of Tourmaline", in Stow, *A Counterfeit Silence*, p. 75.
23. Stow, *To the Islands*, rev. ed., p. 60.
24. Stow, *A Counterfeit Silence*, p. 37.
25. Taylor, "Bosom of Nature or Heart of Stone", p. 152.

2 A Bitter Heritage

1. Randolph Stow, *The Merry-go-Round in the Sea* (London: Macdonald, 1965), p. 213. Cf. Donald Horne: "Australia was an inadequate country, not written about in good literature." *The Education of Young Donald* (1967; rpt. Ringwood: Penguin, 1975), p. 195.
2. Veronica Brady and Peter Cowan point out that: "The richness and confidence of the early letters and diaries of the colony and the journals and written accounts of actual experience for a long time remained in odd contrast with the paucity of fictional writing in Western Australia". "The Novel", in *The Literature of Western Australia*, ed. Bruce Bennett (Perth: University of Western Australia Press, 1979), p. 49. The tradition such as it was would include the novels of E.L. Grant Watson, whose keen sense of the landscape anticipates the vision of Stow and Patrick White; *The Boy in the Bush* by D.H. Lawrence and Mollie Skinner; Kenneth (Seaforth) Mackenzie's *The Young Desire It* (referred to in *The Merry-go-Round in the Sea*), and the novels of Katharine Susannah Prichard.
3. Patrick White, "The Prodigal Son", *Australian Letters* 1, no. 3 (April 1958): 39.
4. Randolph Stow, Foreword to *Poetry Australia* no. 12 (October 1966), West Australian Issue: 4.
5. Geoffrey Dutton, "The Search for Permanence: The Novels of Randolph Stow", *JCL* 1 (1965): 137.
6. Stow, *The Merry-go-Round in the Sea*, p. 102.
7. Ibid., pp. 78-79.
8. William Faulkner, *Requiem for A Nun* (London: Chatto & Windus, 1957), p. 85.
9. Randolph Stow, *A Haunted Land* (London: Macdonald, 1956), p. 108. All

quotations are from this edition, and subsequent references are included in the text.

10. Leonie Kramer, "The Novels of Randolph Stow", *Southerly* 24 (1964): 81.
11. See, for example, Kramer, "The Novels of Randolph Stow"; G.K.W. Johnston, "The Art of Randolph Stow", *Meanjin* 20 (1961): 139-43; and Ray Willbanks, *Randolph Stow* (Boston: Twayne, 1978), pp. 26-28.
12. Malin Pool is based on Ellendale Pool, and Malin on Ellendale homestead, in the Geraldton hinterland.
13. The scene is reminiscent of Catherine Linton's deathbed scene in *Wuthering Heights*.
14. Randolph Stow, *The Bystander* (London: Macdonald, 1957), pp. 194-95. All quotations are from this edition, and subsequent references are included in the text.
15. Cf. Henry Lawson's "On the Night Train", and Kenneth Slessor's "The Night-Ride".
16. Dutton, "The Search for Permanence", p. 142.
17. Randolph Stow, *To the Islands*, rev. ed. (London: Secker & Warburg, 1982), p. ix.
18. Daniel Defoe, *Robinson Crusoe*, ed. Michael Shinagel (New York: Norton, 1975), p. 264.
19. G.A. Wilkes, *Australian Literature: A Conspectus* (Sydney: Angus & Robertson, 1969), p. 97. Cf. Jennifer Wightman's comment on *A Haunted Land* and *The Bystander*: "Stow avoids what is obviously for him the imaginative or technical difficulty of conveying inner states of being directly", in "Waste Places, Dry Souls: The Novels of Randolph Stow", *Meanjin* 28 (1969): 243.
20. Stow, *To the Islands*, p. ix.

3 Lost Man's Country

1. Stow's *To the Islands* won the Melbourne Book Fair Award and the Australian Literature Society Gold Medal for 1958, as well as the Miles Franklin Award.
2. Vincent Buckley, "In The Shadow of Patrick White", *Meanjin* 20 (1961): 144-54.
3. On "The Unprofessed Factor" see Peter Beatson, *The Eye in the Mandala: Patrick White: A Vision of Man and God* (Sydney: A.H. & A.W. Reed, 1977), p. 167.
4. Preface to the revised edition of Randolph Stow, *To the Islands* (London: Secker & Warburg, 1982), p. ix.
5. Patrick White, "The Prodigal Son", *Australian Letters* 1, no. 3 (April 1958): 39.
6. Randolph Stow, *Midnite* (London: Macdonald, 1967), p. 108.
7. As K.G. Hamilton observed: "the late fifties saw the end of the socialist-realist hegemony over Australian fiction". See *Studies in the Recent Australian Novel* (St Lucia: University of Queensland Press, 1978), pp. 14-15.
8. See, for example, Grahame Johnston's review in *Quadrant* 3, no. 4 (Spring, 1959):87-89; David Martin, "Among the Bones: What are our Novelists looking for?" *Meanjin* 18 (1959): 52-58; and Leonie Kramer, "Heritage of Dust: Randolph Stow's wasteland", *Bulletin,* 6 July 1963, p. 41.
9. Preface to the revised edition of Stow, *To the Islands,* p. ix. See note 13.
10. J.J. Healy, *Literature and the Aborigine in Australia 1770–1975* (St Lucia: University of Queensland Press, 1978), p. 227.

11. Quoted in *Crime and Punishment and the Critics*, ed. E. Wasiolek (Belmont: Wadsworth, 1961), p. 21. Cf. O.N. Burgess who argues that "Stow's first two novels create a baroque genre in the Australian novel . . . because life presents itself to this novelist as twisted and violent, not because he is fantasising at a deliberate remove from life as he genuinely sees it", in "The Novels of Randolph Stow", *Australian Quarterly* 37 (1965): 74.

12. John Hetherington, "Randolph Stow: Young Man in No Hurry", in *Forty-Two Faces* (Melbourne: Cheshire, 1962), p. 246.

13. This is true of the first edition as well as of the revised edition. In the discussion which follows I have considered both editions while accepting, for the most part, the second as the author's preferred version. Unless otherwise indicated, page references are to the revised edition. The fullest account of the revisions, which is spoiled somewhat by its sour tone, is Sue Thomas, "Randolph Stow's Revision of *To the Islands*", *Southerly* 42 (1982): 288-94.

14. Buckley, "In The Shadow of Patrick White", p. 145.

15. In his perceptive essay on the book, L.T. Hergenhan argues against the view that there is a split between the story of Heriot and the background of the mission. See "Randolph Stow's *To the Islands*", *Southerly* 35 (1975): 234-47.

16. Leonie Kramer, "The Novels of Randolph Stow", *Southerly* 24 (1964): p. 87. This article is the most influential of the social realist attacks on Stow.

17. First edition, pp. 113, 11, 76.

18. Revised edition, p. 1.

19. The footnote in the text states that: "the names of people concerned and most place names have been altered" (29). For the original account see Randolph Stow, "The Umbali Massacre: As told to him by Daniel Evans", *Bulletin*, 15 February 1961, pp. 45-46. For an account of the Royal Commission into the massacre see Royal Commission of Inquiry into Alleged Killing and Burning of Bodies of Aborigines in East Kimberley, in *Minutes and Votes and Proceedings* of the 13th Parliament of Western Australia, 28 July–9 December 1927, vol. I (Perth: Government Printer, 1929). See also "Massacre at Oombulgurri", *West Australian*, 2 June 1984, p. 157. I am indebted to Randolph Stow for the information that "Onmalmeri" is an invented name, which means "the place of white ochre", and that white ochre is associated with death and ghosts (letter to the author 13 November 1981). Peter Biskup's *Not Slaves Not Citizens* (St Lucia: University of Queensland Press, 1976) incorrectly refers to the "Onmalmeri" massacre instead of to the Umbali massacre (pp. 84-85).

20. Randolph Stow, *Visitants* (London: Secker & Warburg, 1979), p. 187.

21. See Martin, "Among the Bones", p. 52.

22. Alain Robbe-Grillet and Claude Simon are novelists whose work Stow admires. On the "cinematic structure" of Stow's earlier books see John B. Beston, "An Interview with Randolph Stow", *WLWE* 14 (1975): 224-26.

23. Randolph Stow, *The Girl Green as Elderflower* (London: Secker & Warburg, 1980), p. 68.

24. The sentiment is Pascal's. John B. Beston identifies the allusions in the book in "Heriot's Literary Allusions in Randolph Stow's *To the Islands*", *Southerly* 35 (1975): 168-77.

25. Olive Schreiner, quoted in Patrick White, *The Aunt's Story* (London: Routledge & Kegan Paul, 1948), p. 1.

26. John B. Beston argues that reconciliation is "the main theme" of the book. His praise for *To the Islands* as "one of the very best Australian novels" is vitiated by his dismissal of *Visitants* and *The Girl Green as Elderflower* as "slight works". See "The Theme of Reconciliation in Stow's *To the Islands*", *MFS* 27, no. 1 (Spring 1981): 95-107.

27. Cf. Robyn Wallace: "Heriot's journey is not an allegorically mapped out pilgrim's progress through sequential illuminations, but a tension of opposites, in landscape, in feeling, in concepts", in "Messiahs and Millenna in Randolph Stow's Novels", *Kunapipi* 3, no. 2 (1981): 59.
28. Hergenhan, "Randolph Stow's *To the Islands*", p. 243.
29. In a letter to the author (5 July 1983) Randolph Stow has suggested the following as "a good economical definition" of heriot:
    > *Heriot.* An obligation, derived from Saxon times, on an heir to return to the lord the war apparel of the deceased tenant which had been originally supplied by the lord. The military gear, depending on the status of the tenant, included a horse, harness and weapons. This obligation applied to both freeman and villein. At about the time of the Norman Conquest the custom was being superseded by a tenant's heir giving his lord the best beast of the dead tenant, and later this became simply a money payment and, in effect, a fee to enter into the estate.
    > John Richardson, *The Local Historian's Encyclopedia* (New Barnet, Herts: Historical Publications Ltd, 1975), p. 32.
    Cf. Beston, "Heriot's Literary Allusions", p. 176.
30. Preface to the revised edition, p. ix.

4 The Single Soul – A Derelict Independence

1. See John Hetherington, "Randolph Stow: Young Man in No Hurry", in *Forty-Two Faces* (Melbourne: Cheshire, 1962), p. 243; and Anthony J. Hassall, "Interview with Randolph Stow", *ALS* 10 (1982): 312-13.
2. Hetherington, "Young Man in No Hurry", p. 247.
3. See Beston interview, p. 224. The Secker & Warburg edition (London, 1983) reproduces the Macdonald edition (London, 1963) without revision.
4. Barry Pree, for example, reviewed the book enthusiastically in *London Magazine*, NS 3, no. 3, June 1963, pp. 87-88. More typical, however, were such hostile reviews as Keith Thomas, "Eternity In The Never-Never", *Nation* (Aust.), no. 123, 13 July 1963, pp. 22-23; R. Taubman in *New Statesman* 65, 24 May 1963, p. 802; and David Hutchison in *Westerly* 8, no. 3 (September 1963): 77-79.
5. A.D. Hope, "Randolph Stow and the Tourmaline Affair", in *The Australian Experience*, ed. W.S. Ramson (Canberra: ANU Press, 1974), pp. 249-68. See also Hope's "Randolph Stow and the Way of Heaven", *Hemisphere* 18, no. 6 (June 1974): 33-35.
6. David Williamson, "Failed Footballer", *Kunapipi* 1, no. 2 (1979): 126-27.
7. Cf. Dostoevsky's "The Grand Inquisitor": "This craving for *community* of worship is the chief misery of every man individually and of all humanity from the beginning of time . . . man is tormented by no greater anxiety than to find some one quickly to whom he can hand over that gift of freedom with which the ill-fated creature is born", in *The Brothers Karamazov*, trans. Constance Garnett (New York: Macmillan, 1912), pp. 267-68.
8. Kylie Tennant, review of *Voss*, *SMH*, 8 February 1958, p. 12.
9. Dorothy Green, *Ulysses Bound* (Canberra: ANU Press, 1973), p. 15.
10. Two popular recent accounts of Taoism by Western writers are: Raymond M. Smullyan, *The Tao is Silent* (New York: Harper & Row, 1977); and Fritjof Capra, *The Tao of Physics* (London: Fontana, 1976). Stow's Taoism is "philosophical Taoism" not the popular religion: see Helen Tiffin, *"Tourmaline* and the *Tao Te Ching*: Randolph Stow's *Tourmaline"*, in *Studies in the*

Recent Australian Novel, ed. K.G. Hamilton (St Lucia: University of Queensland Press, 1978), pp. 84-120.

11. Leonie Kramer, review of *Tourmaline*, *Bulletin*, 6 July 1963, p. 41.

12. Ibid. Cf. David Martin, "Among the Bones: What are our Novelists looking for?" *Meanjin* 18 (1959): 52-58.

13. Leonie Kramer, "The Novels of Randolph Stow", *Southerly* 24 (1964): 80, 90, 91.

14. Ibid., p. 79.

15. See Hope, "Randolph Stow and the Tourmaline Affair"; and Randolph Stow, "Babbitt Eats Babbitt", *Nation* (Aust.), no. 153, 19 September 1964, pp. 11-12. See also "Professor Plonk's Epistle to Dr Edna Everage", *ABR* 5, no. 8 (June 1966):152.

16. Stow, "*From* The Testament of Tourmaline: Variations on Themes of the *Tao Teh Ching*" was first published in *Poetry Australia*, no. 12 (October 1966): 7-10, and was reprinted in *A Counterfeit Silence* (Sydney: Angus & Robertson, 1969), pp. 71-75. Stow told John Beston that the poem was "a key to the novel. It could be considered as written by the people of Tourmaline", Beston interview, p. 228. The best discussions of the Taoism of *Tourmaline* are: Helen Tiffin, "*Tourmaline* and the *Tao Te Ching*"; and Paul D. Higginbotham, "'Honour the Single Soul': Randolph Stow and His Novels", *Southerly* 39 (1979): 378-92.

17. Randolph Stow, *Tourmaline* (London: Macdonald, 1963), p. 13. All quotations are from this edition, and subsequent references are included in the text. Page numbers are the same in the Secker & Warburg edition.

   Stow has said of his own beliefs: "I tend to adhere to Taoism, which is a very pragmatic religion concerned mostly with time and change, action and inaction. That warped kind of Christianity which the Diviner brings into Tourmaline is the absolute opposite of this". Pons and Keeble interview, p. 77.

18. Beston interview, p. 223.

19. Stow, *To the Islands*, p.v.

20. For a discussion of the metaphysical world of the novel see Helen Tiffin, "Melanesian Cargo Cults in *Tourmaline* and *Visitants*", *JCL* 16 (1981): 113-17.

   Stow has said of the narrator: "he is quite a useful observer, because he doesn't know what's right or wrong, he doesn't know what to think about things". Pons and Keeble interview, p. 78.

21. Stow, *A Counterfeit Silence*, pp. 71-73.

   Random's attempt to "come true" prefigures the search by Cawdor/Clare in *Visitants* and *The Girl Green as Elderflower* for a way to live, to be real, in an alien world.

22. Ibid., p. 72.

23. Stow, *To the Islands*, p. 90.

24. Cited from the draft for *Virgin Soil* by Ralph E. Matlaw, in "Turgenev's Novels and *Fathers and Sons*", in Turgenev, *Fathers and Sons*, ed. & trans. Ralph E. Matlaw (New York: Norton, 1966), p. 277.

25. Cf. Tiffin, "Melanesian Cargo Cults in *Tourmaline*", p. 115.

26. Matthew Arnold, "To Marguerite — Continued", in *The Poetical Works of Matthew Arnold*, ed. C.B. Tinker and H.F. Lowry (London: Oxford University Press, 1950), p. 182. Cf. A.D. Hope, "The Wandering Islands", in *Collected Poems 1930–1965* (Sydney: Angus & Robertson, 1966), pp. 26-27.

27. Stow, "The Land's Meaning", in *A Counterfeit Silence*, p. 36.

28. In *Background to The Long Search* (London: BBC, 1977), Ninian Smart describes the Tao as "almost the antithesis of how Christianity has been interpreted. It is the opposite of the Protestant ethic", p. 258.

29. Cf. Marlow's description of Jim in Joseph Conrad, *Lord Jim* (Harmondsworth: Penguin, 1949), pp. 38-40.
30. The Taoist vision is closer to the "negative" mysticism of works like *The Cloud of Unknowing* than to earlier "positive" Christian mysticism.
31. *Rasselas*, ed. J.P. Hardy (London: Oxford University Press, 1968), p. 20.
32. Stow, *A Counterfeit Silence*, p. 41. For a full discussion of this poem see pp. 78-79.
33. Stow, *Visitants*, p. 185.
34. Cf. O.N. Burgess: "The narrator is meant to be confused and wavering, nebulously regretful and prayerfully hopeful, lost and divided of mind", in "The Novels of Randolph Stow", *Australian Quarterly* 37 (1965): 80.
35. Dorothy Hewett adapts these lines, and Byrne's earlier song "New Holland is a barren place" (p. 15), in *The Man From Mukinupin* (Perth: Fremantle Arts Centre Press, 1979), p. 62.
36. Hetherington, "Young Man in No Hurry", p. 243.

5   Grievous Music

1. For the sake of convenience all of the poetry, including the Music Theatre, is discussed here in a single chapter, which is situated between the chapters on *Tourmaline* and *The Merry-go-Round in the Sea* because of the strong links with these two novels.
2. He receives only the scantiest of mentions, for example, in the "Poetry" section of *The Oxford History of Australian Literature*, ed. Leonie Kramer (Melbourne: Oxford University Press, 1981), pp. 415, 425; and in "Australian Poetry since 1920", in *The Literature of Australia*, revised edition, ed. Geoffrey Dutton (Ringwood: Penguin, 1976), p. 114. The treatment in *The Literature of Western Australia*, ed. Bruce Bennett (Nedlands: University of Western Australia Press, 1979), pp. 163-68, is more generous. Apart from reviews there has been little discussion of the poetry in journals. Among the few perceptive accounts are Brandon Conron, "Voyager from Eden", *Ariel* 1, no. 4 (1970): 96-102; and Artur Lundkvist, "Företal" to *Tystnadens landskap* (Gävle: Cikada, 1981), pp. 5-7. An earlier draft of the present chapter, "The Poetry of Randolph Stow", appeared in *Southerly* 42 (1982): 259-76.
3. The four books are: *Act One* (London: Macdonald, 1957); *Outrider* (London: Macdonald, 1962); *A Counterfeit Silence* (Sydney: Angus & Robertson, 1969); and (in Swedish) *Tystnadens landskap*, trans. Gun Ursing and David Harry (Gävle: Cikada, 1981). For the uncollected poems see bibliography, pp. 199-200. Where the dates of writing are cited, these have been supplied by the author.
4. A.J. Hassall, "Interview with Randolph Stow", *ALS* 10 (1982): 324.
5. Cf. Rodney Hall: "An overwhelming proportion of white Australian poetry has been, and still is, preoccupied with statements about the land, attempting just such a spiritual control as the Aborigines have", introduction to *The Collins Book of Australian Poetry* (Sydney: Collins, 1981), p. 3. By contrast, there has been relatively little love poetry written by Australian poets, especially male poets. See Chris Wallace-Crabbe, "The Absence of Love", in *Three Absences in Australian Writing* (Townsville: Foundation for Australian Literary Studies, 1983), pp. 1-14; and Fay Zwicky, "Speeches and Silences", *Quadrant* 27, no. 5 (May 1983):40-46.
6. *A Counterfeit Silence* (hereafter *CS*), p. 36. References, wherever possible,

are to *A Counterfeit Silence*, which is the most readily available and the most complete collection. Subsequent references are included in the text.

7. The Stow–Nolan collaboration was published separately as *Australian Artists and Poets Booklets No. 9* (Adelaide: Australian Letters, 1963), which reproduced pp. 2-12 of *Australian Letters* 5, no. 2 (December 1962), though the colours of the Nolan paintings in the booklet varied a good deal from the journal reproductions. Stow has described the collaboration in a letter to the author (13 November 1981):

> The *Australian Letters* series first put Sidney Nolan and me in touch with one another. Geoff Dutton suggested that we should collaborate – probably because we were both in England. But I think it might have come to nothing if Macdonalds hadn't become keen on the idea of having him do the book. He worked closely with the printer and was able to supervise every stage of the plates. I don't remember that we ever talked in detail about particular poems or paintings, but we talked a lot in general. We were pretty much on the same wave-length in those days, and started ideas in each other. He called it "cross-fertilization".

   In "The Land's Meaning" the poet refers directly to the Nolan paintings which show camels kneeling in the heat haze and cockatoos lying dead in the air, as Bruce Bennett has pointed out in a radio script on Stow's poetry, ABC, 1982. A.D. Hope has suggested that Nolan's "strange, beautiful and haunting pictures" are evocative of Stow's novels rather than his poems, though he sees "The Land's Meaning" as an exception to this: "Randolph Stow and the Way of Heaven", *Hemisphere* 18, no. 6 (June 1974): 34. In *Australia Fair: Poems and Paintings* (Sydney: Ure Smith, 1974), Douglas Stewart juxtaposes Russell Drysdale's *Anthills on Rocky Plains* and Stow's "Strange Fruit", pp. 74-75.

8. "Outrider", *CS*, p. 45.

9. Stow, *To the Islands*, rev. ed., p. 78. The Law in *Tourmaline* also fears drowning, in a sea of dust like the lava which covered Pompeii, p. 13.

10. "The Singing Bones", *CS*, p. 52.

11. Letter to the author, 5 July 1983. Fay Zwicky discussed the poem perceptively in "Speeches and Silences", p. 45.

12. John B. Beston, "The Love Poetry of Randolph Stow", *ACLALS Bulletin*, fourth series no. 5 (1977), p. 12. Cf. Zwicky, "Speeches and Silences", pp. 44-45.

13. Beston, ibid., p. 12.

14. "The Recluse", *CS*, p. 8.

15. Stow, *The Merry-go-Round in the Sea* (London: Macdonald, 1965), pp. 234-37.

16. As Stow explains in the notes to *A Counterfeit Silence*, p. 76, a Jimmy Woodser is "a solitary drink". It also means a solitary drinker.

17. Miss Sutherland MacDonald was the original for Aunt Kay in *The Merry-go-Round in the Sea* (letter to the author 23 January 1982).

18. Kiriwina is one of the larger Trobriand Islands.

19. "Thailand Railway", *CS*, p. 67.

20. Stow discusses "one pair of opposed myths . . . the myth of Australia as prison, and . . . the other of Australia as Eden", in "The Southland of Antichrist: The *Batavia* Disaster of 1629", in *Common Wealth*, ed. Anna Rutherford (Aarhus: Akademisk Boghandel, 1971), pp. 160-67. Cf. James McAuley's *Captain Quiros* (Sydney: Angus and Robertson, 1964). The city of Petra was chosen: "because it seemed safe and snug but wasn't and because the ruins of a city built of bales of hay would be all light-catching sharp edges like that rock, but yellow (as a first draft of the poem I did a painting

influenced by memories of the great blocks of red rock which strew the canyons of the North Kimberley, as described in *To the Islands*)". Letter to the author, *23 February 1982.*

21. Preface to *Sandgropers*, ed. Dorothy Hewett (Nedlands: University of Western Australia Press, 1973), p. ix.

22. The selection includes fifteen of the original forty-three poems in *Act One*, twenty-three of the original twenty-four poems in *Outrider*, and ten new poems, nine in "Stations" and "For One Dying", which is added to the poems from *Act One* in "Juvenilia". Two of the poems from *Outrider*, "The Recluse" and "The Ship Becalmed", are relegated to "Juvenilia".

23. Hassall interview, p. 324.

24.   Western wind when will thou blow
        (That) the small rain down can rain?
        Christ, that my love were in my arms,
        And I in my bed again!

                            Anon.

25. The poem was first published in *SMH*, 17 August 1974, p. 13; and reprinted in *Kunapipi* 1, no. 1 (1979): 30.

26. Beston, "Love Poetry of Randolph Stow", p. 19.

27. *SMH*, 23 December 1978, p. 16.

28. Stow has described the context of the poem in a letter to the author (13 November 1981). The poem appeared in *SMH*, 12 April 1975, p. 13.

29. The poem was first published in *Westerly* 15, no. 3 (October 1970): 10, and reprinted in *Twelve Poets*, ed. A. Craig (Milton: Jacaranda, 1971), p. 174.

30. Beston, "Love Poetry of Randolph Stow", p. 18.

31. The poem appeared in *The Bulletin Literary Supplement*, 30 September 1980, p. 23.

32. The poem appeared in *Sandgropers*, ed. Hewett, p. 2.

33. Andrew Porter traces Music Theatre back as far as Monteverdi's *Tancredi e Clorinda* (1624) in *The New Grove Dictionary of Music and Musicians*, ed. Stanley Sadie (London: Macmillan, 1980), vol. 12, p. 863. Monteverdi is a favourite composer of Stow's: describing his use of loose pairs of lines that are not exactly couplets in his poetry, he has said: "if there is a composer whose music I try to emulate it is Monteverdi – that long loose music – I love the way he handles words. I love for instance Otorne's opening aria in *The Coronation of Poppaea*". Unpublished section of Hassall interview.

34. See, for example, his *Hymn to Saint Magnus*, based on a twelfth-century original from Saint Magnus Cathedral, Kirkwall, Orkney.

35. James Murdoch, "Music in Theatre", *Theatre Australia*, March 1982, p. 59.

36. Hassall interview, pp. 322-23.

37. The works were performed together in April 1974 at the Queen Elizabeth Hall, London. See Ray Willbanks, *Randolph Stow* (Boston: Twayne, 1978), p. 137. On their success, see Murdoch, "Music in Theatre", p. 59.

38. *Eight Songs for a Mad King*: Music by Peter Maxwell Davies. Words by Randolph Stow. Full Score (London: Boosey & Hawkes, 1971), n. pag.

39. See Davies's note on "The Music" on the sleeve of *Eight Songs for a Mad King*, Unicorn RHS 308, 1972; and the fuller notes in the *Full Score*.

40. Full Score.

41. Ibid.

42. From the Musica Viva programme for the first performance at the Adelaide Festival of Arts, 9 March 1974. Like "A Pomegranate in Winter", "Miss Donnithorne's Maggot" is dedicated to Patrick White. Stow cites J.S. Ryan's "A Possible Australian Source for Miss Havisham", *ALS* 1 (1963): 134-36, as identifying Miss Donnithorne.

43. *Miss Donnithorne's Maggot*. Music by Peter Maxwell Davies. Text by Randolph Stow (London: Boosey and Hawkes, 1977), n. pag.
44. The poem is subtitled: "For Russ Braddon: Your memories, not mine; a debt to acknowledge a debt". Russell Braddon wrote of Australian prisoners-of-war and the Thailand railway in *The Naked Island* (London: Werner Laurie, 1952).
45. Rodney Hall, ed., *The Collins Book of Australian Poetry* (Sydney: Collins, 1981), p. 439.
46. *Twelve Poets: 1950-1970*, ed. Alexander Craig (Milton: Jacaranda Press, 1971), p. 175. Cf. Hassall interview, p. 324.

6   Circling Days

1. 1965 was a good year for autobiographies of childhood. It saw the publication of D.E. Charlwood's *All the Green Year* (Sydney: Angus & Robertson), Graham McInnes's *The Road to Gundagai* (London: Hamish Hamilton) and Thomas Keneally's *The Fear* (Melbourne: Cassell) – which has a significant autobiographical component – as well as *The Merry-go-Round in the Sea*. Reviewing *The Road to Gundagai*, Hal Porter wrote that: "autobiography seems, at any rate just now, the liveliest and most telling way to perform the literary chore of wiping the mallee dust and gum leaves and swaggie gobs off the windscreen so that one can really see". *Bulletin*, 3 July 1965, p. 50.
2. Richard N. Coe, "Portrait of the Artist as a Young Australian: Childhood, Literature and Myth", *Southerly* 41 (1981): 127. Cf. John Colmer, "Australian Autobiography: Flawed and Fortunate Lives", *Meridian* 3 (1984): 135-41.
3. Beston interview, p. 224.
   Stow has rearranged his factual material more extensively than this comment might suggest. To take just one example, Eric Sewell, the main model for Rick Maplestead, was not a prisoner-of-war of the Japanese. The prisoner-of-war memories came from Russell Braddon.
4. Anna Rutherford and Andreas Boelsmand, "Interview with Randolph Stow", *Commonwealth Literature* 5 (December 1973): 19. It must be said that Jane Austen's novels are also deliberately structured.
5. The manuscript of *Tourmaline* includes a graph of the fortunes of Kestrel and Random showing them to be symmetrically opposed throughout. The manuscript is held in the National Library of Australia, Canberra (MS 4912).
6. Randolph Stow, *The Merry-go-Round in the Sea* (London: Macdonald, 1965), p. 269. Subsequent references are to this edition and are included in the text.
7. Stow, "Him", *Overland*, no. 59 (Spring 1974): 19. The poem has an epigraph from the Trobriand Island Diary of the anthropologist Bronislaw Malinowski in which he describes a "strangely autoerotic" dream, similar to the dream described in the poem. Cf. The striking lines from "Enkidu": "Our king builds a shrine to his shadow./The temple mirrors are empty when he looks in." Cf. also Rimbaud's "Conte" in *Les Illuminations*.
8. In his preface to the revised edition of *To the Islands*, Stow speaks of the author of the first edition "who no longer seems to be myself", p. vii.
9. National Library of Australia (MS 4912).
10. Stow has said that "the world of childhood as a source of inspiration is written out for me now", and if that is so he may not return to the theme. See Beston interview, p. 229.

11. "Advance Australia Fair" is now the official Australian anthem.
12. These lines from Laurence Binyon's "For the Fallen" are a traditional feature of Anzac ceremonies.
13. The poems referred to include Henry Lawson, "Middleton's Rouseabout", and Mary Hannay Foott, "Where the Pelican Builds".
14. Randolph Stow, *To the Islands* (London: Macdonald, 1958), p. 76. The passage was omitted from the revised edition (1981).
15. Cf. Stow, "The Singing Bones", in *A Counterfeit Silence*, p. 52.
16. See, for example, Andrew Gurr, *Writers in Exile: The Identity of Home in Modern Literature*.
17. The standard account of Australia's isolation is Geoffrey Blainey, *The Tyranny of Distance* (Melbourne: Sun Books, 1966).
18. Stow, *A Counterfeit Silence*, p. 42.
19. Cf. the early part of Joyce's *A Portrait of the Artist as a Young Man*.
20. McInnes, *Road to Gundagai*, p. 40.
21. Henry Handel Richardson, *Myself When Young* (London: Heinemann, 1948), pp. 70-71.
22. National Library of Australia (MS 4912).
23. Patrick White, *The Aunt's Story* (London: Routledge, 1948), p. 154.
24. Beston interview, p. 224.
25. Kenneth Mackenzie, *The Young Desire It* (London: Cape, 1937).
26. As a commentary on the Australian suburban ugliness this final scene loses nothing by comparison with Patrick White's more strident attacks on Sarsaparilla and Barranugli.
27. S.A. Ramsey, " 'The silent griefs': Randolph Stow's *Visitants*", *Critical Quarterly* 23, no. 2 (1981): 74.
28. Stow is depicting the failure of a tentative attempt at a mature relationship between two overgrown children. He is not attempting to portray an adult relationship. As Jack Speed says in *Tourmaline*. "That's the trouble, in this place. You get old without growing up" (p. 176).
29. Stow, *A Counterfeit Silence*, p. 34.

7   Bushranging

1. Stow, *The Merry-go-Round in the Sea*, p. 218.
2. The exploits of Moondyne Joe, one of Western Australia's better known bushrangers, are recounted by Ian Elliot in *Moondyne Joe: The Man and the Myth* (Nedlands: University of Western Australia Press, 1978); on bushranging in general see Bill Wannan, *Tell 'em I died game* (Melbourne: Lansdowne Press, 1963). Contemporary views of the bushrangers were more divided and less flattering than they have since become. Many of them were murderers as well as thieves, and if they were romanticized by some they were also widely hated.
3. Elliot, *Moondyne Joe*, pp. 137-44.
4. Ibid., p. xii.
5. Randolph Stow, *Midnite: The Story of a Wild Colonial Boy* (London: Macdonald, 1967), p. 16. All quotations are from this edition, and subsequent references are included in the text.
6. Beston interview, p. 226.
7. See, for example, Dennis Dugan, "White and Might", *Age Literary Review*, 16 September 1967, p. 22; and Jennifer Kimber, "Children's Books", *ABR* 6,

no. 10 (August 1967): 162. For a contrary view see Gwen Hutchings, "Legend Lampoon", *Canberra Times*, 6 July 1968, pp. 13-14; and Barbara Buick and Maxine Walker, "Books for Children", in *The Literature of Western Australia*, ed. Bruce Bennett (Nedlands: University of Western Australia Press, 1979), pp. 234-37.

8. The incident of the Governor's bet with Midnite, on which the Governor reneges (93), is based on an agreement between Moondyne Joe, the Governor, Dr J.S. Hampton, and the Governor's son, Acting Comptroller-General George Hampton, as reported in the *Perth Gazette* (see Elliot, *Moondyne Joe*, pp. 89-90). The epigraph to this chapter is a popular refrain of the time which expresses the discomfiture Moondyne Joe caused the Governor and his son (ibid., p. 96).

9. Stow treats the same poem more seriously in "The Singing Bones", *A Counterfeit Silence*, p. 52.

10. Beston interview, p. 226.

11. "Magic" appeared in *Modern Australian Writing*, ed. Geoffrey Dutton (London: Fontana, 1966), pp. 106-19; "Dokonikan" appeared in *Australian Writing Today*, ed. Charles Higham (Harmondsworth: Penguin, 1968), pp. 287-96.

12. The myth is told by Metusela/Taudoga, *Visitants*, pp. 157-58.

13. See note in "Magic", p. 106; and Bronislaw Malinowski, *The Sexual Life of Savages in North-Western Melanesia*, 3rd ed. (London: Routledge, 1932), pp. 456-74. The village is Kumilabwaga on Boyowa Island.

14. Cf. Malinowski: "The taboo against incest between brother and sister is the most important and most dramatic feature of the Trobriand social organization", ibid., p. 451.

15. Tudava, one of the legendary Trobriand heroes, is believed to be the child of a virgin birth. His mother Bulutukwa was impregnated by a dripping stalactite. See Malinowski, ibid., pp. 155, 359.

16. In a letter to the author (19 November 1983) Stow has described the Trobrianders' attitude to cannibalism:

> "Dokonikan" is told as a comic story, and I don't think the Trobrianders considered him or his victims as quite the same people as themselves — though Tudava is their culture-hero. When I was shown Dokonikan's cave, and came back carrying a skull, like Hamlet, the old ladies weeding the gardens laughed and asked what I wanted with the "bone". I formed the theory, though I've no evidence other than their indifference to those human remains, that they were the dead of an earlier immigration. A token, ritual cannibalism was practised by them once, and Malinowski suspected it survived in his day, though outlawed by the administration. It used to be a pious duty to swallow a little of the putrescent flesh of close relations. They told Malinowski that they didn't like doing it, and usually vomited. In *Sexual Life of Savages* I think you'll find a photograph of a widow wearing her husband's jaw-bone round her neck [plate 34; between pp. 252-53]. However, Dokonikan's cannibalism was altogether a different matter; he was merely a comic ogre.

17. "The Arrival at the Homestead: A Mind-Film" has appeared in two forms: in *Kunapipi* 1, no. 1 (1979): 31-36, and in *Bulletin*, 29 January 1980, pp. 164-66. The latter version, which includes an additional introductory sequence, is the basis of the following discussion.

18. There are many correspondences between the disappointed brides in "A Rose for Emily" and "Miss Donnithorne's Maggot". Cf. also James McQueen's "Holding Hands", in *The Electric Beach* (Wynyard, Tasmania: Robin Books, 1978), pp. 93-100.

8 Going Troppo

1. Perhaps the best known of Bronislaw Malinowski's books on the Trobriand Islanders is *The Sexual Life of Savages in North-Western Melanesia*, 3rd ed. (London: Routledge, 1932).
2. Stow was for a time assistant to Dr Charles Julius, the government anthropologist. See Hassall interview, p. 312.
3. Randolph Stow, *Visitants* (London: Secker & Warburg, 1979), p. 187. Subsequent references are to this edition, and are included in the text.
4. Hassall interview, p. 312.
5. In the Beston interview, Stow says: "I'm more attracted to the novella now than to the novel" (224).
6. Cf. Hassall interview, p. 319.
7. The manuscript of the novel held in the National Library of Australia in Canberra has a cancelled epigraph from Blake: "A Last Judgement is necessary because Fools flourish" (MS 4912).
8. The Boianai incident is described as "one of the great classics in UFO history" by Jacques Vallee in *Anatomy of a Phenomenon* (London: Neville Spearman, 1966), p. 145, a work Stow refers to in his note, p. 191.
9. "They wanted facts", says the narrator. "Facts! They demanded facts from him, as if facts could explain anything!" Joseph Conrad, *Lord Jim* (Harmondsworth: Penguin, 1949), p. 27.
10. Hassall interview, p. 317.
11. Ibid.
12. Russell Soaba has praised Stow as "a poet of perception working carefully with local idioms and sentiments, and bringing home to the reader his feeling for the Kiriwina language – its sense of humor, its richness of imagery and its insistent use of symbolic expressions". See "Of Kiaps and Cargo Cults", *Overland*, no. 80 (1980), p. 65. Cf. Stow's own comments, Hassall interview, p. 315.
13. Hassall interview, p. 315.
14. Hemingway's *For Whom the Bell Tolls* is one of the more celebrated and controversial examples.
15. Cf. Norman Talbot's review of *Visitants*, *CRNLE Reviews Journal*, no. 2 (1981), p. 52.
16. See Laszlo Legeza, *Tao Magic: The Secret Language of Diagrams and Calligraphy* (London: Thames and Hudson, 1975), p. 110, diagram 6; and Max Kaltenmark, *Lao Tzu and Taoism* (Stanford: Stanford University Press, 1969), p. 26.
17. This information is contained in a letter to the author (26 February 1981). I am indebted to Randolph Stow for his comments and suggestions in this letter and elsewhere on the original version of this chapter, published in *ALS* 9 (1980): 449-59.
18. Letter of 26 February 1981. The line comes from the *Pervigilium Veneris*.
19. Stow describes this condition in the Hassall interview, p. 318.
20. Stow's use of the cargo cult is discussed by Helen Tiffin in "Melanesian Cargo Cults in *Tourmaline* and *Visitants*", *JCL* 16 (1981): 109-25; and by Robyn Wallace in "Messiahs and Millennia in Randolph Stow's Novels", *Kunapipi* 3, no. 2 (1981): 56-72.
21. Dame Julian of Norwich's "Sin is behovely, but all shall be well, and all shall be well, and all manner of thing shall be well" is perhaps best known as quoted in "Little Gidding". See Julian of Norwich, *Revelations of Divine Love*,

trans. Clifton Wolters (Harmondsworth: Penguin, 1966), pp. 35, 104; and T.S. Eliot, *Collected Poems 1909–1962* (London: Faber, 1963), p. 219.

22. Hassall interview, pp. 318-19.

23. For an account of this condition see R.D. Laing, *The Divided Self* (Harmondsworth: Penguin, 1965), p. 58.

24. Marvin Mudrick's description of Conrad's use of the "double plot" applies, *mutatis mutandis*, to Stow's parallelling of Cawdor's psychic condition and the events on Kailuana: "the fictional technique that [Conrad] exploited . . . is the double plot: neither allegory (where surface is something teasing, to be got through), nor catch-all symbolism (where every knowing particular signifies some universal or other), but a developing order of actions so lucidly symbolic of a developing state of spirit . . . as to suggest the conditions of allegory without forfeiting or even subordinating the realistic 'superficial' claim of the actions and their actors", "The Originality of Conrad", in *Conrad: A Collection of Critical Essays*, ed. Marvin Mudrick (Englewood Cliffs: Prentice-Hall, 1966), p. 38.

25. The two Trobriand stories Stow has published concern the breaking of cannibalism and incest taboos. See pp. 124-25.

26. S.A. Ramsey, "'The silent griefs': Randolph Stow's *Visitants*", *Critical Quarterly* 23, no. 2 (1981): 73.

27. T.A.G. Hungerford, Review of *Visitants*, *Westerly* 25, no. 1 (1980): 107. The dedication of *Visitants* to T.A.G. Hungerford, encoded in Pidgin, may be translated as: "I want to send this book to my friend". The word for friend, "wantok", is particularly appropriate, as it means a fellow tribesman, one who speaks the same local language. The dedication recalls the Spanish epigraph to *Outrider*, "yo no digo esta canción/sino a quien conmigo va" (literally "I do not tell this song except to one who goes with me").

9   Seely Suffolk

1. Stow, *A Counterfeit Silence*, p. 10.

2. Hassall interview, *ALS* 10 (1982), 319.

3. Stow, *The Girl Green as Elderflower* (London: Secker & Warburg, 1980), p. 30. Subsequent references to this edition are included in the text.

4. The card depicts a live man hanging upside down by his foot, not a man hanged by the neck. After his fortune is told by Amabel, Clare examines the card: "Calm and content, hands behind his back, he dangled . . . It's the wrong way up in every kind of way. He must be upside down, because of his hair. But that doesn't look like a gibbet. He seems to be hanging from the earth, between two trees . . . it reminded me of things I've been reading lately. Things they thought they knew, in the Middle Ages, about the Antipodes and their land" (19-20). When he is tortured by Corporal Snart, the merman of the second legend is hung up by the feet.

5. Cf. Stow, "Stations", *A Counterfeit Silence*, p. 62:
   War blacks out the land,
   that knew before us neither hearth nor lamplight,
   only the last lost tremor of nomad fires.

6. "The classic Australian writers", according to A.A. Phillips, "produced a literature of loneliness". "Australian Image: 2) The Literary Heritage Reassessed", *Meanjin* 21 (1962): 176.

7. "A pity that you huddle," says Voss to Laura, "your country is of great subtlety." Patrick White, *Voss* (London: Eyre & Spottiswoode, 1957), p. 13.

8. See "The Singing Bones", *A Counterfeit Silence*, p. 52.
9. Robyn Wallace, "Messiahs and Millennia in Randolph Stow's Novels", *Kunapipi* 3, no. 2 (1981): 70.
10. Dante, *Purgatorio*, 27.
11. Helen Watson-Williams, "Randolph Stow's Suffolk Novel", *Westerly* 25, no. 4 (1980): 71.
12. See Stow, "The Land's Meaning", *A Counterfeit Silence*, p. 36.
13. Hassall interview, p. 321. Brouček is not, in fact, the innkeeper, but a standing guest at the Vikára Inn.
14. A number of reviewers commented on the success of the book's method. Bruce King, for example, says that "without trying", *The Girl Green as Elderflower* "makes many attempts at experimental fiction appear self-conscious, mechanically contrived, and unimaginative", *Sewanee Review* 89 (1981): 464. John Hanrahan agrees, despite a contrary initial impression: "at first this novel seems a muddle of fragments", but it "develops as a finely integrated world that absorbs and convinces", *ABR* no. 27 (December 1980): 8-9.
15. Stow began the writing of *The Girl Green as Elderflower* on New Year's Day 1979. It was completed by 1 February 1979. See Hassall interview, pp. 311-12.
16. In an interview with Bruce Bennett, Stow describes the first paragraph of the book as "rather Jamesian". "Discussions with Randolph Stow", *Westerly* 26, no. 4 (1981): 59.
17. Stow, *A Counterfeit Silence*, p. 51.
18. Clare again attempts to explain Amabel's message at the end of the book: "She knew, without knowing, what I expected to see, and wrote it" (142).
19. Thomas Shapcott, radio review for the ABC's "Books and Writing" no. 125, 1 September 1980.
20. Stow, *A Counterfeit Silence*, p. 40.
21. Hassall interview, p. 312.
22. Bennett interview, p. 58.
23. Ibid., p. 55.
24. See pp. 136-37, 140.

10   A Privee Theef

1. In a letter to the author (31 October 1983).
2. Randolph Stow, *The Suburbs of Hell* (London: Secker & Warburg, 1984), pp. 1-2. Subsequent references are to this edition, and are included in the text.
   On death as a thief, cf. this fourteenth-century lyric:
   Sum men sciþ þat deþ is a þef,
     And al vnwarned wol on him stele,
   And I sey nay, and make a pref,
     Þat deþ is studefast, trewe, and lele,
   And warneþ vche mon of his greef,
     Þat he wol o day wiþ him dele.
   Religious Lyrics of the XIVth Century, ed. Carleton Brown, 2nd ed., rev. G.V. Smithers (Oxford: Clarendon Press, 1952), p. 148.
3. The suggestion that the ideal criminal is the reader is Charles Rycroft's, cited by Julian Symons, *Mortal Consequences: A History — From the Detective Story to the Crime Novel* (New York: Schocken, 1973), pp. 6-7.

4. John Webster, *The Duchess of Malfi*, ed. John Russell Brown (London: Methuen, 1964), 5, ii, 337-38, p. 157.
5. John Webster, *The White Devil*, ed. John Russell Brown (London: Methuen, 1960), 1, i, 31-33, p. 9.
   Epigraphs are quoted as they appear in *The Suburbs of Hell*. References to editions of the original works identify the location of the quotations, but not necessarily their form.
6. *Beowulf*, trans. David Wright (Harmondsworth: Penguin, 1957), p. 30. The epigraph is quoted incorrectly by Stow, *Suburbs of Hell*, p. 1.
7. The "Nedlands Monster", who terrorized Perth for eight months in 1963, was Eric Edgar Cooke. He murdered six people altogether, both men and women, chosen seemingly without motive, though one of the women was raped. Cooke was hanged on 26 October 1964, the second last person to be hanged in Australia. See Jack Coulter, *With Malice Aforethought* (Perth: St George Books, 1982), pp. 108-22. In a letter to the author (22 December 1983), Stow has said that Cooke's murders, and the atmosphere they created, were "the genesis" of *The Suburbs of Hell*.
8. John Gardner suggests in *Grendel* (London: Picador, 1973) that the monster of *Beowulf* learned the more bloodthirsty of his ways from men.
9. Christopher Marlowe, *The Jew of Malta*, ed. N.W. Bawcutt (Manchester: Manchester University Press, 1978), 2, iii, 176-209, pp. 115-17. Stow, *Suburbs of Hell*, p. 59.
10. Letter to the author (12 June 1984).
11. This tattoo, which is not uncommon, was used allegorically in Charles Laughton's 1955 film *Night of the Hunter*. Robert Mitchum who played the psychopathic preacher Harry Powell, had L-O-V-E and H-A-T-E tattooed on his fingers. See François Truffaut, *Hitchcock* (London: Panther, 1969), p. 397.
12. William Shakespeare, *King Richard III*, ed. Antony Hammond (London: Methuen, 1981), 5, iii, 185, p. 318; and *Titus Andronicus*, ed. J.C. Maxwell (London: Methuen, 1953), 5, i, 125-28, p. 108.
13. Thomas Kyd, *The Spanish Tragedy*, ed. Philip Edwards (London: Methuen, 1959), Fourth Additional Passage between 3, xii and 3, xiii, 162-63, p. 133. Stow, *Suburbs of Hell*, p. 77.
14. Stow has described *The Secret Agent* as the novel of Joseph Conrad's to which *The Suburbs of Hell* "comes closest". Letter to the author (21 May 1984).
15. Letter (12 June 1984).
16. There is only one entry under the letter Y in *The Murderers' Who's Who* by J.H.H. Gaute and Robin Odell (London: Pan, 1980). It describes the career of Graham Young, who poisoned his workmates at a Hertfordshire firm with thallium. When he was tried, he "denied killing anyone and claimed that the notes in his diary [which contained the names of his victims] were for a novel he intended to write. The jury found him guilty" (p. 353).
17. The original form is:
    al to late, al to late,
    wanne þe bere ys ate gate.
    See "Proprietates Mortis", in *English Lyrics of the XIIIth Century*, ed. Carleton Brown (Oxford: Clarendon Press, 1932), p. 130.

Afterword

1. Stow, "Stations", in *A Counterfeit Silence*, p. 60.

Bibliography

Works of Randolph Stow

Poetry

Act One: Poems. London: Macdonald, 1957.
Outrider: Poems, 1956–1962. With paintings by Sidney Nolan. London: Macdonald, 1962.
Poems from "The Outrider" and other Poems. Illus. Sidney Nolan. Australian Artists and Poets Booklets No. 9. Adelaide: Australian Letters, 1963.
A Counterfeit Silence: Selected Poems. Sydney: Angus & Robertson, 1969.
Eight Songs for a Mad King. Music by Peter Maxwell Davies. Words by Randolph Stow. London: Boosey and Hawkes, 1971. Recording: With Julius Eastman, voice. Cond. Peter Maxwell Davies, The Fires of London. Unicorn, 1972.
Miss Donnithorne's Maggot. Music by Peter Maxwell Davies. Text by Randolph Stow. London: Boosey and Hawkes, 1977. Recording: With Mary Thomas, soprano. Cond. Peter Maxwell Davies, The Fires of London. Unicorn-Kanchana, 1985.
Randolph Stow Reads From His Own Work. Ed. Thomas W. Shapcott. Poets on Record Series No. 11. St Lucia: University of Queensland Press, 1974.
Tystnadens landskap. Trans. into Swedish by Gun Ursing and David Harry. Gävle: Cikada, 1981.

Editorial Work

Australian Poetry 1964. Selected by Randolph Stow. Sydney: Angus & Robertson, 1964.

Novels

A Haunted Land. London: Macdonald, 1956; New York: Macmillan, 1957.
The Bystander. London: Macdonald, 1957.
To the Islands. London: Macdonald, 1958; Boston: Little, Brown, 1959; Melbourne: Penguin, 1962.

Revised Edition. London: Secker & Warburg, 1982; New York: Taplinger, 1982; Sydney: Angus & Robertson, 1981; Sydney: Picador, 1983.

Tourmaline. London: Macdonald, 1963; Melbourne: Penguin, 1965.

Reissued. London: Secker & Warburg, 1983; New York: Taplinger, 1983; Sydney: Angus & Robertson, 1983; Harmondsworth: Penguin, 1984.

The Merry-go-Round in the Sea. London: Macdonald, 1965; New York: Morrow, 1966; Melbourne: Penguin, 1968.

Reissued. London: Secker & Warburg, 1984; New York: Taplinger, 1984; Sydney: Angus & Robertson, 1984.

Midnite: The Story of a Wild Colonial Boy. Illus. Ralph Steadman. London: Macdonald, 1967; Melbourne: Cheshire, 1967; Harmondsworth: Penguin, 1969; Melbourne: Penguin, 1970.

Illus. Joan Sandin. Englewood Cliffs: Prentice-Hall, 1968.

With new illustrations by Ralph Steadman. London: Bodley Head, 1984.

Visitants. London: Secker & Warburg, 1979; New York: Taplinger, 1981; London: Picador, 1981.

The Girl Green as Elderflower. London: Secker & Warburg, 1980; New York: Viking, 1980.

The Suburbs of Hell. London: Secker & Warburg, 1984; New York: Taplinger, 1984; Melbourne: Heinemann, 1984.

Short Stories

"Magic". In *Modern Australian Writing*, edited by Geoffrey Dutton, 106-19. London: Fontana, 1966.

"Dokonikan". In *Australian Writing Today*, edited by Charles Higham, 287-96. Harmondsworth: Penguin, 1968.

"The Arrival at the Homestead: A Mind-Film". *Kunapipi* 1, no. 1 (1979): 31-36. Expanded version, *Bulletin*, 29 January 1980, 164-66.

Uncollected Poems

"Ecco La Vita". *Winthrop Review* 1, no. 2 (1953): 20.

"Cartoon Parade". *Winthrop Review* 1, no. 2 (1953): 35.

"Lament For Dylan Thomas". *Winthrop Review* 2, no. 1 (1954): 25.

"All Hallows Eve". *Bulletin*, 20 July 1955, 24.

"Metamorphosis". *Bulletin*, 14 September 1955, 2.

"Guildford". *Bulletin*, 14 December 1955, 32.

"Three Poems by Clement Marot". Trans. Randolph Stow. *Westerly* 1, no. 1 (1956): 48-49.

"Aboriginal Dream-Song". *Bulletin*, 4 July 1956, 23.

"Montebellos". *Meanjin* 15 (1956): 332.

"The Infanta Betrayed". *Australian Letters* 1, no. 1 (June 1957): 32.

"Black Jack's Doppelganger". *Prospect* 1, no. 1 (1958): 13.

"Jabulmara Dancing". *Prospect* 2, no. 2 (1959): 14-15.

"Thank God The West Australian Is On Our Side". *Australian Book Review* 2, no. 11 (September 1963): 186.

"The Tender Trap", *Australian Book Review* 3, no. 2 (December 1963): 58. Rpt. in *Wide Domain*, edited by Bruce Bennett and William Grono, 180-81. Sydney: Angus and Robertson, 1979.

"The Lamentable History of Dr Verwoerd's Aunt". *Australian Book Review* 3, no. 10 (August 1964): 180.

"Penelope". *Westerly* 15, no. 3 (1970): 11. Rpt. in *Sandgropers: A Western Australian Anthology*, edited by Dorothy Hewett, 1. Nedlands: University of Western Australia Press, 1973. For revised version see John B. Beston. "The Love Poetry of Randolph Stow". *ACLALS Bulletin* 5 (1977): 12.

"Enkidu (Gilgamesh Laments)". *Westerly* 15, no. 3 (1970): 10. Rpt. in *Twelve Poets, 1950–1970*, edited by Alexander Craig, 174-75. Brisbane: Jacaranda Press, 1971.

"Incubus to Virgin". In *Sandgropers: A Western Australian Anthology*, edited by Dorothy Hewett, 2. Nedlands: University of Western Australia Press, 1973.

"The Wind-rose". In *Sandgropers: A Western Australian Anthology*, edited by Dorothy Hewett, 3. Nedlands: University of Western Australia Press, 1973.

"Simplicities of Summer". *Sydney Morning Herald*, 17 August 1974, 13. Rpt. in *Kunapipi* 1, no. 1 (1979): 30.

"Him", *Overland* 59 (Spring 1974): 19.

"Efire". *Sydney Morning Herald*, 12 April 1975, 13.

"Jasmine of Madagascar". *The Literary Half-Yearly* 16, no. 2 (July 1975): 124.

"A Pomegranate in Winter". *Sydney Morning Herald*, 23 December 1978, 16.

"Frost-Parrots". *The Literary Half-Yearly* 20, no. 1 (January 1979): 1.

"Playing with My Coronet". *Kunapipi* 1, no. 1 (1979): 27.

"Alof De Vignacourt Sits For His Portrait". *Age*, 21 January 1978, 26. Rpt. in *Kunapipi* 1, no. 1 (1979): 29.

"Orphans betrothed". *Bulletin Literary Supplement*, 30 September 1980, 23.

Manuscripts

Keithy Farnham [*The Bystander*]. NLA MS 4912.

Outrider. NLA MS 4912.

Tourmaline. NLA MS 4912.

The Merry-go-Round in the Sea. NLA MS 4912.

Midnite. NLA MS 4912.

Miss Donnithorne's Maggot. NLA MS 4912.

Visitants. NLA MS 4912.

The Girl Green as Elderflower. NLA MS 4912.

The Suburbs of Hell. NLA MS 4912.
(All manuscripts are typescripts except for the final section of *Visitants*
("Troppo"), *The Girl Green as Elderflower* and *The Suburbs of Hell.*)

Articles

"A New Look at Religion". *Advertiser* (Adelaide), 9 November 1957, 16.

"Our Children in Cole Land". *Australian Letters* 1, no. 3 (April 1958):
14-22. Rpt. in *The Vital Decade: Ten Years of Australian Art and
Letters*, selected by Geoffrey Dutton and Max Harris, 18-25.
Melbourne: Sun Books, 1968.

"Wrap me up with my Portable Gramophone". *Australian Letters* 2, no. 1
(June 1959): 5-13.

"The Umbali Massacre: As told to him by Daniel Evans". *Bulletin*, 15 February 1961, 45-46.

"Raw Material". *Westerly* 6, no. 2 (1961): 3-5. Rpt. in *Westerly 21*, edited
by Bruce Bennett and Peter Cowan, 47-49. Fremantle: Fremantle
Arts Centre Press. 1978.

"Australian Men of Letters". *ABR* 1, no. 5 (March 1962): 58.

"Babbitt Eats Babbitt". *Nation* (Aust.), 19 September 1964, 11-12.

"Negritude for the White Man". In *Aborigines Now*, edited by M. Reay,
1-7. Sydney: Angus & Robertson, 1964.

"Foreword". *Poetry Australia*, West Australian Issue, no. 12 (October
1966): 4-5.

"The Southland of Antichrist: The *Batavia* Disaster of 1629". In *Common
Wealth*, edited by Anna Rutherford, 160-67. Aarhus: Akademisk
Boghandel, 1971. Paper delivered at the Conference of Common-
wealth Literature, Aarhus University, 26-30 April 1971.

"Afterword". In *Twelve Poets: 1950–1970*, edited by Alexander Craig, 175.
Milton: Jacaranda Press, 1971.

"Two Letters of 1629 on the *Batavia* Disaster". *Westerly* 17, no. 1 (April
1972): 7-11.

"Victorian Legs: A Footnote". *ABR* 11 (November 1973): 132-34.

"The Australian Miss Havisham". *ALS* 6 (1974): 418-19.

"Transfigured Histories: Recent Novels of Patrick White and Robert
Drewe". *ALS* 9 (1979): 26-38.

"Denmark in the Indian Ocean, 1616–1845: An Introduction". *Kunapipi*
1, no. 1 (1979): 11-26.

Reviews

"Kings in Grass Castles". Review of *Kings in Grass Castles*, by Mary
Durack. *Overland* 18 (Winter-Spring, 1960): 52-53.

Review of Nene Gare: *The Fringe Dwellers*. *ABR* 1, no. 1 (November
1961): 3-4.

"From Bundaberg to the Rex". Review of *The Delinquents*, by Criena
Rohan. *ABR* 1, no. 5 (March 1962): 60.

"The Primitives Around Us". Review of *Art of the World: Oceania and Australia*, by A. Buhler, T. Barlow, and C.P. Mountford. *ABR* 2, no. 4 (February 1963): 64.

"Sir Perceval in the Outback". Review of *The Letters of F.W. Ludwig Leichhardt*, edited by M. Aurousseau. *ABR* 7, no. 10 (August 1968): 177-78.

"Epic of Capricorn". Review of *Poor Fellow My Country*, by Xavier Herbert. *TLS*, 9 April 1976, 417.

Review of *Poor Fellow My Country*, by Xavier Herbert. *National Times*, 2-7 August 1976, 28-29.

"In the boundless garden". Review of *A Fringe of Leaves*, by Patrick White and *The Eye in the Mandala*, by Peter Beatson. *TLS*, 10 September 1976, 1097.

Review of *A Fringe of Leaves*, by Patrick White. *National Times*, 11-16 October 1976, 25.

"A Sad, Tough, Lonely Pioneer". Review of *To Be Heirs Forever*, by Mary Durack. *National Times*, 17-22 January 1977, 17-18.

"Suffocation in Sydney". Review of *Water Under the Bridge*, by Sumner Locke Elliott, *Escape to Reality*, by D.M. Foster and *The Most Beautiful Lies*, edited by Brian Kiernan. *TLS*, 4 August 1978, 897.

"The naturally reckless life". Review of *Adam Lindsay Gordon*, by Geoffrey Hutton. *TLS*, 25 August 1978, 944.

"Fully versed". Review of *Puddin' Poems*, by Norman Lindsay. *TLS*, 29 September 1978, 1084.

"Going bush". Review of *The Trackers*, by B. Wongar. *TLS*, 21 December 1979, 150.

"The beauties of the bush". Review of *Billabong's Author: The Life of Mary Grant Bruce*, by Alison Alexander. *TLS*, 28 March 1980, 374.

"Orphan of the Sydney surburbs". Review of *Unreliable Memoirs*, by Clive James. *TLS*, 25 April 1980, 469.

"The voracious virgin". Review of *Travels with Dr Leichhardt in Australia*, by Daniel Bunce. *TLS*, 12 September 1980, 999.

"Picnics and fibreglass pumpkins". Review of *Their Chastity was not too Rigid: Leisure Times in Early Australia*, by J.W.C. Cumes and *Treasury of Australian Kitsch*, by Barry Humphries. *TLS*, 13 February 1981, 173.

"Of O. and the General's stock". Review of *Les Géorgiques*, by Claude Simon. *TLS*, 4 December 1981, 1412.

"The model of manliness". Review of *A Soldier's View of Empire: The Reminiscenses of James Bodell 1831–92*, ed. Keith Sinclair. *TLS*, 13 August 1982, 874.

"Irrupting into the inland". Review of *The Cry for the Dead*, by Judith Wright and *Aboriginal Australians*, by Keith D. Suter and Kaye Stearman. *TLS*, 15 October 1982, 1123.

Review of *Where the Green Ants Dream*, film by Werner Hertzog. *TLS* 9 November 1984, 1284.

Letters to the Editor

"Victorian Legs". Letter. *TLS,* 26 January 1973, 94.
"Victorian Fevers". Letter. *TLS,* 3 October 1975, 1141.
"Australian Experiences". Letter in answer to Warwick Gould's review.
    TLS, 23 April 1976, 491.
"Adam and Eve and Pidgin". Letter. *TLS,* 2 December 1977, 1420.
"Edwin Drood". Letter. *TLS,* 25 November 1983, 1321.

Works about Randolph Stow

Bibliographies

O'Brien, Patricia. *Randolph Stow: A Bibliography.* Bibliographies of
    Australian Writers. Adelaide: Libraries Board of South Australia,
    1968.
Index to Australian Book Reviews. Adelaide: Libraries Board of South
    Australia, 1965–1981. This supplements O'Brien annually
    1968–1975.
Randolph Stow (1935–   ). Fryer Library, University of Queensland, St
    Lucia, 1972. This supplements O'Brien to 1972.
Beston, Rose Marie. "Principles of Selection of Bibliographical Items".
    The Literary Half-Yearly 16, no. 2 (July 1975): 137-44.
Stenderup, Vibeke. "Randolph Stow in Scandanavia". *Kunapipi* 1, no. 1
    (1979): 37-40.
"Annual Bibliography of Studies in Australian Literature". *ALS,*
    1964–   ). Annual in May issue.

Biographies

Beston, John B. "The Family Background and Literary Career of
    Randolph Stow". *The Literary Half-Yearly* 16, no. 2 (July 1975):
    125-34.
Hetherington, John. "Randolph Stow: Young Man in No Hurry". In
    Forty-Two Faces, 242-47. Melbourne: Cheshire, 1962.
Willbanks, Ray. *Randolph Stow.* Twayne's World Author Series. Boston:
    Twayne, 1978. Includes biographical sketch.

Interviews

Bennett, Bruce. "Discussions with Randolph Stow". *Westerly* 26, no. 4
    (December 1981): 52-61.
Beston, John B. "An Interview with Randolph Stow". *WLWE* 14 (1975):
    221-30.

Hassall, Anthony J. "Interview with Randolph Stow". *ALS* 10 (1982): 311-25.

Pons, Xavier, and Neil Keeble. "A Colonist with Words: An Interview with Randolph Stow". *Commonwealth (Rodez): Essays and Studies Mélanges* 2(1976): 70-80.

Rutherford, Anna, and Andreas Boelsmand. "Interview with Randolph Stow". *Commonwealth Literature* 5 (December 1973): 17-20.

Criticism

The following is a selective list of the more useful studies of Stow, and does not include all the works cited in the text. Reviews have not been included unless they are of particular interest. For comprehensive listings including reviews see *Bibliographies* above.

Bennett, Bruce. "Australian Perspectives on the Near North: Hal Porter and Randolph Stow". In *South Pacific Images*, edited by Chris Tiffin, 124-44. South Pacific Association for Commonwealth Literature and Language Studies, 1978.

_____. ed. *The Literature of Western Australia*. Perth: University of Western Australia Press, 1979.

_____. "Randolph Stow's Poetry". *Radio Script*, ABC, 1982.

Beston, John B. "Heriot's Literary Allusions in Randolph Stow's *To the Islands*". *Southerly* 35 (1975): 168-77.

_____. "The Love Poetry of Randolph Stow". *ACLALS Bulletin* 5 (1977): 12-25.

_____. "The Theme of Reconciliation in Stow's *To the Islands*". *MFS* 27, no. 1 (Spring 1981): 95-107.

Brady, Veronica. *A Crucible of Prophets*. Sydney: Theological Explorations, 1981.

Buckley, Vincent. "In The Shadow of Patrick White". *Meanjin* 20 (1961): 144-54.

Burgess, O.N. "The Novels of Randolph Stow". *Australian Quarterly* 37 (1965): 73-81.

Clarke, Donovan. "My Soul is a Strange Country". *The Bridge* 2, no. 1 (September 1965): 37-43.

_____. "The Realities of Randolph Stow". *The Bridge* 2, no. 2 (February 1966): 37-42.

Coe, Richard N. "Portrait of the Artist as a Young Australian: Childhood, Literature, and Myth". *Southerly* 41 (1981): 126-62.

Conron, Brandon. "Voyager from Eden". Review of *A Counterfeit Silence*, *Ariel* 1, no. 4 (1970): 96-102.

Cotter, Michael. "The Image of the Aboriginal in Three Modern Australian Novels". *Meanjin* 36 (1977): 582-91.

Curle, J.J. "Randolph Stow: Poet and Novelist". *The Poetry Review* 49, no. 1 (January-March 1958): 17-19.

Dilnot, A.F. "The Australian Miss Havisham: Some Reservations". *ALS* 7 (1975): 206-8.

Dutton, Geoffrey, ed. *The Literature of Australia*. Rev. ed. Melbourne: Penguin, 1976.

_____. "The Search for Permanence: The Novels of Randolph Stow". *JCL* 1 (1965): 135-48.

Geering, R.G. *Recent Fiction*, 3-30. Australian Writers and Their Work. Melbourne: Oxford University Press, 1974.

Goulder, Gina. Review of *Visitants. Westerly* 29, no. 3 (October 1984): 91-93.

Hamilton, K.G., ed. *Studies in the Recent Australian Novel*. St Lucia: University of Queensland Press, 1978.

Hassall, Anthony J. "The Alienation of Alistair Cawdor in Randolph Stow's *Visitants*". *ALS* 9 (1980): 449-59.

_____. "Full Circle: Randolph Stow's *The Merry-go-Round in the Sea*". *Meanjin* 32 (1973): 58-64.

_____. "The Poetry of Randolph Stow". *Southerly* 42 (1982): 259-76.

_____. "Randolph Stow's *The Merry-go-Round in the Sea*". In *Perspectives 79*, edited by J. Fox and B. McFarlane, 163-69. Melbourne: Sorrett, 1978.

_____. "Seely Suffolk: A Reading of Randolph Stow's *The Girl Green as Elderflower*, *LiNQ* 11, no. 2 (1983/84): 5-17.

Healy, J.J. *Literature and the Aborigine in Australia 1770–1975*. St Lucia: University of Queensland Press, 1978.

Hergenhan, L.T. "Randolph Stow's *To the Islands*". *Southerly* 35 (1975): 234-47.

Heseltine, H.P. "Australian Image: 1) The Literary Heritage". *Meanjin* 21 (1962): 35-49.

Hewett, Dorothy. Preface to *Sandgropers*, edited by D. Hewett, ix-xiii. Nedlands: University of Western Australia Press, 1973.

_____. "Stow Comes Home". Review of *The Merry-go-Round in the Sea*. *The Critic*, 31 December 1965, 86-87.

Higginbotham, Paul D. " 'Honour the Single Soul': Randolph Stow and His Novels". *Southerly* 39 (1979): 378-92.

Hope, A. D. "Randolph Stow and the Tourmaline Affair". *The Australian Experience*, edited by W.S. Ramson, 249-68. Canberra: ANU Press, 1974.

_____. "Randolph Stow and the Way of Heaven". *Hemisphere* 18, no. 6 (June 1974): 33-35.

Hungerford, T.A.G. Review of *Visitants. Westerly* 25, no. 1 (March 1980): 105-7.

Johnston, G.K.W. "The Art of Randolph Stow". *Meanjin* 20 (1961): 139-43.

Keesing, Nancy, ed. *Australian Postwar Novelists: Selected Critical Essays*. Brisbane: Jacaranda Press, 1975.

_____. "Stow, (Julian) Randolph". In *Contemporary Poets*, edited by James Vinson, 1507-9. 2nd ed. London: St James Press; New York: St Martin's Press, 1977.

Koch, C.J. "Literature and Cultural Identity". *The Tasmanian Review*, no. 4 (1980): 2-5.

Kramer, Leonie. "The Novels of Randolph Stow". *Southerly* 24 (1964): 78-91.

———. ed. *The Oxford History of Australian Literature*. Melbourne: Oxford University Press, 1981.

Martin, Philip. "Randolph Stow as Poet". *Twentieth Century (Aust.)*, 12 (Winter 1958): 349-52.

Moore, T. Inglis. *Social Patterns in Australian Literature*. Berkeley and Los Angeles: University of California Press, 1971.

New, William H. "Outsider Looking Out: The Novels of Randolph Stow". *Critique* 9 (1966): 90-99.

Newby, P.H. "The Novels of Randolph Stow". *Australian Letters* 1, no. 2 (1957): 49-51.

Oppen, Alice. "Myth and Reality in Randolph Stow". *Southerly* 27 (1967): 82-94.

Perkins, Elizabeth. "Randolph Stow and the Dimdins". *Quadrant* 26, no. 7 (July 1982): 28-33.

Ramsey, S.A. " 'The silent griefs: Randolph Stow's *Visitants*". *Critical Quarterly* 23, no. 2 (Summer 1981): 73-81.

Ryan, J.S. "A Possible Australian Source for Miss Havisham". *ALS* 1 (1963): 134-36.

Tanner, Godfrey. "The Road to Jerusalem". *Nimrod* 2, no. 1 (1964): 33-39.

Taylor, Andrew. "Bosom of Nature or Heart of Stone: A Difference in Heritage". In *An Introduction to Australian Literature*, edited by C.D. Narasimhaiah, 144-56. Brisbane: John Wiley, 1982.

Thomas, Sue. "Randolph Stow's Revision of *To the Islands*". *Southerly* 42 (1982): 288-94.

Tiffin, Chris. "Mates, Mum, and Maui: The theme of maturity in three antipodean novels". In *Awakened Conscience*, edited by C.D. Narasimhaiah, 127-45. New Delhi: Sterling, 1978.

Tiffin, Helen. "Melanesian Cargo Cults in *Tourmaline* and *Visitants*". *JCL* 16 (1981): 109-25.

———. "*Tourmaline* and the *Tao Te Ching*: Randolph Stow's *Tourmaline*". In *Studies in the Recent Australian Novel*, edited by K.G. Hamilton, 84-120. St Lucia: University of Queensland Press, 1978.

Wallace, Robyn. "Messiahs and Millennia in Randolph Stow's Novels". *Kunapipi* 3, no. 2 (1981): 56-72.

Watson-Williams, Helen. "Randolph Stow's Suffolk Novel". *Westerly* 25, no. 4 (December 1980): 68-72.

Whitehead, Jean. "The Individualism of Randolph Stow". In *Sandgropers*, edited by Dorothy Hewett, 181-87. Nedlands: University of Western Australia Press, 1973.

Wide Domain: Western Australian Themes and Images. Selected by Bruce Bennett and William Grono. Sydney: Angus & Robertson, 1979.

Wightman, Jennifer. "Waste Places, Dry Souls: The Novels of Randolph Stow". *Meanjin* 28 (1969): 239-52.

Wilkes, G.A. *Australian Literature: A Conspectus.* Sydney: Angus & Robertson, 1969.

Willbanks, Ray. *Randolph Stow.* Boston: Twayne, 1978. Twayne's World Authors Series.

Zwicky, Fay. "Speeches and Silences". *Quadrant* 17, no. 5 (May 1983): 40-46.

Index